AGING AND ADULT DEVELOPMENT IN THE DEVELOPING WORLD

Applying Western Theories and Concepts

Frank E. Eyetsemitan
and
James T. Gire

Westport, Connecticut
London

Library of Congress Cataloging-in-Publication Data

Eyetsemitan, Frank E., 1955–
     Aging and adult development in the developing world : applying Western
theories and concepts / Frank E. Eyetsemitan and James T. Gire.
        p. cm.
     Includes bibliographical references and index.
     ISBN 0-89789-925-3 (alk. paper)
        1. Aged—Developing countries.   I. Gire, James, T.   II. Title.
HQ1064.D44 E96   2003
305.26'09172'4—dc21   2002021572

British Library Cataloguing in Publication Data is available.

Library of Congress Catalog Card Number: 2002021572
ISBN: 0–89789–925–3

First published in 2003

Praeger Publishers, 88 Post Road West, Westport, CT 06881
An imprint of Greenwood Publishing Group, Inc.
www.praeger.com

Printed in the United States of America

The paper used in this book complies with the
Permanent Paper Standard issued by the National
Information Standards Organization (Z39.48–1984).

10 9 8 7 6 5 4 3 2

This book is dedicated to our spouses for their inspirations and to our children to whom we sometimes have to explain both worlds:

Francisca and Tosan
and
Mbarumun, Dooter, and Sechivir

Contents

Preface

This book came about as a result of the experiences of both authors who grew up and worked in a developing society but are now living and working in a developed society. For those of us who have lived in and experienced both worlds, there is that feeling of burden—or call it responsibility—to explain each side to the other, and sometimes to serve as a "moderator." We have seen tour guides serve as interpreters to visitors. We have also witnessed in the literature indigenous non-Western intellectuals trying to play the roles of "tour guides" and "interpreters" to their Western colleagues. Because most theories and perspectives on human behavior are developed in the West, the interpretation of these theories and perspectives by non-Western intellectuals in their local contexts is sometimes perceived as defensive. Therefore, we have not seen much of the role of a "moderator," someone who acknowledges the strengths and weaknesses that both sides bring to the understanding of human behavior. Given our experiences in both worlds, we hope we have attempted to serve in the role of "moderators." We have tried to do this, by first presenting Western theories and concepts and then discussing their appropriateness or inappropriateness in the developing world—a term we carefully chose instead of non-Western because of our desire to emphasize common global developmental objectives in human development and aging while also acknowledging cultural relativity.

According to the United Nations, the developing world comprises Asia (excluding Japan), North America (excluding Canada and the United States), South America, Africa, and Oceania (excluding Australia and New Zealand). All the nations of the developing world are not at the same level of development and neither are those of the developed world. For example, within the developing world, there is the category of the least developed countries (LDCs) made up of nations like Afghanistan, Cambodia, Samoa, Sao Tomé and Príncipe, Sierra Leone, Solomon Islands, and Uganda. Likewise, within the developed world category there are the most developed nations—the United States, Japan, Canada, Germany, France, England, and Italy. Thus, there is a hierarchy and a continuum of development from the least to the most developed nations but all are striving toward a common goal—DEVELOPMENT! The United Nations uses the following as criteria for development: per capita gross domestic products (GDP), share of manufacturing in total GDP, adult literacy rate, augmented quality of life index, economic diversification index, and population size.

Understandably, most studies on human development in developing societies have focused on the childhood stage, with a few studies sometimes extending the range to cover processes in adolescence. After all, children under 14 years of age not only make up almost half of the population, but their needs are also tremendous. Studies on early and middle adulthood stages are therefore rare, and those on late adulthood are mostly anthropological, focusing on roles, the adult's changing nature as a result of Westernization, and intergenerational helping relationships. Our book attempts to fill this void through an exhaustive discussion of the later part of the life span, thereby providing an important step toward diversifying the application of various Western theories and perspectives on adult development and aging, and evaluating their appropriateness or inappropriateness to the developing world. We must admit, however, that in some areas, especially having to do with the physical and psychological aspects of aging and adult development, it was a challenge to find existing literature that pertains to the developing world. Therefore, we had to use extrapolations, and in some cases our experiences, to discuss the appropriateness or inappropriateness of Western theories and concepts with suggestions made for future studies. From our field studies in seven developing countries in Africa, the Middle East, Asia and south America, we were able to identify age parameters and typical roles associated with the early, middle, and late adulthood stages, thereby adding to the scarce existing literature. But more empirical work is still needed. Hopefully, this book will help the reader in identifying those areas where research is still lacking.

The book is divided into ten chapters. Chapter 1 is the introductory chapter that lays the background for the need to study aging and adult development in the developing world, especially with 55 percent of older adults currently living in the developing world. This figure is likely to increase to 65 percent by the year 2020, and if 60 years is used as the lower benchmark for old age, as is sometimes the case, then this number will significantly rise. The chapter also defines and clarifies relevant concepts like development and Western; indigenous versus universal psychologies, aging and human development; and acculturation. The cultural context in which aging and human development occur is the focus of Chapter 2, with a suggestion for cross-cultural context as a more appropriate paradigm for understanding aging and human developmental trajectories in the developing world.

In Chapters 3, 4 and 5, pertinent Western theories and perspectives on the physical, psychological and social aspects of aging and adult development are first presented and then discussed within the context of the developing world. In Chapter 6, the primary data collected from seven developing nations and from different regions of the world on the psycho-social markers of the early, middle and late adulthood stages are presented. As mentioned earlier, they add to the scant existing literature and also help to enrich our discussions on the appropriateness or inappropriateness of Western theories and perspectives.

Chapters 7, 8, and 9 focus on some of the peculiarities that come with aging: health, retirement and social/public policies, and death and dying. Here, again, Western theories and perspectives are first presented followed by a discussion of their appropriateness or inappropriateness in the developing world. In chapter 10, the concluding chapter, we make general conclusions on the appropriateness or inappropriateness of pertinent Western theories and perspectives presented in previous chapters and on the seven-nation study, with suggestions made on aging and adult developmental pathways for the peoples of the developing world.

Because of the scope and depth of this book, it could be used either as a stand-alone text or as a supplementary text in courses in adult developmental psychology, gerontology, cross-cultural psychology, cultural anthropology, international business, marketing, and family studies.

We would like to extend our gratitude to all those who, in one way or another, have been instrumental in bringing this book about. We especially want to thank Greenwood Press and our editor Jane Garry; Angela Williams Urquhart at Thistle Hill Publishing Services; and our employers McKendree College and Virginia Military Institute for various types of support received. Our gratitude also goes to colleagues around the world: Angela Biaggio and Sergio Luis Tesche in Brazil, Omar Haroon in Bahrain, Monty Satiadarma in Indonesia, Nazmul Haq in Bangladesh, John Kyeleve in Botswana, and Alejandra Vargas in Chile for their help with data collection.

During the four years we worked on this book, we have come to appreciate our families more; we lack the words that can aptly describe the sacrifices they have made, and we thank them heartily for their patience and understanding.

Frank Eyetsemitan
James T. Gire

1

Introduction

The population under age five has been shrinking worldwide over the past two decades. At the same time, adults are enjoying increased longevity. While it is projected that the elderly population worldwide will more than double in the next 25 years if this trend continues, the greatest relative increase will occur in the developing world. This growth will range from 106 to 174% compared to the United States and other more developed nations where the increase will be just over 50%. Thus by 2025 over two-thirds of those 65 years and over will be living in the developing world (U.S. Census Bureau, 1999). Improved sanitation, immunization, better nutrition, health care, and education are some of the reasons responsible for this projected growth. As a result, there is a compelling need both to understand the aging process and the potentials of later life in the developing world. Unfortunately, this impending population explosion has not been matched by a corresponding increase in research on aging and adult development.

This chapter examines the scarcity of research on aging and adult development in developing societies and draws attention to the need for studies on the later part of the life span. Concepts, as well as their definitions, that will offer a better understanding of the developing world, and a better understanding of aging and adult development, will be introduced in summary form and utilized appropriately in later chapters.

RESPONSE TO POPULATION GROWTH

In response to the population growth trend in developing societies, governments of these countries, nongovernmental organizations (NGOs), and scholars have so far made issues pertaining to children and adolescents take center stage. Programs sponsored by the Ford Foundation, the Carnegie Foundation, and other similar organizations typically target children and adolescents in the developing world, and this is understandable because children still constitute a large number of the total population.

Nonetheless, the elderly population is growing at a phenomenal rate, yet the issues concerning adults and the elderly still receive little attention (Gardiner, Mutter, & Kosmitzki, 1998). Whether for children or adults, there is even a general dearth of psychological studies in the developing world. For example, Bauserman (1997) reviewed 113 countries based on the American Psychological Association electronic PsycLit records from 1975 to 1990 and found that the developing nations of Southeast Asia, Latin America, and sub-Saharan Africa were poorly represented in the psychological literature. To understand aging and adult development in developing societies, therefore, one typically has to extrapolate and use the processes and perspectives formulated and tested mainly in the developed world. This process, which Berry, Poortinga, Segall, and Dasen (1992) referred to as "transport and test," is devoid of the ecocultural environment of the developing world. The need to understand human behavior within a cultural context is not just for adults but also for children who are still undergoing biological maturation (Kagitcibasi 1996b). Therefore, the aims of this book are to:

1. discuss the aging process and adult development using Western theories and concepts, highlighting both their appropriateness and inappropriateness to the developing world;

2. through primary data collection, identify some psycho-social developmental milestones that delineate the early, middle, and late adulthood stages in developing societies; and

3. suggest new perspectives for understanding aging and adult development in the developing world.

This book discusses the appropriateness or inappropriateness of Western theories and perspectives in the developing world. To approach this discussion in an organized manner, subsequent chapters, after Chapters 1 and 2, offer a separate section on the developing world, following the discussion of Western theories and perspectives. But first, what is the developing world? What societies and characteristics make up the developing world? We will now consider these questions.

THE DEVELOPING WORLD

According to the United Nations, the developing world, or less developed regions comprises Asia (excluding Japan), North America (excluding Canada and the United States), South America, Africa, and Oceania (excluding Australia and New Zealand). All the nations of the developing world are not at the same level of development and neither are those of the developed world. Within the developing world, there is the category of the least developed countries (LDCs) made up of countries like Afghanistan, Cambodia, Samoa, Sao Tomé and Príncipe, Sierra Leone, Solomon Islands, and Uganda. The African region contributes more than two-thirds of the nations in this category. These countries, with a combined population of 570 million people, are the poorest in the world. The criteria the United Nations uses for belonging to this category are as follows: per capita gross domestic product (GDP), share of manufacturing in total GDP, adult literacy rate, augmented quality of life index, economic diversification index, and population size. Likewise, within the developed world there are the most industrialized nations comprising the United States, Japan, Canada, Germany, France, England, and Italy. Thus, there is a hierarchy and a continuum of development from the least to the most developed nations.

High in the hierarchy, the developed world, made up mostly of Western countries, has been used as a standard of development for the developing world. However, the standard or criteria for human development put forth by the United Nations, representing the international community, will be adopted in this book. The developed world will only provide a model for achieving those standards, which may or may not apply to the ecocultural contexts of the developing world.

STANDARD MODEL OF HUMAN DEVELOPMENT

In the choice of a standard model of human development, the following questions are pertinent: 1) should there be a universal standard for human development? and, if so, 2) should each society determine its own trajectory for achieving those standards? While the United Nations agrees on a universal standard of human development, the process for achieving the standard can vary from one society to another. Indeed, the United Nations through its agency, the United Nations Development Programme (1997), has set *standard criteria* but not *standard process(es)* for human development. Though different, human development objectives could be confused with the following:

1 Economic growth: There is an erroneous assumption that the economic growth of a country is automatically translated into progress in human development. Human development issues may not be a priority to the government, especially in developing societies where military expenditure could take priority over education.

2. Theories of human capital formation and human resource development: In this approach, human beings are viewed as a means to increasing the income and wealth of a society, but not as beneficiaries in terms of priorities. Another way of looking at it is using human beings as "slave laborers."

3. The human welfare approach: This is the opposite of number 2 above. With this approach human beings are beneficiaries, but they are denied the opportunities to participate in the development process.

4. The basic needs approach: The focus is on providing a deprived group of basic needs such as food, shelter, clothing, health care, and water. While the eradication of poverty is approached from an economic perspective only, *psychological poverty* is not approached, and choices that reflect the values and beliefs of a people are ignored. We shall address this issue further under our concept of *supply* and *demand*.

UNITED NATIONS ANALYTICAL TOOLS FOR HUMAN DEVELOPMENT

The United Nations' analytical tools for human development are used for gauging policy choices by governments of countries and by practitioners in human development. Researchers can also use them to explain and predict human development. The following are some of the tools used.

Human Development Index (HDI)

This is a measure of the average achievement of a country in basic human capabilities, for example, whether people lead a long and healthy life, are educated and knowledgeable, and have a decent standard of living. There is a minimum and a maximum dimension, expressed as a value between 0 and 1. For example, with a minimum adult literacy rate of 0% and a maximum of 100%, a country with an adult literacy rate of 65% would be 0.65 on the HDI. Also, with a minimum life expectancy at 25 years and maximum at 85, a country with a life expectancy of 65 would be 0.67. For income, the minimum is $100 and the maximum is $40,000. The scores of the three dimensions are averaged into an overall HDI index. However, *Disaggregated HDI* has been used to account for differences within a country, for example, the disparities among different regions, between sexes, between rural-urban dwellers, and among ethnic groups. It can also be used for different age groups.

The Gender-Related Development Index (GDI)

This index is the same as HDI, but specifically deals with inequality between men and women. GDI falls either when the levels of achievement of both men and women in a country go down or when the disparity of achievement levels between men and women goes up. There is a penalty for gender inequality in the overall HDI score. The GDI focuses on the expansion of capabilities.

Gender Empowerment Measure (GEM)

The GEM evaluates the extent to which men and women are able to actively take part in political and economic life, and in decision making. The GEM focuses on how men and women take advantage of the opportunities with which they have been provided in order to better their lives.

Excerpts of the 1998 United Nations' indexes of human development from Chile, Bahrain, Brazil, Indonesia, Botswana, Nigeria, and Bangladesh are presented in Tables 1.1 and 1.2. These are developing nations in Asia, Africa, the Middle East, and South America from which we obtained primary data on aging and adult development. The data are presented in Chapter 6. Based on the Human Development Index table, Chile, Bahrain, and Brazil fall under the

Table 1.1
United Nations Human Development Index for 1998

Country	Life Expectancy at Birth (years)	Adult Literacy Rate (%)	Life Expectancy Index	Education Index	HDI Value	World Ranking
High Human Development						
Chile	75.1	95.2	0.836	0.877	0.893	31
Bahrain	72.2	85.2	0.787	0.847	0.872	43
Brazil	66.6	83.3	0.693	0.795	0.809	62
Medium Human Development						
Indonesia	64.0	83.8	0.649	0.766	0.679	96
Botswana	51.7	69.8	0.446	0.702	0.678	97
Low Human Development						
Nigeria	51.7	57.1	0.440	0.546	0.391	142
Bangladesh	56.9	38.1	0.531	0.376	0.371	147
All Countries						
ADC	62.20	70.44	0.620	0.661	0.586	
LDC	51.16	49.20	0.436	0.449	0.344	
Industrial Countries	74.17	98.63	0.820	0.934	0.911	

ADC – All Developing Countries

LDC – Least Developed Countries

HDI – Human Development Index

Source: United Nations Development Programme (1998). *Statistics from the 1998 Human Development Report*. New York: Author.

"high category" of human development, Indonesia and Botswana fall under the "medium category," while Nigeria and Bangladesh fall under the "low category."

Similarly in the area of gender-related development, Chile, Bahrain, and Brazil fall under the "high category," Indonesia and Botswana into the "medium category," and Nigeria and Bangladesh under the "low category." Whereas Bahrain is in the "high category," the country has an adult female literacy rate that is comparable to the literacy rates of countries in the "medium" and "low" categories, but its "share of earned income for females" compared to the countries in the "medium" and "low" categories is relatively low. While both literacy rate and earned income are important for gender empowerment, the latter seems to be more important.

Although the United Nations standard of human development is adopted in this text, Western theories and perspectives will provide a framework on how to achieve the standard because 1) the Western industrial countries have better human development scores than the developing countries, and 2) there is a current dearth of theories and perspectives on aging and adult development in the developing world.

Table 1.2
United Nations Gender-Related Development Index, 1998

Country	GDI Rank	Life Expectancy at Birth		Adult Literacy (%)		Share of Earned Income		HDI Rank minus GDI Rank
		Female (%)	Male (%)	Female (%)	Male (%)	Female (%)	Male (%)	
High Human Development								
Chile	46	78.01	72.16	94.96	95.4	22.02	77.98	-16
Bahrain	60	74.72	70.40	79.39	89.05	14.98	85.02	-19
Brazil	56	70.72	62.76	83.21	83.32	29.27	70.73	-1
Medium Human Development								
Indonesia	88	65.75	62.19	78.00	89.64	32.98	67.02	0
Botswana	85	53.14	50.06	59.91	80.52	38.86	61.14	4
Low Human Development								
Nigeria	133	53.03	49.84	47.30	67.34	30.01	69.99	-1
Bangladesh	140	57.01	56.85	26.14	49.37	23.08	76.92	-3
All Countries								
ADC	-	63.67	60.78	61.82	78.86	32.42	67.58	-
LDC	-	52.30	50.03	39.30	59.19	34.29	65.71	-
Industrial countries	-	77.90	70.36	98.50	98.76	38.02	61.98	-

GDI – Gender-Related Development Index
Source: United Nations Development Programme (1998). *Statistics from the 1998 Human Development Report.* New York: Author.

THE INTERCHANGEABLE USE OF "WESTERN" AND "DEVELOPED"

The term "developing countries" assumes that these societies are in the process of becoming "developed." Since most "developed" societies are Western, "developed" and "Westernization" have come to be used interchangeably. When this happens, Western societies take on the status of standards for development, and constitute the "end" rather than a means to that end.

Unfortunately, in this light, Western standards have been used to examine, explain, and predict the different facets of human development in developing societies, including political, social, economic, and psychological. While it is true that the developed world is made up mostly of Western societies, Japan, a non-Western society, also belongs to this category. Therefore, Japan is an example that illustrates that "Western" is not the same as "developed," nor should it be the standard for "developed."

There are value systems that delineate Western and non-Western societies, and certain studies have linked those value systems to human and societal developments. One such influential study was Hofstede's (1980) research on work values among IBM employees in Western and non-Western countries. Hofstede identified Western societies as being individualistic and non-Western societies as collectivist. Hofstede's individualism and collectivism concept has become the basis on which societies are compared (Kim et al., 1994) with a lot of research interests generated in diverse domain areas. The notion of whether or not Western and non-Western societies fit into Hofstede's individualism and collectivism classification is still a subject of serious scholarly debate. Yet Hofstede's concept still remains popular.

INDIVIDUALISM AND COLLECTIVISM

Hofstede (1980, 1983) surveyed IBM employees from 50 countries and 3 multicountry regions and constructed an index of individualism and collectivism along with three others: power and distance, uncertainty and avoidance, and masculinity and femininity. Although interest in individualism and collectivism preceded Hofstede's work (Barry, Child, & Bacon, 1959), his contribution has led to a resurgence of interest in this construct in more recent times, and in diverse areas (Gudykunst, Ting-Toomey, & Chua, 1988; Schwartz, 1990; Smith & Bond, 1993, but see Triandis, 1995 for details). The appeal of individualism and collectivism is in providing a neat paradigm around which most societies and cultures are organized. Yet, individualism and collectivism still faces conceptual and measurement challenges (Kagitcibasi, 1997; Schwartz, 1990).

In societies that tend toward individualism, the emphasis is on being independent, self-contained, and autonomous (Markus & Kitayama, 1991), and these characteristics are said to represent Western values. In those societies that tend toward collectivism, mostly non-Western, the emphasis is on interdependence, relatedness, and social obligations (Church & Lonner, 1998). Furthermore, while individualists value equality, freedom, and an exciting life, collectivists value social order, honoring of parents and elders, and self-discipline (Schwartz & Bilsky, 1987, 1990).

Triandis (1995) and also Triandis and Bhawuk (1997) reviewed diverse works on this construct and identified four universal dimensions of individualism and collectivism:

1. Definition of self: Whereas collectivists view self in relation to others with interdependency in resource sharing, individualists view self as autonomous from groups, and are not obligated to share resources, but such decisions are made individually (Markus & Kitayama, 1991; Reykowski, 1994).

2. Structure of goals: Whereas in collectivist cultures, the individual's goals are subsumed within the in-group's goals, in individualist cultures the individual's goals are not often related to those of the in-group (Shwartz, 1992, 1994; Triandis, 1988). Triandis (1995) says that the in-group is made up of sets of individuals with whom a person feels similar, and that similarity may come from common fate or some other attributes. In general, while collectivist in-groups are ascribed, for example, caste, kin, race, tribe, religion, village, nation individualist in-groups are achieved, for example, similar beliefs, attitudes, values, actions, programs, occupation. However, in some cases, some attributes are both achieved and ascribed, for example, nationality.

3. Emphasis on norms versus attitudes: Whereas norms, duties, and obligations determine social behavior in collectivist cultures, attitudes, personal needs, perceived rights, and contracts determine social behavior in individualist cultures (Diaz-Guerrero, 1993).

4. Emphasis on relatedness versus rationality: Whereas in collectivist cultures the emphasis is on relatedness, in individualist cultures it is on rationality. With relatedness, the individual gives priority to relationships even if it is not to his or her advantage. With rationality, however, emphasis is on the costs and benefits of relationships (Kim, Triandis, Kagitcibasi, Choi, & Yoon, 1994).

The goals and values of individualists and collectivists are not so clear-cut. For example, there are findings that were opposite of the hypothesized direction. Triandis, McCuster, and Hui (1990) observed that Americans scored higher than Chinese samples on values that have implications for social connections.

Because the research based on individualism and collectivism is so expansive, when covering cognitive, behavioral, motivational, and emotional domains, caution is required in the imputation of differences between the developed and developing worlds. There are various individualism and collectivism instruments that have emerged with some similar dimensional themes like self-reliance, social obligations or interdependence, distance, or separation from in-groups, but their replicability and convergence across and even within cultures are still questionable. For example, a concept like self-reliance, long considered a distinguishing characteristic of individualist cultures (Triandis, 1990), is also an important attribute of collectivist cultures (Niles, 1998). But part of the problem with individualism and collectivism is that researchers indirectly assume differences in participants based on their national and ethnic status without establishing a causal relationship (Kagitcibasi, 1997). Kagitcibasi (1997) suggested the need to study background variables like education, income, rural-urban standing, and type of employment in individualism and collectivism measures. Even at the societal level, the levels of technological and economic advancement, of secularity and openness, and of citizen participation, are additional dimensions to consider (Triandis, McCuster, & Betancourt, 1993). The study of individualism and collectivism has been carried out in diverse domains, but of particular interest to this book is how it has been applied to human developmental trajectories.

INDIVIDUALISM AND COLLECTIVISM AND
HUMAN DEVELOPMENTAL TRAJECTORIES

From reviewing their works and those of others, Keller and Greenfield (2000) posited two types of developmental trajectories that are based on individualism and collectivism. They suggested that divergent developmental pathways from childhood through adolescence are predicated on early conceptions of self and relationships (Greenfield & Suzuki, 1998). For example, development in middle childhood in a collectivistic context is expressed in unconditional in-group helpfulness, whereas in an individualistic context it is expressed in conditional or negotiated helpfulness (Mundy-Castle & Bundy, 1988). Furthermore, while the collectivistic model encourages socially shared knowledge, the individualistic model highlights individually possessed knowledge (Greenfield, 1997a, 1997b). In addition, emphasis on being a part of a group will be fostered under collectivism while separation from the group will be emphasized under individualism (Markus & Kitayama, 1991).

With collectivism, therefore, based on preceding childhood experiences, the transition from adolescence to adulthood will be short, characterized by early marriage, childbearing, and responsibilities for the economic support of the family. On the contrary, in an individualistic context adolescence will be relatively longer and reserved for education and other forms of self-development.

Keller and Greenfield (2000) did not, however, state whether there were gender differences in both collectivistic and individualistic societies. For example, most care providers for elderly parents in the United States are females. Furthermore, in collectivist cultures, there is a likely interface between religion and gender on the one hand and early marriage on the other. Also, the notion of self-development (for example, education) proceeding sequentially may not be accurate. It can proceed concurrently with raising a family, working, or taking care of significant others. These issues need to be considered carefully, according to Kagitcibasi (1997), to avoid the temptation of treating individualism and collectivism as opposite constructs and making predictions from them.

Another danger in using individualism and collectivism occurs when an evolutionary approach is taken and a suggestion is made that human development should proceed from collectivism to individualism. While the characteristics of individualism and collectivism seem to be at odds with each other (Schwartz, 1990), they are not necessarily so, and may affect what is looked for or even what research questions are asked. Therefore, questions like the following do not readily come to mind: can a person be assertive (individualism) and yet be dependent (collectivism)? Also, can a person be competitive (individualism) and yet be dutiful (collectivism) at the same time?

To answer these questions, let's take the example of adult children's caring responsibilities toward their parents in developing societies. Because children are the "social security" or the "walking sticks" of their parents, there is a psychological contract between children and their parents on this issue. Therefore, when adult children fall short of their expectations, parents assert their rights to be dependent. For example, Rosenberg (1997) noted that care is perceived as a right by the Ju/'hoansi elderly of Botswana and they do not have to negotiate their dependence. In other words, elderly parents are "assertively dependent." Also, adult children compete with each other to provide care to elderly parents and, in some cases, this competition extends to "who does the most" for his or her family, for the village, or the community. Cattell (1997) reported a case in Kenya where adult children implored their elderly father to give up his job so that others would not think that they (the children) were not providing for him. The adult children's behavior may be based on the desire to fulfill a filial responsibility (duty), or a desire to outdo their peers (competition).

Studies on individualism and collectivism should not only explore differences in goals and values or personal motivation (Phalet & Claeys, 1993), but should also measure the perceived pressure to conform or not to conform in individualist and collectivist cultures. For example, do individualists perceive less pressure to conform than collectivists? And what roles do gender, level of education, age, rural or urban residence play in such perception?

There should be caution also in associating individualism and collectivism with societal development because there are collectivist societies that have achieved high economic and technological advancement while still remaining largely collectivistic. As noted by Kagitcibasi (1996b): "The achievement of high economic technological development in collectivistic cultures, such as Japan and the 'four tigers' [Korea, Taiwan, Hong Kong, and Singapore] challenge the assumption that collectivism is incompatible with development and that an individualistic 'human model' is necessitated by industrialization" (p. 44). While this assertion is true, Kagitcibasi has suggested three types of socialization patterns: pattern X (collectivistic), pattern Z (individualistic), and Y (a dialectical synthesis of patterns X and Z), and noted that developing countries with pattern X are shifting to pattern Y occasioned by modernization.

A major problem with individualism and collectivism that researchers and commentators point to is methodology. For example, the differences made between Western and non-Western societies are based on national averages (Hofstede, 1980). Therefore the issue of methodology has brought to the forefront the question of how best to study and compare psychological phenomena within and across cultures. Two schools of thought have emerged from this debate: the indigenous (relativistic) and the universal school of thought.

INDIGENOUS VERSUS UNIVERSAL PSYCHOLOGIES

There is a clamor for an "indigenous" psychology approach among cross-cultural psychologists (Sinha 1986) in order truly to understand human behavior. The proponents of "indigenous" psychology believe that only when each culture is studied, taking into consideration the peculiarities in each culture, can we fully understand human developmental trajectory. They maintain that material culture, symbols, and history of a people are important antecedents to the development of behavior. Indigenous psychology is native to the people (Kim, 1990), and is rooted in a particular cultural tradition (Enriquez, 1990).

Furthermore, it matches the sociocultural realities of the native society (Berry, Poortinga, Segall, & Dasen, 1992). Therefore, true psychological knowledge is not externally imposed (*etic*) and experimentally contrived, but rather is based on the daily activities of the people using relevant local frames of reference and categories (*emic*) (Azuma, 1984; Berry, Poortinga, Segall, & Dasen, 1992). Even when psychological knowledge is imported, more attention should be paid to the unique elements within the local culture (Adair, 1992), thus resulting in a process of *indigenization* (Berry, Poortinga, Segall, & Dasen,1992; D. Sinha, 1965). In explaining *indigenization* within the Indian society, D. Sinha (1965) suggests "an integration of modern psychology with Indian thought" (p.6). Such *indigenization* process is however gradual (D. Sinha, 1986), and involves changes to the foreign discipline first, in order to make it suitable to the local sociocultural context.

It is important to distinguish between *indigenization* and *indigenous*, the later referring to a psychology that is locally generated with its own constructs and categories. There is a misconception that *indigenous* psychology is opposed to the discovery of universal facts and principles and, therefore, *indigenization* seems to be preferred. But to the contrary, *indigenous* psychology sets out to challenge (Western) universal facts and principles that are simply assumed (Diaz-Guerrero, 1993; Ho, 1993; D. Sinha, 1993) rather than established through cross-cultural and cross-indigenous studies.

Nevertheless, there is evidence that both indigenous, non-Western psychology and Western psychology can coexist and that both approaches can offer perspectives that are complementary and not antagonistic to each other. For example, coexistence is described in such concepts as the "nurturant-task leader" (J. B. P. Sinha, 1980); in "socially oriented achievement motivation" (Agarwal & Misra, 1986; Yu & Yang, 1994); in "relationship harmony" (Kwan, Bond, & Singelis, 1997); and in "autonomous-relational self" (Kagitcibasi, 1996a). Similar to the arguments made between universal and indigenous psychologies are those made between cultural and cross-cultural psychologies.

CULTURAL AND CROSS-CULTURAL PSYCHOLOGIES

The arguments for and against cultural and cross-cultural psychologies, also referred to as relativistic and universalistic approaches (Berry, Poortinga, Segall, & Dasen, 1992), are similar in some respect to those advanced for universal and indigenous psychologies. Likewise, there are various arguments against the relativistic position but a complementary approach of combining cultural context (cultural psychology) with universal standards of human development (cross-cultural psychology) has been posited (Aycan, 2000; Kagitcibasi, 1996b; Singelis, 2000). Universalism, also referred to as absolutism, assumes a pan-cultural presence of psychological phenomena, while cultural relativism assumes a context that varies for the expression of such phenomena (Lightfoot & Valsiner, 1992). Therefore, both similarities and differences should be sought in cross-cultural studies. Unfortunately, however, too much attention has been paid to differences. There are cross-cultural similarities in emotion and cognition, and different societies display similar social-structural mechanisms for regulating behavior, and yet these are not usually explored in cross-cultural studies (van de Vijver & Leung, 2000). These cross-cultural similarities are aided by global travel and communication, which have made defining cultural boundaries more difficult. But similarities in emotion and cognition, as well as in social-structural mechanisms across cultures, are also triggered by shared biological experiences like senescence and death. This oversight in looking for cross-cultural similarities is partly due to methodology problems (van de Vijver & Leung, 2000), and/or to the implicit assumption that each culture is unique.

In a pancultural situation, however, individuals from one society experience the cultures of individuals from other societies (acculturation). Although this experience has been of much interest to cross-cultural psychologists, much of the studies done are with minority populations in mostly Western societies (Berry & Sam, 1997). But the interaction of individuals with a foreign culture takes a different dimension in developing societies. Therefore, we have proposed a psycho-economic model as being more appropriate in understanding the interaction dynamics between Western cultural elements and individuals in the developing world.

PSYCHO-ECONOMIC MODEL OF ACCULTURATION

Acculturation is defined as cultural change at both societal and individual levels as a result of cultural encounters (Graves, 1967). Most research on acculturation has focused on peoples in the Western Hemisphere. Therefore, existing models of acculturation have been developed from studies on immigrants, sojourners, refugees, and minority indigenous peoples in Western societies (Berry & Sam, 1997). Yet, as Berry and Sam (1997) note, "[A] good deal of the impact of acculturation on indigenous peoples is to be found in Asia, Africa, and Oceania" (p. 312). We, therefore, suggest that existing models of acculturation are not suitable for explaining the impact of Western acculturation on the indigenous peoples living in the developing world. The process of choice making during acculturation by the indigenous peoples living in the developing world is likely to be different from those of immigrants, sojourners, and refugees in developed societies. People who relocate to foreign societies may be more motivated or feel more pressured to integrate the culture of their host societies. For example, it is almost impossible to get by in the United States without being able to communicate in English or by being communicated to in English. Foreign students whose first languages are not English are required to learn English as a second language. There are aspects of Western culture that enhance or facilitate human development, but even so developing world people can exercise more choices in interacting with them, for example, education, language, and health care. Thus, when acculturation models developed in Western societies were used with the indigenous people in the developing world, it was hard to know whether the indigenous people shifted toward the Western acculturation experience or not. For example, in their study of Indian tribe groups, Mishra, Sinha, and Berry (1996) noted the importance of considering the "values, beliefs and attitudes of the individuals and whether they had moved in the direction of the dominant group" (p. 246). We, therefore, propose an alternative model of acculturation based on a *supply* and *demand* dynamic. It assumes a more voluntary interaction between the individual (or group) with a foreign cultural element that is "consumable" by that individual or group, for example, language, Western education, and Western medicine. As opposed to cultural contact, this model emphasizes cultural utility. Triandis (1990) suggests that it is best to consider culture in discrete forms or as elements rather than as wholesale units. The term *supply* represents both an awareness of, and the accessibility—cost, distance—of a foreign cultural element, while *demand* reflects the levels of desire—need, value, beliefs—for that foreign cultural element. The term "consumable" represents the extent to which a foreign cultural element meets the *demand* of the individuals or groups of the culture with which it comes in contact. Therefore the individual, or group, in exercising agency, has the choice to "consume" that cultural element or not. Using the psycho-economic model shown in Table 1.3 it becomes easier

Table 1.3
Psycho-Economic Model of Acculturation

Cultural Elements	Levels of Supply/ Demand Interactions	Consumption Outcomes
Supply Dimensions	High Supply / High Demand	High
Economic	Low Supply / Low Demand	Low
Psychological	Low Supply / High Demand	Low
Social	High Supply / Low Demand	Low
Political	Moderate Supply / Moderate Demand	Moderate
Demand Dimensions		
Economic	Moderate Supply / High Demand	Moderate
Psychological	Moderate Supply / Low Demand	Low
Social	High Supply / Moderate Demand	Moderate
Political	Low Supply / Moderate Demand	Low

to predict different consumption levels of a foreign cultural element, based on a *supply* and *demand* dynamic.

Both the *supply* dimensions of a foreign culture and the *demand* dimensions of the indigenous people living in the developing world could be classified as economic (wage employment), as psychological (values), as social (technology), and as political (political system). The left side of the model contains the *supply* dimensions of the foreign culture and the *demand* dimension of the individual and group followed by the possible interactions (based on the level of *supply* of the cultural element and the level of *demand* for it) leading to various consumption outcomes for that particular cultural element, as shown on the far right. The premise here is that the values, beliefs, and attitudes of individuals (and groups) constitute an internal mode that defines their different levels of *demand* for a foreign cultural element being "supplied."

Using the psycho-economic model to access the level of acculturation for English language, for example, would require a question like this: "How important is the English language to you?" Or "How often do you communicate in English in a week?" Asking an individual to rate his or her knowledge of the English language on a four-point scale of "good knowledge," "working knowledge," "little knowledge," and "no knowledge" (Mishra, Sinha & Berry, 1996) tells us about the different levels of contact with that foreign cultural element, but not its "consumption" level. While it is possible for an individual to have a "good knowledge" of the English language, the language could still be of little importance to that individual's daily life in terms of usage.

However, existing needs, values, and beliefs (or demand) do change, and such changes may be triggered from either within or outside of the individual and/or group (Eyetsemitan, 1997). Acculturative intervention from outside the individual is sometimes important for human development to occur. For example, in order to enhance development in the "High Supply/Low Demand" interaction scenario, the level of *demand* can be increased through change in attitudes and values in order to match a high *supply,* or *supply* can be modified in order to accommodate that low *demand* level. Therefore, the *supply* of a cultural element should always consider the *demand* level of the individual (or group). Furthermore, interaction outcomes suggest both the efforts and directions that would be required in any intervention effort. For example, more intervention efforts would be required in a "High Supply/Low Demand" scenario than in a " High Supply/Moderate Demand" scenario.

Although a low consumption level for a foreign cultural element is the result of various interaction antecedents, this model also helps to point to where appropriate intervention is required. For example, which of the following interaction outcomes explains why an African mother did not seek the help of Western medical care for her sick child: Low Supply/Low Demand; High Supply/Low Demand; Low Supply/High Demand; Low Supply/Moderate Demand; and Moderate Supply/Low Demand? All these various interaction outcomes signify a low consumption level for Western medicine, but to conclude that the low consumption level for Western medicine was entirely due to the woman's cultural beliefs (low *demand*) or to unavailable Western medicine (low *supply*) may be inaccurate. Nor would it be accurate to conclude that two individuals are at the same level of *demand* or even have the same level of perception of *supply* of Western medicine. Thus both *supply* and *demand* are best measured *subjectively*.

The "Low Supply/High Demand" interaction outcome would lead to a low consumption from a foreign culture as a result of a restricted *supply* of that foreign cultural element, for example, Western medicine, Western education, wage employment, electricity, etc. However, where *demand* is higher than *supply*, this could also lead to acculturation-seeking behavior. Acculturation-seeking behavior may take the form of rural-urban migration commonly seen among young people leaving rural areas to seek wage employment and other cultural opportunities in the cities and may also lead to international migration, for example, migrant workers and international students. Acculturation-seeking behavior also can be predicted in a Low Supply/Moderate demand interaction outcome, but to a lesser degree.

A High Supply/Low Demand interaction scenario may not yield a high consumption level either, for example, making Western education accessible to females in predominantly Islamic northern Nigeria has not yielded a high consumption level for Western education. In one study, Denga (1983) compared 184 Fulani parents who received counseling with 166 Fulani parents who received no counseling on attitude toward formal education. The Fulanis are a nomadic group in northern Nigeria. The experimental group received counseling on the value of formal education over a nine-month period, and results from both pre- and postcounseling questionnaires revealed that parents increased their acceptance of formal education only slightly. Thus, Denga recommended that schooling must be arranged in a way that will be acceptable to the Fulanis and that will be respectful of their culture.

Interaction with a foreign culture may not only lead to behavioral changes, but may also lead to stress. While "behavioral shifts" lead to changes in cognition, attitudes, values, and in interpersonal relationships (which may be developmental), "acculturative stress" produces psycho-pathological symptoms (Mishra, Sinha & Berry, 1996). But as noted also by Mishra, Sinha & Berry (1996) and by our *supply* and *demand* paradigm, each cultural contact is unique and, therefore, may or may not lead to behavioral changes and to stress.

So far, concepts that are of particular interest to cross-cultural psychologists have been discussed and, in some cases, clarifications have been made to concepts that appear similar and confusing, for example, "developed" and "Westernization," "individualism and collectivism," "indigenous and universal psychologies," and "cultural and cross-cultural psychology." In aging and adult development, such clarifications are also required. For example, concepts like aging, senescence, and development appear similar but are different and could be confusing.

AGING AND DEVELOPMENT: WHAT ARE THEY?

Traditionally, both aging and adult development are thought to be two separate phenomena with aging succeeding development at around age 30 (maturity), the age considered to be the apex of transition. While development is synonymous with incremental positive changes (biological growth), aging is likened to decremental negative changes (senescence) (Schroots, 1991; Schroots & Yates, 1999).

In more recent times, however, there has been a better understanding that suggests that psychological changes do not necessarily parallel biological changes. A good example that challenges this traditional viewpoint is wisdom, a progressive change that typically occurs around middle and late adulthood stages (Sternberg, 1990). Therefore, development and aging occur simultaneously.

AGING VERSUS SENESCENCE

It is important to make a distinction between the terms "aging" and "senescence." While aging (or to age) applies to both animate and inanimate systems, and is associated with the passage of external, geophysical time, that is, calendar or clock time, the changes that come from aging are not necessarily bad. They may be good or neutral (Schroots & Yates, 1999). On the other hand, senescence is a unidirectional phenomenon, implying damage, loss, harm, or failure—as a result of aging (Yates & Benton, 1995a). Therefore, aging (or to age) is a broader term while senescence is a subterm under aging.

DEVELOPMENT VERSUS SENESCENCE

Development and senescence are different in their pathways, with development proceeding in more than one direction and senescence proceeding in only one direction. Unlike development, however, senescence is slow and uniform and the physiological losses, which are present from the beginning of the life span, become dominant and manifest after maturity is reached at age 30, and the losses from senescence ultimately lead to system failure (Yates & Benton, 1995b).

Although senescence spans the entire life span, it is, however, masked prior to maturity, which is suggested to be age 30, after which a linear loss of 0.50% per year occurs for the healthiest people (Bortz & Bortz, 1996), but this rate of loss is slowed by exercise training (Davies, 1979; Heath, Hagberg, Ehrani, & Holloszy, 1981; also Polack, Foster, Knapp, Rod, & Schmidt, 1987). The role of exercise in slowing down senescence is still controversial and contradictory

(Suominen, Heikkinen, Parkatti, Forsberg, & Kiiskinen, 1980) because the extent of an individual's biological loss limits cultural interventions (Baltes, Staudinger, & Lindenberger, 1999). For example, an eye that has gone blind cannot be trained to see unlike one that still has some residual vision.

The transition point from development to senescence (at around age 30) would however vary from one individual to another and even within the same individual from one organ system to another. However, not all transitions and transformations from development to senescence lead to destruction. Some would, but others would evolve and become more coherent at a higher level of organization (Baltes, Staudinger, & Lindenberger, 1999). In each individual's life trajectory there are a series of transformations that are nonlinear, ending up in both lower order and higher order behaviors (Schroots, 1995). Examples of lower order behaviors are morbidity, disease, and disability while examples of the higher order behaviors are good quality of life, life satisfaction, healthy life expectancy, and wisdom. Whereas the lower order behaviors manifest *senescence*, we can suggest that the higher order behaviors are some forms of *human development*.

Interestingly, the relationship between development and aging is based on the principle of iteration. This means that the next ontogenetic state of the system, that is, the level of developmental and aging phenomena, will be contingent upon the previous ontogenetic state of the system (Schroots & Yates, 1999). In other words, lifestyles or life experiences in the early phase of the life span do contribute to aging and developmental outcomes in the later phase of the life span. Because both *development* and *senescence* take place within a cultural context, however, there would be both cultural universals and cultural peculiarities in the expressions of these phenomena. In Chapter 2, more details will be provided on how aging and development occur in both cultural and cross-cultural contexts.

SUMMARY

In this introductory chapter, concepts and perspectives that are considered relevant to the subject of aging and adult development in the developing world were introduced. Because some of these concepts are the subject of much research, for example, individualism and collectivism, only a summary review could be permitted due to space constraints.

The characteristics of the developing world as delineated by the United Nations were discussed, and the United Nations standards of development were discussed as separate from Westernization. Clarification was provided for other concepts that are similar but confusing, such as indigenous and universal psychologies; culture and cross-cultural psychology; and aging, senescence, and human development.

Because of the inadequacy of existing acculturation models, a new approach for understanding cultural contact between the developed and the developing worlds, based on a *supply* and *demand* paradigm, was introduced.

2

Aging and Adult Development in Context

Each one of us develops and functions within a cultural milieu. It is therefore difficult, if not impossible, to discuss human development devoid of the cultural environment within which it occurs. In this chapter, related perspectives that will help us understand the importance of aging and human development within both cultural and cross-cultural contexts will be presented. Aging and human development are life-span phenomena on which biological and cultural factors play important roles at different times.

As biological declines become more prominent in later life, the role that culture plays becomes even more important than before. Human development (ontogenesis) proceeds from conception to old age (Baltes, Reese, & Lipsitt, 1980; Dixon & Lerner, 1988; Neugarten, 1996) but in a multidimensional, multifunctional, and dynamic manner (P. B. Baltes, 1997; Magnusson, 1996; Lerner, 1991). It means, therefore, that ontogenetic trajectory varies at both intra- and interindividual levels.

Generally, life-span theorists conceptualize life-span development under two dimensions: Functional (Baltes, Staudinger, & Lindenberger, 1999) or Socio-logical typologies (Dannefer & Uhlenberg, 1999), stressing both person and societal levels' contributions to aging and human development.

THE FUNCTIONAL DIMENSION OF AGING AND HUMAN DEVELOPMENT

The Functional dimension identifies a category of behavior for study, (for example, perception, information processing, and identity), and then explains the mechanisms responsible for the changes experienced. From this perspective, researchers have described human development as involving both gains and losses in functional areas, and intelligence is one of such areas where both gains and losses have been identified (Baltes, Staudinger, & Lindenberger, 1999).

Biological Basis of Functional Dimension

As mentioned earlier, there is the saliency of biological impetus in devel-opment during the early stages of the life span. One reason for this occurrence is that the benefits of evolutionary selection decrease with age (Finch, 1996; Jazwinski, 1996). For example, human functioning, especially reproduction, is at its prime during the early part of the life span. After maturity, which occurs around 30 and with aging, the functional quality of the genes, both in expression and mechanisms, decreases (Baltes, Staudinger, & Lindenberger, 1999). The waning of biological impetus after maturity is only one aspect of the functional approach. Another aspect is the negative biological degradation, (e.g., as a result of wear and tear, which we shall discuss in detail in the next chapter), that occurs from the beginning of the life span but becomes more prominent in later life.

Cultural Basis for the Functional Dimension

As biological impetus begins to decline and negative biological effects begin to set in more prominently, the impact of culture, more than ever before, becomes very important (Valsiner & Lawrence, 1997). Culture helps to augment or attenuate losses that come from biological weakening and aging, as is evidenced from cognitive training and support to maintain previous levels of performance into old age (Dixon & Backman, 1995; Hoyer & Rybash, 1994). As Baltes, Staudinger, & Lindenberger (1999) noted, the increase in the average life expectancy witnessed in industrialized societies in the second half of the twentieth century was not due to changes in genetic make-up but to advances in culture, especially biomedical technology.

But how much culture is able to accomplish in augmenting or reducing losses that come from biological declines will be affected by the amount of physiological decline that has already taken place in the individual (Baltes, Staudinger, & Lindenberger, 1999). This is because an asymptote level is reached beyond which it becomes difficult to maintain the same level of performance even with more training (P. B. Baltes, 1997; P. B. Baltes & Smith, 1997).

At both intra- and interindividual levels, physiological declines do vary (Hoyer & Rybash, 1994; Lindenberger & Baltes, 1997; Schaie, 1996); therefore, in order to adapt to these declines, older people need to reallocate their resources either for growth, for maintenance and resilience, or for regulation of loss. While those for growth obviously decline, resources for maintenance and resilience and for the regulation of loss increase, or should increase (Staudinger, Marsiske, & Baltes, 1995). Growth behaviors are defined as those aimed at reaching higher levels of functioning or adaptive capacity, (for example, increasing perceptual speed), whereas maintenance behaviors are those intended to keep the same levels of functioning after a loss has occurred or in the face of new challenges. However, when it is not possible to maintain or recover losses, there is organization or mobilization of lower level functioning, (for example, dependency). It is important to note that in all of these responses to age-related declines, there is always the potential for the development of new behaviors, new knowledge and values, and new environmental features. Invariably, such responses will lead to better ways of adapting to changes (P. B. Baltes & Baltes, 1990; Brandtstadter, 1998; Dixon & Backman, 1995), and sometimes to *development;* in other words, deficits or losses can constitute a momentum for human development in later life. For example, they could lead to a heightened sense of religion, the meaning of life, and one's finitude. All these are areas of *development* that come from losses and they lend credence to the multidirectional pathway of the human state in later life (M. M. Baltes & Carstensen, 1999).

The Sociological Dimension

The Sociological dimension, on the other hand, involves the periodization of development (Darling & Lawrence, 1994), largely aided by society. The approach examines life structures at different times of the life span, but without explaining the mechanisms that bring about such changes. For example, marriage typically occurs earlier in the life span, perhaps due to an internal biological mechanism within the individual or to societal norm. Sometimes societal norms are biologically driven as seen in age periodization (Valsiner & Lawrence, 1997), but not necessarily so. For example, the typical age for girls to marry in one society may be 16 whereas in another society it is 25 (due to differences in educational opportunities), and even within the same society this could differ across different generations.

In both the *Functional* and *Sociological* dimensions of aging and human development, culture plays either an interventionist role, as in the case of the Functional dimension, or a co-constructivist one, as in the case of the Sociological dimension. In either case, culture provides a context for aging and human development to occur.

THE CULTURAL ENVIRONMENT AS CONTEXT FOR AGING AND ADULT DEVELOPMENT

Bronfenbrenner (1979) proposed a schema for understanding the child's interactions beyond the immediate environment, which is usually the home. The child's environment is conceived as going beyond the people with whom the child interacts on a face-to-face basis or the objects with which the child directly comes into contact. Also important is the interconnectedness within and between the different levels of the environment that influence the child's development.

Although Bronfenbrenner (1979) essentially described the world of the child, we believe that his principle is also relevant to the world of an adult. Apart from the immediate environment called the *microsystem* (for the adult, this would include members of his or her household), the next layer of environment, in which the adult can also participate, is the *mesosystem* (the workplace). The *exosystem*, the following layer, is that environment which the person never enters, but is, however, affected by what happens there (for the adult, this would include the government or bureaucracy). Bronfenbrenner (1993) defines the *macrosystem*, the outermost layer, as consisting of "the overarching pattern of micro-, meso-, and exo-systems characteristic of a given culture, subculture, or other extended social structures" (p. 25). This layer is made up of the belief systems, resources, hazards, lifestyles, opportunity structures, life course options, and patterns of social interchange found in any group. In Bronfenbrenner's model, culture plays an interventionist role, but there are other models that point to a co-constructivistic relationship between the individual and his or her environment.

In Valsiner and Lawrence's (1997) model, the directional path of development occurs as a result of regulators that are both external and internal to the individual. Examples of external regulators are social class membership, ethnic group membership, gender, and religion, and based on these external regulators, it is possible to predict how the individual would behave. But the individual has internal regulators also, which are the internalized ideals of how to behave fostered by that individual's historical antecedents (family or ethnic group membership). For example, an individual learns how to behave as a member of his or her family or ethnic group. While both external and internal regulators complement each other, they could also contradict each other in the course of fostering development. Age periodization is an example. It is formulated by society, perhaps based on biological development and/or the perceived competencies and expectations for individuals in a particular culture (Goodnow, Cashmore, Cotton, & Knight, 1984), or across different cultures (Schlegel & Barry, 1991). However, how each individual constructs his or her own experience (or personal culture) within each age period or social structure could vary (Valsiner, 1989). For example, within the domains of marriage and family, multiple trajectories are possible (Bhatt, 1991), with some women choosing to be home full time while others choose to work. Also, some choose to have children, no children, many children, or few children. Therefore, the nexus of internal and external forces provides opportunity for multiple developmental trajectories to develop and also for culture to be reorganized (Devereux, 1963), allowing the individual to become more open to new ideas or ways of being.

As discussed earlier, individual abilities, needs, and values influence the choices people make within a particular social structure, and even when the social structure is very rigid, they can still exert their own goals to change their life trajectories. For example, Wikan (1982) describes how women with authoritarian husbands within a strict Muslim community were still able to create their own experiences by asking their husbands to change houses or jobs. We suggest that the type of interaction that takes place between the individual and the social structures within a particular culture is similar to that which occurs between the individual and a foreign cultural element, as espoused in our *supply* and *demand* model in Chapter 1. But the social environment is only one aspect of the ecology of the individual. The physical environment is another and there are models like Berry's (1976, 1979) that recognize this aspect of the ecology.

Berry's (1976, 1979) co-constructivist model explains how the individual and populations "adapt" to their environment through reciprocal actions. But Berry's model identifies essentially two levels of the human ecology (the physical and sociopolitical contexts). The physical environment, for example, temperature and soil quality, is more or less constant whereas the sociopolitical context, type of government and educational system is subject to changes. As the two levels influence the individual (and group) and vice-versa, biological and cultural adaptations will emerge. Biological adaptation is seen in genetic transmission while cultural adaptation is accomplished through cultural transmission.

THE CROSS-CULTURAL ENVIRONMENT AS CONTEXT FOR AGING AND ADULT DEVELOPMENT

Except for explaining differences and similarities in peoples of different cultures (Greenfield, 1994; Mundy-Castle, 1974), it is difficult to find models explaining cross-cultural contributions to human development and aging. This is perhaps due to the belief that human development can only be understood within a particular cultural context such as in an indigenous and relativistic psychology school. And when cross-cultural contacts occur they lead to changes and most researchers are more interested in how the individual, and group, adjust to such changes, as a result of acculturation (Mishra, Sinha & Berry, 1996).

Yet the cross-cultural environment provides a more fitting framework for explaining the different developmental trajectories of people in developing societies, including members of ethnic minority groups in developed societies. Due to the relatively high level of development of the developed world and of the dominance of Western culture, Western education, wage employment, Western medicine, the developed world provides a model for the developing world on how to develop. It therefore invariably constitutes an environmental dimension that is likely to influence human developmental trajectory in the developing world. But there are other environmental dimensions of the cross-cultural environment of the developing world that would influence aging and human development. These are the Global dimension, the developed (Western) dimension, and the developing (non-Western) dimension (Eyetsemitan, 2002a). Examples of items that characterize each environmental dimension are presented in Table 2.1.

Table 2.1
Examples of Items in the Global, Developed, and Developing Dimensions of the Cross-Cultural Environment

Global	Developed	Developing
High Life Expectancy	Western Medicine	Native Medicine
High literacy rate	Western Education	non-Western Education
Gender equity	Christianity	non-Christian religions
Senescence	Advanced technology	Simple Technology
Death	Industrialization	Small scale / family businesses
	Urbanization	Rural
	Democracy	Authoritarianism; respect for age
	English / French languages	Native languages
	Individualism	Collectivism

The Global dimension represents the universal cultural indexes that the United Nations identifies as important for high-level human development. Using its Human Development Index (HDI) tools, the United Nations measures the performance of countries in areas such as literacy rate, life expectancy, and gender equity. The United Nations does not prescribe a particular route for achieving these global standards of development but uses its agencies such as WHO and UNESCO to create a global culture especially in the less developed countries of the world. These agencies have country and regional offices around the world pushing the agenda of the United Nations.

The United Nations is not alone in creating a global environmental dimension. There are several Western nonprofit organizations like the Carnegie Foundation, the Ford Foundation, the Rockefeller Foundation, and World Vision that supplement the efforts of the United Nations. It is, however, difficult to determine if their efforts fit under a global environment or under the developed world dimension. As mentioned in Chapter 1, while the United Nations sets standards of development, it does not prescribe the route through which those standards should be met. As long as Western nonprofit organizations meet these criteria, then they would, along with the United Nations, be creating a global environment. However, if a Western approach (literacy in English as opposed to literacy in the mother tongue) is presented as the equivalent of the global environment (literacy), then the efforts of these nonprofit organizations would fit under the developed world environment dimension.

In addition to cultural change, biological changes that are universally shared (senescence) help to create a global environment. The experience of death is universally shared, and each society has practices in place to recognize such end-of-life experience. Thus in a way biological changes help to periodize aging and human development more or less uniformly across different societies. For example, the typical age to marry, to have children, and to start a career would biologically favor the early adulthood stage rather than the late adulthood stage

(Baltes, Staudinger, & Lindenberger, 1999), while retirement timing would typically occur in the late adulthood stage when biological declines become more pronounced. Not surprisingly, therefore, in most societies, the workforce is dominated by young people, and even employers' hiring practices are somewhat geared toward ensuring this. Although life expectancy generally varies between the developed and developing worlds, the influence of biology (Baltes, Staudinger, & Lindenberger, 1999) is still prominent across cultures. Therefore the global environment results from both cultural and biological imperatives.

Another environmental dimension is the developed world, made up of Westernization influences—education, language, technology, medicine, and individualism (Cowgill & Holmes, 1972: modernization influences). Cowgill and Holmes (1972) suggest that the elderly in developing societies lose their high status and respect as a result of modernization influences—urbanization, education, medical technology. However, modernization influences could positively affect aging and development in the developing world as they have done in the industrialized world during the second half of the twentieth century (Baltes, Staudinger, & Lindenberger, 1999).

The dimension of the developing world includes native medicine and spiritualism, local languages, non-Western education system, simple technology, and collectivism (see Eyetsemitan 2002a, for details). There is the temptation to understand aging and human development only from this dimension (Azuma, 1984; Bronfenbrenner, 1979; Enrique, 1990; Kim, 1990; D. Sinha, 1986; 1993: "indigenous psychology"). However, the other dimensions of the cross-cultural environment discussed earlier do have influences on aging and human development trajectories, and to restrict our understanding of aging and human development to only this dimension would be limiting.

In conceptualizing three dimensions of the cross-cultural environment, it becomes easier to comprehend the range of possible interactions (based on our *supply* and *demand* model) between the individual and his or her environment. For example, the Hindu religion believes in the cyclical nature of existence but Christianity does not (LeGoff, 1984). Therefore, a Hindu religion adherent (a reflection of the developing world dimension) would have a different cognitive style and developmental trajectory than a Christian (a reflection of the developed world dimension). And both individuals will have a different developmental trajectory and cognitive style than another individual who accommodates the two religions. "Accommodation behavior" is a phenomenon described among Indians (see Mishra, Sinha & Berry, 1996; but also see Harmon, 1996, and Steen & Mazonde, 1999 for their studies in other societies). Steen and Mazonde (1999) studied the health-seeking behavior and attitudes of 212 tuberculosis (TB) patients in Botswana. They reported that patients who believed that TB was caused from the breaking of taboos (Tswana) used modern medicine for symptom relief, but sought traditional treatment for the perceived cause of the disease. In another study reflecting "accommodation" behavior in the South Pacific, Harmon (1996) reported that traditional paganism continued to prosper in the islands of the South Pacific despite the people's supposed conversion to Christianity. While Christianity was invoked for public consumption, paganism still ran deep in all the clans and generations, and in conversions.

Because the individual's interaction with his or her cross-cultural environment will be influenced by a *supply* and *demand* dynamic, we propose the following interaction outcomes:

1. The Individual and the Developing World dimension: An example would be a Botswana native who only seeks the help of a native healer for medical treatment.

2. The Individual and the Developing and Developed World dimensions: An example would be a Botswana native who seeks both Western and native medical treatments (accommodation behavior).

3. The Individual and the Developing and Global World dimensions: An example would be a Botswana native who is literate only in his or her native language.

4. The Individual and the Developed and Global World dimensions: An example would be a Botswana native who is literate only in a Western language (e.g., English).

5. The Individual and the Developing, Developed, and Global World dimensions: An example would be a Botswana native who is literate in both English and his or her native language.

Although we might say that every society, both developed and developing, is influenced by other cultures, the cross-cultural environment has had more influence on the worldview of non-Westerners than on Westerners (Sodowsky, Maguire, & Johnson, 1994). For example, as a result of urban residency, English language fluency and Western education individualist behaviors have been predicted among Sri Lankans (Freeman, 1997).

A distinction, however, has to be made between Western individualism and non-Western individualism; a distinction based primarily on the respective environments. Whereas in Western societies, the different layers of the environment—government, larger society, work, family (Bronfenbrenner, 1979)—reinforce individualistic values, this could not be said for non-Western societies. In Western developed societies, from government policies to child-raising styles there is consistency in individualistic pursuits. In non-Western societies, on the other hand, this consistency is not there; a person with individualist values might be forced to behave as a collectivist because of the different demands of his or her environmental layer (Bronfenbrenner, 1979). While the work environment might reinforce individualist values, the home environment might require collectivist behaviors. For instance, there are no laws and/or general societal expectations in the United States requiring an adult child to take care of his or her frail elderly parent, but there are such laws and especially such expectations of adult children to take care of their parents in most developing societies. For example, in Singapore, the government housing policy and the normative patterns of care obligation are influential in the coresidency arrangements found between an adult child with his or her elderly parent (Mehta, Osman, & Alexander, 1995). Therefore, to discuss individualistic and collectivistic values at the personal level without scrutinizing how the different layers of the environment within each society might reinforce those values will be insufficient.

In the next chapter, theories and perspectives on the biology of aging and adult development are presented. Although the theories and perspectives represent Western views, biological changes (senescence) fit into the Global dimension. Given the likely influence of the Developing world dimension, however, the manifestations of some biological changes in the developing world might be different.

SUMMARY

Life-span researchers approach studies in aging and development essentially from two perspectives. One perspective looks at the mechanism behind changes in functional areas like intelligence, memory, and perceptual speed. Most researchers in this area note that the changes involve both losses and gains, and intelligence is one of such areas. Whereas biology is largely responsible for the losses that come with aging, culture is largely responsible for the gains. This approach to the study of the life span is known as the Functional approach or the Sociological approach.

The other perspective considers the effect of societal structures on aging and development. Unlike the first perspective, this approach does not consider the mechanisms behind change, but rather it emphasizes the interface between the individual and culture. While various dimensions of culture within a particular society will influence aging and development, the individual and society affect each other in a co-constructivistic manner. But the individual's environment is also cross cultural and includes the global, developed, and developing dimensions. The interaction between the individual and the cross-cultural environment also occurs in a co-constructivistic manner.

3

Physical and Biological Aspects of Aging and Adult Development

Aging begins from the day we are born, but the changes that come with aging (senescence) are gradual and become more pronounced in the adult years. Fortunately, normative changes that accompany senescence do not imply that our entire organ system has considerably declined once we have passed the age of 30. There is a wide variation among different systems and organs in our bodies, as well as among individuals, in terms of whether or not we will age rapidly. Our sociocultural environment is one of the main factors that affect the aging process. It is thus important to distinguish between *primary aging*, which represents the inevitable physical changes that are universally shared as a result of aging, and *secondary aging*, which may result from environmental events that are widely shared, and are not inevitable (Busse, 1969).

In this chapter, some theories and perspectives of biological and physical aging will be reviewed. These theories and perspectives help us to appreciate the basic declines that accompany senescence and also to recognize that aging is a universal phenomenon. We will then identify normal changes that occur in several organ systems in the body following senescence. Where necessary, we will discuss some of the deviations from the normal aging process that arise from diseases in these systems. Before we briefly review these theories, we would like to emphasize two key points. First, physiological changes do not automatically result in functional changes. Therefore, a person's bodily system may undergo considerable physical change and yet the person's functioning may not be noticeably affected. Second, we support the position proposed by some earlier contributors (Whitbourne, 1985) that the impact of physiological change cannot be truly understood devoid of its psychological context. A person who believes that he or she is losing his eyesight and interprets this to mean that he or she is helpless will be more incapacitated by the decline in eyesight than someone in a similar physical condition who does not feel incapacitated. The point that will be stressed throughout this chapter is that the physical and social elements of culture (Berry, 1976, 1979) play a significant role in defining this psychological context.

BIOLOGICAL THEORIES OF SENESCENCE

Like many phenomena of this nature, no single cause or mechanism has been proposed that fully accounts for senescence. In fact, approximately 300 different theories have been proposed to explain senescence (Medvedev, 1990). The theories that we will briefly discuss in this chapter represent some of the more commonly used theories and encompass the salient points espoused by many other theories of senescence. They also satisfy the four minimum requirements that Strehler (1986) suggests must be met before any biological theory can be considered viable:

1. The process must be universal; that is, all members of the species must experience the phenomenon.

2. The process must result in physiological decline.

3. The process must be progressive; that is, losses must be gradual over time.

4. The loss must be intrinsic; that is, it cannot be corrected by the organism.

These guidelines help to distinguish between the degeneration that comes from diseases like arthritis and Alzheimer's and those that result from normal aging.

Wear-and-Tear Theory

This theory contends that organisms age because their organ systems accumulate damage from the frequent abuse they face in the course of daily functioning. Thus, like a machine that eventually wears out after extensive use, our bodies, too, gradually deteriorate over time. Because the several organs and systems in the body are not subject to the same rate of usage and abuse, both the onset and magnitude of deterioration in the aging process vary from one organ system to another. Stress and other environmental conditions such as air and noise pollution, may, for instance, exacerbate the regular wear and tear of organ systems and thus affect the respiratory and hearing systems respectively.

Age-related processes such as *osteoarthritis* seem to validate the claim by the wear-and-tear theory of problems that can result from lifelong use. However, these kinds of effects may be the results of aging, and may not adequately explain why we age (Hayflick, 1994). According to Hayflick, even if wear and tear represents a fundamental cause of senescence, it likely would operate at the molecular level; though even at this microscopic level, these changes could still be a sign of another cause of aging.

Autoimmune Theory

The immune system acts as an important defense against any foreign substances that may invade the body. According to the autoimmune theory of senescence, the immune system becomes not only less efficient in producing antibodies to fight foreign invaders, but also develops a propensity, with age, to attack the body's own proteins. This theory is predicated on two main findings. First, as we age, the immune system is no longer able to produce antibodies in sufficient quantities. Because of the decline in the ability of the immune system to produce antibodies, we are more likely to acquire and manifest diseases of old age that an efficient immune system, perhaps in our youth, may have kept in check.

Second, the declining immune system may become defective and produce antibodies that attack not just foreign bodies, but also mistakenly attack and damage the body's own proteins. A possible candidate for the decline in immune system functioning is the thymus gland, located in the upper part of the chest, that produces disease-fighting white blood cells (T cells), a vital component of the immune system. The thymus gland begins to wither after adolescence and by middle- to late-adulthood, the shrinkage is considerable. By age 50, humans are said to retain only 5 to 10 percent of the thymus gland's original mass (Hayflick, 1994). Proponents of the autoimmune theory suggest that it is this deterioration of the thymus that triggers the eventual decline of the entire immune system.

The autoimmune theory is intuitively appealing, but has a number of drawbacks. One problem is that we can only indirectly infer the decline of the immune system from the greater incidence of disease in old age. However, disease is pathological and not a normal condition of senescence. There is no independent evidence to show that decrements in the immune system affect normative senescence. Also, like the wear-and-tear theory, the autoimmune theory does not explain why the immune system declines with age. It is also unable to explain why more older adults do not suffer from autoimmune diseases.

Cross-Linkage Theory

The cross-linkage theory (Bjorksten, 1974) focuses on age-related changes that occur to the protein called collagen. Collagen is an important connective tissue found in most organ systems; in fact, almost one third of all the protein in our body is collagen. Cross-links are essential in joining parallel molecules of collagen together. Proponents of this theory argue that with age, cross-links form some kind of a scaffold that connects a larger number of neighboring molecules, a process that may impede the metabolic process by obstructing the passage of nutrients and wastes in and out of cells. Consequently, the tissue becomes less pliable and may indeed shrink. Wrinkling of the skin is a clear example of changes in our collagen, but collagen changes also occur in the lens of the eyes, the blood vessels, muscle tissues, and other internal organs not outwardly seen as the body's skin.

Cellular Aging Theory

This theory is based on the premise that there is a limit to the number of times cells can divide, supposedly limiting the life span of complex organisms. Hayflick and Moorehead (1961) reported from laboratory studies that cells undergo a finite number of replications, indicating that cells appear to be programmed to follow a biological clock. The number of possible divisions depends on the age of the donor organism, a process known as the Hayflick phenomenon (Hayflick, 1994). Cells from human fetal tissue, for instance, are capable of 40 to 60 divisions, but those from human adults are capable of only approximately 20 divisions. Some researchers initially believed that the Hayflick limit could account for why cells eventually die. However, some research evidence has shown that cells from some older adults sometimes double as often as those of younger adults (Harrison, 1985). Thus, at least in humans, the exact role of the Hayflick limit in senescence remains inconclusive. The most that can be said at this point is that the theory indicates that aging is possibly genetically programmed.

The Rate of Living Theory

The theory is based on the notion that we are born with a limited amount of some substance, potential energy, or physiological capacity that can be used up at various rates (Hayflick, 1994). If it is expended early, one dies young; if the rate of expenditure is slow, aging will be slowed and one will live longer.

Some variation of the rate of living theory suggests that the amount of calories a person consumes has a great influence on senescence. Laboratory experiments with animals (e.g., mice) have demonstrated that reducing caloric intake by 65% increased an animal's life span by as much as 35%. Although controlled experiments on humans have not been performed, there are some cross-cultural data that provide some credence to this viewpoint. For example, Okinawa, where people eat only 60% of the normal Japanese diet, has 40 times as many centenarians per capita as elsewhere in Japan. In addition, Okinawans also have only about half the incidence of cardiovascular disease, diabetes, and cancer, diseases that tend to increase with age (Monczunski, 1991). However, these data are correlational only, and thus should be interpreted with caution.

The main problem with the crux of the rate of living theory is that the substance or physiological capacity that supposedly becomes depleted in animals is unknown, and there is no evidence to indicate that it even exists. Also, there is not even anecdotal evidence to suggest that people whose rate of living or energy expenditure is high age at an accelerated pace.

PHYSIOLOGICAL CHANGES IN SENESCENCE

We shall discuss both primary and secondary aging in developed societies based on these theories. Although these biological theories provide ways to describe physiological forces, we have to emphasize that these in turn interact with the psychological and sociocultural forces. In the next section, we will discuss some of the normal changes that occur in several systems of the body. The initial discussion under each system will be based on research that has been conducted in the developed world. Next, we will attempt to discuss research evidence from the developing world with the view to identifying some of those processes in senescence that are culture-general or culture-specific. Where such empirical research is not available, we will attempt to, on the basis of extrapolation, and, in some cases our personal observations, generate some viable hypotheses that may, hopefully, serve as possible research agenda items for future researchers. The following systems will be discussed: body mass, the skin, hair, musculoskeletal system, the nervous system, vision, hearing, taste and smell, respiratory system, urinary system, and sex life.

Aging and Body Mass

There are changes in both body mass and composition as a result of aging. A major cause of lowered weight observed in most older people is the loss of water, which makes up, on the average, 54 to 60% of the body mass for males, and 46 to 52% for women (Blumberg, 1996). Fat is substituted for lean body mass, a condition known as sarcopenia, which usually accelerates after menopause and when a person is very old (Rosenberg, 1989). The decline in elasticity of muscle tissue due to collagen loss results in weight gain, beginning from the middle years up to about age 55, when it begins to drop (Hayflick, 1994). However, a vigorous exercise regimen can prevent a significant loss of muscle tone. Many elderly in the developed world are aware of the benefits of regular exercise and generally have reasonable access to exercise facilities.

Aging of the Skin

Changes in the texture and appearance of the skin and hair are perhaps the most visible signs of senescence. It is the appearance of the skin that very often determines our stereotyped conclusions about a person's age. As stated earlier, almost one third of all the protein in our body is collagen. With age, collagen fibers that make up the connective tissue lose much of their flexibility, resulting in the wrinkling of the skin. However, the ultraviolet light from the sun itself also has adverse effects on the skin leading to wrinkles, dryness, and toughness of the skin. In response, the body produces melanin, a dark pigmentation, which helps to protect the skin from the damaging effects of sunlight, particularly from the sun's ultraviolet rays.

The skin is able to shed the dry and flaky outer skin layer caused by adverse environmental factors with new cells. This process is carried out by the *dermis*, a layer of connective tissues located under the outer skin. However, the dermis loses its own elasticity with age, thus causing the outer skin to sag and wrinkle and to not replace the dead cells as often. This problem with the dermis is seen earlier in women than in men and may begin in their 20s or 30s because women have less oil in the sebaceous glands, which helps to make the skin elastic.

Also, the skin heals slowly from cuts due to the declines in elasticity. Gilchrest (1982) reports that it will take 50% more time for those over age 65 to heal from a wound than for those under 35 years.

Changes in the Hair

Gradual thinning and graying of the hair for both men and women are some of the obvious changes that occur with age. Graying of hair is usually caused by the loss of melanin-producing cells and the subsequent loss of melanin, a pigment that gives color to the hair and skin (Hayflick, 1994). Genetics clearly play a part, as some people have gray hair earlier than others; some people start to have gray hair as early as in their early 20s. In the other extreme, as much as 35% of older people are not gray, or do not become gray until they are very old.

Body hairs generally become less numerous with age, although hair growth may, in certain areas such as the ears and nostrils, actually increase with age. The diameter of our hair strands reduces by as much as 20% by the time we are in our 70s. These changes are obviously different in men and women. Pattern baldness, marked by hair loss on the scalp, tends to occur in young men and appears to be genetically determined. In many women, declines in the levels of the female hormone estrogen are believed to result in hair growth above the lip. In general, however, slower growth and loss of hair in both sexes frequently accompany aging and do not seem to be genetically induced.

Changes in the Musculoskeletal System

Changes in height and stature are some of the other manifestations of senescence, with an estimated average decline in height of as much as three inches. According to the Baltimore Longitudinal Studies, height reduction at an average of one-sixteenth inch per year usually begins at age 30. This reduction is attributable to loss of bone mineral, which is related to decline in estrogen levels in menopausal women, and although less pronounced in older men, their decline is due to decreases in testosterone levels (Rudman, Drinka, Wilson, Mattson, Scherman, Cuisinier, & Schultz, 1991). *Osteoporosis*, a disease of the bone found mainly in women, adds to the reduction in height. Vitamin supplements rich in calcium are recommended to help reduce bone loss. Our maximum size and height is reached at about age 25, and thereafter begins to decline. Our strength and stamina also decline as we age; however, being active and exercising helps to reduce these declines.

Changes in the Nervous System

The nervous system is our body's main communication system, made up of billions of interconnected cells called *neurons*. Neurons are the individual cells that receive, integrate, and transmit information. The neuron is the basic building block of the nervous system. Although there are different types of neurons, they are basically variations of the same fundamental process. Each neuron consists of a cell body or soma that contains the nucleus; dendrites, the bushy branches that are specialized to receive information; and the axon, a long thin fiber that transmits signals by releasing chemical substances stored at its terminal endings. These chemical substances, called *neurotransmitters*, are released into a junction, the *synapse*, between the sending neuron and other neighboring neurons. Neurotransmitters are essentially chemical messengers that the nervous system relies upon to communicate information between neurons. This information is fundamental to behavior and plays a key role in everything from muscle movements to moods and mental health.

With the passage of time, some of the neurons begin to die. Neuronal loss commences at about age 30 and is compounded by alcohol consumption, cigarette smoking, and the breathing of polluted air. The brain's size is reduced as we age and changes occur to the neurotransmitters. According to researchers with the Baltimore Longitudinal Study of Aging, the slowing down of reaction time could to be as much as 20% between ages 20 and 60 (Shock, Greulich, Andres, Arenberg, Costa, Jr., et al., 1984). This could be partly attributed to the slower transmission of neurotransmitters between neurons. Slowdown in reaction time requires the elderly to take their time to cross the street, to answer the doorbell or telephone, and to make decisions.

Many older adults adjust to the reduced speed of both motor and cognitive functions by modifying their physical environment or personal routines, such as allocating more time for doing certain tasks and avoiding rush situations. In the developed world where there is greater structure, an older person may, for instance, shop at off-peak hours or at smaller stores.

Changes in the Sensory Functions

Our senses of vision, hearing, smell, taste, and touch all decline as we age, and at a more rapid rate after the ages of 45 to 55. These sense organs help us to interact with our ecocultural environment. The rate of decline varies from individual to individual and is partly due to heredity and to our environment. Furthermore, all the senses may not decline at the same rate.

It is important to understand some concepts that help to explain how our senses function. *Sensation* is the process of receiving information through any of our sense organs, vision, hearing, smell, taste, and touch, while *perception* is the interpretation or processing of the information received through our sense organs. This interpretation occurs in the brain, but our values, beliefs, memory all play a part. Therefore, cultural and ethnic differences play important roles in perception. For example, some Westerners describe non-Western foods as bland and that they are not "sweet"; however, for the non-Westerners the foods are "sweet," and of course not bland. While we understand the sensation of sweetness, the perception of sweetness is relative. The same goes for smell; what stinks for the people in one culture may be a sweet aroma to the people in another culture.

Sensory threshold is the minimum intensity level at which a stimulus is detected. There are both individual and cross-cultural differences in detection threshold, as well as differences among the various organ systems in the individual. *Recognition threshold* is the intensity of the stimulus a person needs in order to recognize the stimulus. For example, from our observation, Westerners have a lower sensory threshold and a higher recognition threshold for spicy, hot foods than non-Westerners. Last, *sensory discrimination* is the minimum difference required to distinguish between two or more stimuli. We will now discuss the senses in turn, beginning with our most influential sense: vision.

Changes in Vision

Our visual sensory organ is the eye, which is often likened to a camera. The visual stimulus, light, first passes through a glass-like, transparent covering of the eye's surface called the *cornea*. The amount of light that passes through the cornea is moderated by the size of the opening of the muscle known as the *iris*, the colored part of the eye. The opening in the iris is called the *pupil*. The size of the pupil adjusts automatically to the amount of available light; the more intense the light, the smaller the opening. From the iris, the light encounters the *lens*, which adjusts to the image by changing its thickness; it thickens in response to nearby objects and flattens when it focuses on distant objects. This process, known as *accommodation*, is intended to project a clearer image of an object onto the *retina*. The actual receptors for vision, known as the *rods*, sensitive to intensity, and the *cones*, responsible mainly for color and acuity, are found in the retina. Once stimulated by light, the rods and the cones send neural messages through the *bipolar* and *ganglion* cells whose axons form the optic nerve to the brain.

Age-related changes in vision are attributed to structural changes affecting the eye. Changes occur to the cornea, making its smooth, round surface flatter and less smooth. The pupil becomes smaller and more fixed in size, thus the individual is less able to dilate his or her eyes and adjust to low light levels.

Therefore, in order to function effectively, older persons may need several times the level of light required by young people.

The lens of the eyes become relatively brittle, making it more difficult to accommodate, or focus on, nearby objects, a condition known as *presbyopia*. This condition begins at about the ages of 38 to 46, and occurs in about 42% of people aged 52 to 64, 73% of people aged 65 to 74, and 92% of those aged 75 and over (Hayflick, 1994). Using reading glasses or bifocals are ways to adjust to this problem.

Cloudiness of the lens is another problem, and when it is severe enough to prevent the lens from refracting light, this condition is known as a *cataract*. Jacques, Chylack, and Taylor (1994) linked the development of cataracts as we grow older to the lack of vitamins A, C, and E. However, removal of cataracts through eye surgery has proven to be highly successful (AHCPR, 1993).

Age-related changes in vision, while a disability, need not be a handicap if people are encouraged to make changes to their usual activities and environment, in order to adapt to their current level of visual functioning and needs.

Changes in Hearing

The auditory sense is very important for communication because we use our hearing for conversation, to localize sound, and to interpret the emotions in people's voices. Our auditory system has an outer part called the *pinna* (the part we see); the pinna gathers and funnels sound waves into the auditory canal to the *eardrum* (the tympanic membrane), a thin membrane that vibrates in response to sound waves, thus transmitting them to the middle and inner ear. The middle ear consists of the eardrum and three small bones: the *hammer*, the *anvil*, and the *stirrup*, collectively referred to as the *ossicles*. The ossicles form a three-stage lever system that converts fairly large movements with little force into smaller motions with greater force. The major function of the middle ear is amplification: it increases the magnitude of the air pressure. The stirrup is attached to the *oval window*, another vibrating membrane. The oval window transmits vibrations into the inner ear, made up of a circular snail-shaped structure called the *cochlea*. The cochlea contains two longitudinal membranes that divide it into three fluid-filled chambers; one of these membranes is called the *basilar membrane*. Vibrations in the fluids of the cochlea, caused mainly by the pressure from the oval window, press thousands of *hair cells* (the actual auditory receptors) to bend. This movement generates neural impulses that are transmitted to the brain for interpretation through the *auditory nerve*.

As we grow older, the pinna becomes elongated and rigid. Structural changes to the cochlea result in a decreased ability to hear higher-frequency sounds, a condition known as *presbycusis*. This decline in our auditory threshold can be detected by age 30 or even earlier. However, exposure to environmental noise over the life span can also cause *presbycusis* (Gordon-Salant, 1996). *Tinnitus,* a condition whereby the individual experiences a high-pitched ringing noise, is related to exposure to long-term environmental noise, especially in noisy work environments. Excessive wax accumulation is another cause of hearing loss. These losses can be mitigated by available aids that enable the individual to effectively cope or adapt to declines in auditory functioning.

In suggesting ways of improving communication between a practitioner and an aged patient, Kiyak (1996) provides the following guidelines for conversation with an elderly person that we think are also applicable in other settings:

1. Face the older person directly and maintain eye contact.
2. Sit somewhat close and maintain the same eye level with the older person.
3. Do not obstruct your face with your hands or objects while speaking.
4. Speak slowly and clearly, but do not exaggerate your speech.
5. Do not shout.
6. Avoid a noisy and distracting background.
7. Speak in a lower, but not monotonic, voice.
8. Repeat key points in more than one way.
9. If conveying specific information, for example, how to take medication, make the message clear and systematic.

Changes in Taste and Smell

Taste and smell are chemical senses in the sense that we sample molecules of the substances being perceived. These two senses are also intricately related, so we will discuss them together beginning with taste. Our sense of taste is important for food intake. Taste is sensed through *taste cells*, receptor neurons that are located on the *taste buds*. There are approximately 10,000 taste buds, most of which are located near the edges and back of the tongue. Taste buds are somewhat specialized; some are responsive to sweetness, others to bitterness, saltiness, sourness, and so forth.

The ability to detect the four primary tastes, salty, sweet, bitter, and sour decreases only slightly with age, and contrary to previous belief, there does not seem to be a loss in the number of taste buds in older people. However, older people may complain that their food has little or no taste. This is most likely due to a decline in smell (Brody, 1992), since the sense of smell is intricately involved in flavor. This process is known as *sensory interaction*. Because flavor provides much of the motivation to eat, older people are sometimes at risk of becoming malnourished. To avert becoming malnourished, older people are often encouraged to spice their food to enhance its flavor (Brody, 1992).

Smell constitutes an important part of our everyday functioning. The nature of an odor can warn us about potentially dangerous events, such as a fire, even before we see or feel it or signal us that a meal is being cooked. Smell also plays an important part in social relations. It is not surprising that billions of dollars are spent yearly on fragrances. Receptor cells for odor are in the *olfactory membrane,* located high up in each nostril. These neurons fire when a few molecules of the substance in gaseous form come into contact with them. Firing transmits information to the brain through the *olfactory nerve.*

Our ability to detect odors remains reasonably intact until in the 60s when it starts to decline rapidly (Murphy, 1986). There is a wide variation among individuals in the degree to which age affects olfactory declines. Even within the same individual, different odors may not be experienced to the same degree (Stevens & Cain, 1987). As stated earlier, one of the major consequences of decrements in olfactory functioning is that it may negatively impact eating, since smell plays an important role in flavor. In addition to affecting nutritional intake, the decline in being able to smell could pose safety hazards to elderly persons, especially in the failure to recognize gas odor or other dangerous substances. In the social arena, a decrease in our ability to detect unpleasant odors may render us unaware that we have body odors, causing serious embarrassment. Older adults who suffer from such conditions as urinary incontinence can easily be vulnerable to this type of embarrassment.

Changes in the Respiratory System

The functioning of the respiratory system declines with age. Our maximum breathing ability requires the functional combination of a variety of organ systems such as the respiratory, nervous, and muscular systems. As our maximum breathing capacity declines, we gradually lose the ability to maintain physical activities for a long time. The average amount of oxygen men between the ages of 25 and 70 can take in by a deep breath declines by 50%. However, this decline is slower for physically active than for sedentary healthy men. Due to environmental pollutants and infections, the respiratory system suffers the most punishment of all the body systems.

Changes in the Urinary System

Both our kidney and bladder change with age. The kidney decreases in weight and volume, and its filtering system, called the *glomeruli,* decreases by 30% between the ages of 30 to 65. By the time we are about 50, our bladder function may be reduced by as much as 50% for some individuals. The sensation for emptying the bladder is affected, leading to *urinary incontinence,* which makes older people avoid social outings for fear that they may not have access to a bathroom.

Changes in Sex Life

There are physiological changes in our sex lives that accompany senescence. Women, as they grow older, experience a reduction in the production of *estrogen* and *progesterone* by their ovaries during *menopause;* the depletion begins in the 40s as menstrual cycles become irregular, and between the ages of 50 to 55 it is usually complete in most women (Rykken, 1987). *Climacteric,* a term that applies to the decline of sexual hormones in both men and women, is marked by a loss of reproductive ability in women, and proceeds in three phases: premenopause, menopause, and postmenopause.

In premenopause, the ovaries stop producing eggs and monthly production of estrogen is significantly reduced. In menopause, there is a gradual cessation of the menstrual cycle; it occurs irregularly and this is related to a loss of the ovarian function. Menopause occurs when 12 consecutive months have passed without a menstrual period, and occurs around the age of 50 (Hayflick, 1994). Like the other systems discussed earlier, the onset of menopause varies form one individual to another. *Hot flashes,* skin flushing, *urogenital atrophy,* urinary tract changes, and bone changes have been associated with menopausal and postmenopausal conditions. However, nutrition, exercise, and herbal treatment have been found helpful in moderating the symptoms of menopause. Sociocultural factors, personality variables, and other cultural influences may play a role, aside from the physiological changes, in women's experiences before and after the climacteric (Jackson, Taylor, & Pyngolil, 1991).

Men also experience physiological changes that are age-related, although unlike the conspicuous reproductive aging that occurs in women, the senescence of the male reproductive system is more gradual. In fact, some question whether male climacteric occurs at all. Nevertheless, there seems to be sufficient evidence to indicate that there is a *male menopause* that starts between the ages of 45 and 54 years, due primarily to a decline in testosterone. Testosterone loss occurs gradually, at an average of approximately 1% a year and leads to reductions in muscle size and strength, adversely affecting the immune system responses and sexual interest and response. It has been found to be associated with increased calcium loss in the bones. Psychological states such as fatigue, depression, poor appetite, and irritability are also associated with male menopause (Diamond, 1997).

Erectile dysfunction can occur in older men. For both men and women, there is a theory of "use it or lose it" that suggests that sustained sexual activity throughout the life course helps to maintain a sexually virile old age; such virility is lost if sexual activity is not sustained.

THE DEVELOPING WORLD

PHYSIOLOGICAL CHANGES IN SENESCENCE

Aging and Body Mass

In developing societies where life expectancy is relatively low, the changes in body mass and composition are due to both primary and secondary aging. Fat infiltration into the body mass that occurs with senescence has been found in both Westerners (Mueller, Deutsch, & Malina, 1986) and among samples from Papua New Guinea (Norgan, 1987). Among elderly samples, a corresponding decline in muscle mass accounts for reduced metabolic rates and energy (Wurtman, Liberman, Tsay, & Nader, 1988).

Weight gain is compounded by a diet rich in fat and a lack of an exercise regimen. Whereas a lack of exercise may be common among urban dwellers, the tendency of older rural dwellers to depend on young people for help and assistance with chores and errands may contribute to a lack of exercise.

Another element of body mass involves its association with socioeconomic status in different cultures. According to Sobal (1991), while the developed world believes that thinness is better, especially for women, the traditional developing world believes that bigness is better than thinness. In West Africa, the term "fat" implies strength and beauty and is a symbol of wealth (Cassidy, 1991). However, it is important to effectively communicate the health risks associated with bigness or "fat" to enable individuals to make appropriate lifestyle changes.

Given the cross-cultural context of the developing world environment, people born in the same society would develop and age differently. For example, Lake, Staiger, and Glowinski (2000) studied the effect of Western culture on women's attitudes to eating and perceptions of body shape among 140 Hong Kong-born and Australian-born women aged 17–42 years. The result showed a significant difference in body shape perceptions with the Australian-born sample reporting greater dissatisfaction. But when separated into two groups, Western acculturized Hong Kong respondents expressed significantly greater displeasure in their eating habits and perceptions of body shape than traditional Hong Kong-born samples. Thus, even though born in the same society, the Western acculturized Hong Kong sample appeared to be influenced by the "Developed world" dimension of their environment while their traditional Hong Kong-born counterparts, by the "Developing world" dimension.

In planning changes, however, it is always important to recognize the *demand* values of the natives. For example, in Latin America, community initiatives in Costa Rica, Chile, and Argentina that empowered older people to plan their own programs, develop services, and advocate change, have been reportedly successful (Checkoway, 1994).

Aging and the Skin

Most of the developing world has tropical or near tropical climates. The inhabitants of Zaire, a country which is closer to the equator, have darker skin color, as a result of an over production of melanin, than the inhabitants of Algeria, which is farther away from the equator but also in Africa. The farther away one is from the equator, the lighter the skin color as we find with those inhabiting Europe. It is possible that the much higher rates of skin cancer among Europeans than sub-Saharan Africans may be due to the protective effect of melanin. Also, while skin flushing is one of the symptoms for light skinned menopausal women in Western societies, this will not be an applicable symptom to dark skinned women of Africa.

Changes in the Hair

The changes to hair in the developing world will be influenced by both genetic and environmental factors. Environmental stress may emanate from jobs, the loss of loved ones, modernization influences, and from other significant life events, just like in the developed societies. However, environmental stressors have to be perceived as either "good' or "bad," and will be influenced by gender, by adulthood stage, and by the perceived available social support. These intervening variables to environmental stress may account for differences among societies, and between the developed and developing societies.

Because the elderly are still venerated in the developing world, gray hair is a "badge" of honor for both males and females. According to Hooyman and Kiyak (1999), there is a stigma attached to the graying of hair in the United States, especially for women. Youthfulness is an advantage in developed societies, except where certain behaviors of young people are legally regulated through age restrictions, for example, purchase of alcohol, voting, and driving. However in developing societies youthfulness may not be an advantage. Apart from the legal age restrictions of certain behaviors, the roles and behaviors of young people are also subject to regulation through traditional customs and beliefs.

Changes in the Musculoskelatal System

The progressive loss of bone appears to be universal with the loss in women being two or three times higher than in men (Plato, 1987), thus osteoporosis, a disease that affects bone density, afflicts women more than men with implications for high financial cost over time (Berg & Cassels, 1992). While there appear to be racial differences in bone loss with non-Whites showing higher rates of declines than Whites (Evers, Orchard, & Haddad, 1985; Solomon, 1979), the cause of the difference may be cultural, as in nutritional deficiencies, or in combination with genetic factors (Albert & Cattell, 1994).

Taking vitamin supplements rich in calcium requires health education, especially for the rural elderly in developing societies. Even with health education, the cost of these supplements may be prohibitive. Young adults also require health education if declines begin at age thirty. A *modification approach* to the *supply* of calcium supplement should be adopted, especially if the *demand* for calcium intake is low. For example, fortifying stable foods such as rice with calcium and other essential vitamins will be one such approach. This way, it becomes easier to ensure a successful intake of vitamin supplements.

The tendency to become less active or to engage in less physical exercises occurs as one grows older because of declines in physical strength and stamina.

However, the tendency for elderly persons in developing societies to depend on their children for their needs exacerbates this situation. Since adult children are often conscious of their obligations toward parents, parental dependency is encouraged and reinforced and parents may in turn exercise their rights to be dependent.

Young adults with siblings and relatives as members of their households may also fall into this dependency trap. Unlike their counterparts in the developed world who do not have such living arrangements, these young adults may come to rely on siblings and relatives for doing the house chores, running errands, and helping to take care of their young children. Therefore, in order to avoid early declines in stamina and strength, physically challenging activities outside of the home may be required. During his early adulthood stage in Nigeria, the first author (Eyetsemitan) experienced firsthand what has just been described. As a young teacher at the university, he lived in a large apartment with a sibling and two relatives, one a young uncle and the other a distant relative. Both relatives were students at the same university, so they conveniently rode with him to and from campus. He also provided for their other needs. In return, the relatives insisted on doing the house chores and running errands. Prior to the arrival of his long-term guests, the author did the house chores and ran errands as a means of exercise. As an alternative, he then took to walking as a means of exercise. Even with walking, people who knew him would often stop and insist on giving him rides, thinking he had a car problem. Apparently, exercise for the sake of exercise was not, and is yet to become, a routine activity. This anecdote, and other similar instances that the authors have noted through casual observation, is one of such hypotheses that needs to be systematically tested in future research. Draper and Harpending (1994) suggest that the concept of "independence," which in the West means self-sustaining, may not apply to developing societies, where such a behavior may result in a person being branded as weird or a "witch," especially when there are others to help. A distinction is noted, however, between the individuals who are forced to be active and those who are active for the sake of being active (Draper & Harpending, 1994). Unlike their counterparts in the developed world, the elderly in developing societies who are "compulsorily active" are more likely to lack available support.

Changes in the Nervous System

Declines in nerve cells are also likely to occur with age, but there are also related ecocultural risk factors. In one study of 388 men and women in a rural area in northern India, neurological factors identified through history of impaired consciousness, gait disturbance, diminished tendon reflexes, and the presence of at least one primitive reflex, were implicated in cognitive impairment. The authors concluded that nutritional deficiencies might be a unique risk factor in these outcomes (Chandra, Dekosy, Pandav, Johnston, Belle, Ratchiff, & Ganguli, 1998).

Loss of neurons may be compounded by air pollution from automobiles and industrial plants and from refuse and forest-burning activities. Although some of these factors are also present in the developed world, we think that the risk is even higher in the developing world where there are very few regulations about emission standards, and even where they exist, they are not strictly enforced. In addition, the consumption of locally brewed alcohol (*ogogoro* or *brukutu* as it is known in some places in West Africa) is commonplace because it is relatively cheaper. Unfortunately the alcoholic content is unregulated. Cheap cost may lead to an over-consumption of locally brewed alcoholic beverages, with a likely higher than normal alcoholic content.

Apart from the cost factor, there are psychological reasons for the consumption of alcohol and other substances. A study conducted among 256 Nigerian motorcyclists, aged 13–70 years, showed that 98.4% of them regularly used alcohol, marijuana, amphetamines, valium, or other psychoactive substances to keep alert and fearless and to fight boredom and fatigue. There was no correlation between the age and education levels of the respondents and drug use.

In coping with declines in nervous system function, particularly reaction time, older people in the developing world may not feel constrained to adjust their time habits. It is more graceful for an elderly person to be slow in his movement. A "walking stick" or cane is even part of the dress code of an elderly person or of someone important, young or old, and does not indicate a handicapped status. On the other hand, to walk briskly reflects a high energy level and youthfulness and is a valued behavior in developed societies.

Changes in the Sensory Functions

Changes in Vision

From a physiological point of view, changes in vision that accompany senescence may be similar to what occurs in the developed world, and to some extent, even the psychological, social, and cultural implications of the changes (Beall & Goldstein, 1986). However, resources for individual adjustment to vision impairment like glasses, magnifying glasses, Braille, audio versions of books, and talking clocks may be inadequate or unavailable; so also is the adequacy or availability of medical attention like surgery for cataracts.

Beall and Goldstein (1986) conducted a cross-sectional study of Nepalese men, aged 50–88 years, and found that vision and hearing impairments affected the frequency of their outings and social contacts. Furthermore, they were less likely to retain their esteemed role as head of household. In the Polynesian society of Niue, Barker also reported the loss of social roles among decrepit elders, especially those who suffer from blindness (Barker, 1997). In this respect, the visual consequences of senescence in these societies may be reasonably negative. However, there are social roles elderly persons might perform in the community and within the extended family that may not be affected by vision loss. For example, visual impairment should not hinder elderly persons from providing words of wisdom and spiritual advice to the young. Barker (1997) noted that political and social influences in Polynesian society are acquired by middle age and maintained into later life by a competent person, even when significant declines in physical and mental abilities set in.

In developing societies, the nature of adjustment to declines in vision that elderly persons require is different. The concerns expressed about driving by older adults in the developed world may not be applicable, as few elderly persons in the developing world own cars, and with adult children and relatives, or paid drivers for the rich, to help with driving, self-driving is less common even among older adults who own cars.

Although government hospitals in the cities may be able to perform cataract surgery, the elderly persons may not be able to separate disease from normal aging, due to a high rate of illiteracy. This situation requires health education. This is another instance in which the demand and supply concept applies. Low demand could account for why more people may not be getting the benefit of effective medical interventions in the form of surgical treatment for conditions such as cataracts, if the lack of utilization is due to a failure to distinguish between normal aging process and disease. On the other hand, hospitals in most of the developing world lack both adequate equipment and qualified personnel. Therefore, a good number of the elderly who seek medical interventions may not be able to receive such help (see discussion of social policies in Chapter 8). In this instance, lower than optimum utilization of medical intervention will be due to a low supply of Western medical facilities.

Changes in Hearing

There is a high level of noise pollution in most urban centers of the developing world. Both industrial plants and traffic contribute to a large proportion of this noise. The noise from industrial plants not only affects the workers but also residents who live close to these plants, because of poor zoning laws or a lack of implementation of existing laws. Used by drivers to navigate through traffic and also by taxicab drivers to attract the attention of potential roadside passengers, horn honking also contributes to urban noise.

Noise pollution is more of an urban phenomenon, and it's likely to affect younger adults than older people, who are mostly rural dwellers.

In reviewing Kiyak's (1996) guidelines for conversation with an elderly person, the following should be noted:

1. In some cultures, a younger person may not maintain eye level contact in conversation with an elderly person. For example, depending on the situation, the Japanese avoid eye contact as a sign of respect and deference (Sue & Sue, 1977). This is a common practice in non-Western societies.

2. In relation to the point made in (1) above, sitting side by side as opposed to sitting directly opposite the elderly person is a more respectful seating arrangement.

3. While speaking in a soft voice is usually perceived as a sign of timidity in Western societies, in non-Western societies it conveys a respectful and nonaggressive posture of the speaker toward the listener.

A problem therefore arises in balancing respect for and communicating with an older person who is suffering from a hearing loss. Thus it is important to emphasize the following of Kiyak's (1996) suggestions:

1. Avoid distracting background noises.
2. Speak slowly and clearly but without exaggerating speech.
3. Repeat key points in several ways.

In addition to the above, we suggest:

1. Use culturally appropriate hand movements, bodily gestures, and facial expressions with speech.
2. If you are not familiar with the elderly, bring along a relative, spouse, friend, or child who is as a go-between for your conversation.

Changes in Taste and Smell

Cooking with spices is commonplace in the developing world. For example, curry powder is a common feature in the cuisine of Indians in Asia and among Jamaicans in the Caribbean. Hot pepper is common in the diets of west Africans and Mexicans. To compensate for declines in smell, perhaps an elevated level of these spices may be necessary for elderly persons. For convenience, if these spices are in table forms the elderly can spice their own food accordingly. For a good number of the spices used in the developing world, research is still required to determine their optimum intake.

Some of the spices are natural, are believed to have medicinal values, and are used not only in foods but also in beverages. For example, the locally brewed west African alcoholic drink, *ogogoro*, mentioned earlier, can be taken with *root*, a special local herb believed to cure malaria fever. Since many of the herbs and other substances used by traditional healers contain many chemicals that are found in Western medicines, this might be another area in which empirical research may be needed to test the validity of these claims.

The danger of not detecting gas odor due to declines in smell is also applicable to elderly persons in the developing world. In places where there is no electricity supply or where there are frequent electricity outages, bottled gas is used for lamps and for cooking. When used for outdoor cooking, bottled gas can be safe, but when used indoors it may be dangerous. However, firewood and kerosene are less expensive and less hazardous alternative means of power supply than gas, and they are more frequently used.

A study of the olfactory acuity between African and American samples found that both African men and women respondents have higher levels of olfactory functioning (Barber, 1997). While Africans may have a relatively low threshold for smell from this study, it is possible that the difference may be due to ecological factors. The reason is that the odor of interest, *androstenone,* is a scent produced by bacteria on the human body and tends to appear in sweat. Given the relatively hotter African climate, the African sample is likely to sweat more often and may become more sensitive to this particular odor. Therefore the perceptual threshold to smell might have been ecoculturally influenced.

Changes in the Respiratory System

Air pollution is rife in developing societies. Pollution comes especially from automobiles, from industrial plants, and from open refuse burning. Poor governmental regulatory controls are mostly responsible for the high level of air pollution, which tasks the respiratory system. Brandon (1996) acknowledged that increasing health costs and mortality are some of the real costs of pollution in Asia. Air pollution seems to be a symptom of "ecocultural stress," or stress to the ecocultural environment, due to modernization effects such as industrialization and urbanization. These pollution problems tend to be more prevalent in urban centers than in rural areas.

Changes in the Urinary System

Incontinence or problems with bladder control may not affect the social outings of the elderly in developing societies as it does in the developed world. The reason is that the concept of public bathrooms or "Johnny-on-the-spot" is novel to most of the developing world, especially in the rural areas. Therefore, it is commonplace to see people taking the liberty to ease themselves by the roadside or nearby bushes. Also, since the developing world consists mostly of societies with high collectivist values, it is not uncommon for people in transit to request the use of a stranger's bathroom, especially if they share a common language, ethnicity, or religion.

Changes in Sex Life

Although we expect physiological changes in the sexual and reproductive system to be the same as in the developed world, the sociocultural contexts of the developing world are likely to affect both the age of onset and the impact of sexual changes following senescence. Depending on a range of genetic and environmental factors, menopausal age varies, with the median age ranging from 42 to 51 years (Beall & Weitz, 1989). Whereas American women reach menopause at an average age of 51 (Crews, 1990), the mean age for the onset of menopause is 40 years for the !Kung women of Africa (Howell, 1979), and 47 years for Tibetan women of Asia (Beall, 1983).

Hooyman and Kiyak (1999) described menopause as a time of respect and status for women in many non-Western cultures, but the following psychosocial factors are likely to cause decline in their sexuality:

1. Lack of a male partner: Females have a higher life expectancy than males in all developing countries, even including the least developed countries. However, the United Nations (1998) gender-related index reports the margin to be smaller in all developing countries combined (63.67 years for females and 60.78 years for males) compared to the developed-industrial countries (77.9 years for females and 70.36 years for males). With a smaller female to male life expectancy difference, the availability of male partners for older women should not be as much of a problem as it is in the developed-industrial countries. Unfortunately, it is still a problem because of the margin in the average age of marriage for women on the one hand, and the average age of the men to whom the women are married, on the other hand. Men are generally older than their wives even in developed societies.

2. Older women married to their deceased husbands' relatives, as the tradition of some African societies require, benefit more from material than sexual accommodations while the younger widows are more likely to benefit from both. However, this practice is changing.

3. Older women in polygamous marriages may lose out to their younger, more attractive mates in terms of getting their husband's sexual attention.

Based on the "use it or lose it" theory, these psychosocial factors will exacerbate the normal process of senescence that affects vaginal elasticity and lubrication, the thinning of the vaginal walls, and the length of the preorgasmic plateau state. Unlike females, males do not experience the problem with lack of partners. Men in developing societies are generally sexually active, as is evidenced by the number of their children and the tendency to continue to have children even in old age. Sexual virility is important to the male self-concept and self-esteem, and it is expressed in having a large number of children, in having male children, in having polygamous marriages, and in engaging in sex with multiple partners. Given these antecedents slower and less full erections and ejaculate coming out in seepage form may be slowed with age. It should be noted, however, that conducting human sexuality research among the elderly in developing societies may be problematic, as sex is still considered a taboo subject especially in Islamic societies.

SUMMARY

The phenomenon of senescence is evident in predictable physiological changes that occur in the individual. Some biological theories have been proposed to explain these changes. The wear-and-tear theory suggests that, similar to any mechanical system, the body simply wears out after extensive use. Although the degeneration in some body systems appears to support this theory, it seems to describe the effects of aging and not what causes senescence. The autoimmune theory proposes that as we age, the immune system becomes less efficient, and may even attack the body itself, resulting in declines that are noticed in aging. The cross-linkage theory posits that aging occurs primarily because of declines in the protein collagen. Cellular theories of aging propose that there is a limit to the number of times that any cell can divide. Aging occurs as the number of divisions declines. Finally, the rate of living theory suggests that people are born with a limited amount of a substance that can be expended at a certain rate. We age as this substance gets increasingly used up. Although these theories play a central role in our understanding of senescence, the picture of aging will be incomplete without the inclusion of the sociocultural and psychological context within which it occurs.

Almost all body systems are affected, to some degree, by the aging process. We experience a loss in body mass mainly due to significant decreases in water, which tends to be replaced by fat. Changes in the skin, such as wrinkles, come about as a result of losses in the protein collagen as well as exposure to ultraviolet rays from the sun. Other visible signs of senescence include the thinning and loss of hair that, in some, results in baldness. Graying of the hair is another characteristic of aging, and it comes about due to losses in melanin. Senescence also brings about a loss in height of as much as three inches, a process that, especially in women, is exacerbated by osteoporosis.

All our sensory systems are affected by aging. With vision, the lens becomes more brittle, affecting our ability to focus on nearby objects, a condition known as presbyopia. Cloudiness in the lens results in cataracts. Deficits in hearing affect our ability to hear high-frequency sounds, a defect known as presbycusis. Losses in taste and smell can diminish appetite and put the elderly at risk of malnutrition. Declines in smell can also pose threats to safety and can cause embarrassment.

Respiratory system declines reduce the ability to engage in physical activities for a prolonged period of time. This problem can be improved by exercise. Reduction in the size of the kidneys results in glomeruli, a condition that is associated with urinary incontinence. Finally, senescence leads to changes in our sexual and reproductive system, caused mainly by declines in estrogen in women and testosterone in men. These declines tend to result in menopause, especially in women. However, men experience a reduction in reproduction and sexual functioning as well. The time of onset and rate of each of these changes, the coping mechanisms adopted to deal with the changes, as well as the psychological impact of the changes and the coping mechanisms are intricately moderated by the ecocultural context.

4

Psychological Aspects of Aging
and Adult Development

As mentioned in the *introductory* chapter, there is a dearth of studies on aging and development in developing societies. Therefore, studies on the developing world, where available, would be reviewed against the backdrop of Western theories and perspectives. However, where studies are not available, Western theories and perspectives would be discussed with a view to making propositions for future studies.

The selection of topics discussed in this chapter is influenced by 1) the current interests shown for them in cultural and cross-cultural research; and 2) the current dearth in cultural and cross-cultural research. First, we will present the Western theories and perspectives, and then review them in the context of developing societies under the section of developing world.

PERSONALITY THEORIES

Personality is that relatively enduring and unique way in which a person thinks or acts. Pervin (1996) defines it as the "complex organization of cognitions, affects, and behaviors that gives direction and pattern to the person's life" (p. 414). There are arguments whether personality exhibits change or stability over the life span or not. A major position argues for change, based on contextual variables (Bloom, 1964; Haan, Millsap, & Hartka, 1986; Helson, 1998) while another argues for stability (Costa & McCrae, 1988).

Erikson's popular theory (Erikson, 1959, 1982; Erikson, Erikson, & Kivnick, 1986) recognizes that development continues into the later part of the life span, and three of his eight stages occur during adulthood. Although Erikson's model presents conflicts and tasks to be accomplished at each stage, it assumes similar life experiences for all people. Erikson called the early adulthood stage, 18 to 24 years, a period of intimacy versus isolation, the middle adulthood stage, 40 to 65 years, he called generativity versus stagnation, and the late adulthood stage, 65 years and on, ego integrity versus despair.

Intimacy versus isolation requires a person to form intimate relationships or risk the feelings of isolation. In the generativity versus stagnation stage, the individual faces the challenge of finding some ways to support the next generation or risks being preoccupied with self. And last, if all the previous stages have been reasonably dealt with, the ego integrity versus despair stage challenges one to accept oneself as is or face being preoccupied with regrets over missed opportunities and accomplishments, which could lead to depression (Ryland & Rickwood, 2001). These stages reflect changes that are developmental. Erikson believes in the interface between genetics and the environment in determining personality development and concludes that each person is pushed through a sequence of dilemmas by both biological pressures and by the demands of the roles that the individual takes.

More recently, however, Erikson's stages have been debated, especially with regard to women in contemporary society. As more women delay marriage in pursuit of career goals, coupled with the advent of the women's liberation movement, women's personality development has been profoundly influenced (Agronick & Duncan, 1998; Helson, Stewart, & Ostrove, 1995). For example, midlife may be a time for the reexamination of their lives, and if they are not satisfied with family life they can move on to other endeavors like work outside the home.

Whereas Erikson implies an abrupt change from one stage to another, Levinson's (1986) model recognizes a transition period. It divides adulthood in men into a sequence of broad periods, or eras, with each period marked by a distinct character, lasting about 20 years, and with a 5-year transition period separating each period or era. A similar situation applies to women (Roberts & Newton, 1987). This transition period allows an individual to reflect on and to recognize the changes about to occur in his or her life as a result of the new environmental demands. For example, does a newly retired individual recognize the change or demand on his or her life in order to effect a change in routine? Levinson suggests that personality development occurs only if the individual is sensitive to changes and is able to respond to them by modifying both self and the environment. A dynamic individual, therefore, is one who strives to maintain a state of equilibrium between the self and the environment. Levenson's model explicitly recognizes the importance of agency in personality development, suggesting that the individual can influence both the self and the environment. Carstensen (1992) makes a similar argument in her social selectivity theory of emotion regulation in older people.

While personality development has been considered from a stage perspective, others have instead considered personality from a trait perspective, suggesting stability across the life span. Traits are those specific attributes that are relatively stable in an individual, and they help to distinguish one individual from another. They are the outcome of both heredity and environment.

McCrae & Costa's trait studies are of particular interest to many scholars because of their cross-cultural validity in Germany, Croatia, Italy, Portugal, and Korea (McCrae, Costa, Pedroso de Lima, Simtes, Ostendorf, et al., 1999). They propose a five-factor model of personality traits, namely neuroticism, extraversion, openness to experience, agreeableness, and conscientiousness, with subcategories within each of the independent trait components. The following are the characteristics of the five-factor (Big-Five) dimensions:

1. neuroticism: anxiety, hostility, self-consciousness, self-pity, touchiness, worry, depression, impulsiveness;

2. extraversion: assertiveness, warmth, gregariousness, activity, excitement-seeking, energetic, enthusiastic, optimistic;

3. openness: openness to fantasy, aesthetics, feelings, actions, ideas, values;

4. agreeableness: trust, altruism, tendermindedness, straightforwardness; also appreciative, forgiving, generous, kind, sympathetic; and

5. conscientiousness: competence, order, dutifulness, achievement, striving, self-discipline, deliberation, efficiency, reliability, responsibleness, and thoroughness.

Studies by Costa and McCrae and others show that personality traits seem to demonstrate a strong intraindividual stability over a long period of time (Costa & McCrae, 1980; Schaie, 1996, Schaie & Willis, 1991), even lasting for as long as 30 years (Costa & McCrae 1994). But with regard to selected personality dimensions, some studies have, however, found consistent age differences. For example, on measures of neuroticism and extraversion, younger adults scored higher than older individuals and on measures of social desirability, older individuals scored higher than younger adults (Eysenck & Eysenck, 1975). Other studies report an increase in responsibility, self-control, good impression, and norm-orientation from the 40s to the 50s (Helson & Wink, 1992) and an increase in responsibility, self-control, and good impression in women in their 30s and 40s (Cartwright & Wink, 1994). But when asked about their perceived personality traits across different target ages, past, present, and future, Fleeson and Heckhausen (1997) reported that respondents ages 26 to 64 indicated both moderate changes and more variability in their personalities than are observed in longitudinal studies. Participants perceived their personalities as characterized by exploration in early adulthood, by productivity in middle adulthood, and by comfortableness in later adulthood; overall, they perceived personality in late adulthood as containing more losses than gains.

There are at least two ways to interpret these age-related changes. They may be developmental or cohort related. For example, there are studies that suggest that older individuals regulate their emotions through the reinterpretation of negative situations into positive affect (Aldwin, 1994; Diehl, Coyle, & Labouvie-Vief, 1996) while others affirm the influence of social context (Maas & Kuypers, 1974; Neugarten, 1968).

Personality dispositions have implications for an individual's well-being. They are linked to life satisfaction and to how individuals handle life events in general. For example, individuals who are high in extraversion are consistently more satisfied with their lives than those who are high in neuroticism (Costa & McCrae, 1984; McCrae & Costa, 1990). On the other hand, those individuals who are high in neuroticism will handle stressful life events more poorly (Liker & Elder, 1983). Other studies have found that the level of optimism—an important personality attribute—that an elderly person displays could affect how losses experienced in later life are perceived. Optimism has been found to make a difference in people afflicted with Parkinson's disease (Shifren, 1996) and in how care providers for people with Parkinson's disease perceive the severity of the disease (Shifren & Hooker, 1995).

In a way, personality disposition consciously or unconsciously helps us to answer the intriguing question of "who am I?"—a question that also draws much attention in cross-cultural research. But if certain dimensions of personality change across the life span, how does the individual continue to maintain a sense of who he or she is? To this and more issues, we now turn to the self.

The Self

The self, an aspect of personality, is an individual's characteristic way of defining himself or herself in the world in which he or she lives. It is a way of answering the question, "who am I?" The self includes a multilevel structure of cognitive, affective, and somatic representations, which have implications for a person's experiences, activities, and well-being. It is a social construction, but it is also a social constructor—actively selecting and ignoring certain experiences and contesting or rearranging others (Herzog & Markus, 1999). The self functions by identifying what the person attends to, what he or she thinks and cares about, or spends time on (Banaji & Prentice, 1994). It also functions in how the person describes himself or herself across the life span in a more or less consistent way (Costa & McCrae, 1988).

But what then is the self rooted in? Markus, Holmberg, Herzog, & Franks (1994) surveyed 1,500 American adults requesting them to "tell me about yourself." Based on an analysis of the responses, they found that respondents rooted their self-concept mainly in attributes and roles—physical attributes, personality attributes, and family roles. Attributes and roles made up 60 to 73% of the responses, while the remainder of responses focused on what the individuals were doing (occupation and leisure). Therefore, the self seems to include personality traits and beyond. It includes social roles but also demographic characteristics (Rentsch & Heffner, 1994).

Because of the ability of the self to select or ignore, and to challenge or rearrange certain experiences (Herzog & Markus, 1999), people can adjust to changes. And such adjustments can take a variety of forms, including the processes of selection, compensation, and optimization (Baltes & Baltes, 1990; but also see Carstensen, 1992), and the ability to set future goals and to adopt new ones (Ryff, 1991). All these adjustments help people to maintain a sense of well-being across the life span.

The ability to make adjustments would vary from individual to individual. Changes resulting from stressful life events and severe hearing loss, and also from significant physical disabilities and social isolation, can affect the self-esteem of elderly people. Nevertheless, it is important to note that to adjust to the changes that occur from both within and outside of the individual, the ability to reinterpret and/or control emotions will be required. As Brandtstadter and Greve (1994) argue, older people maintain a sense of well-being because of their emotional resilience. They are able to move from an "assimilative mode" to an "accommodative mode." "Assimilative mode" is the desire to maintain the status quo, that is to maintain level of competence from young adulthood stage, whereas "accommodative mode" is adjusting to losses. But not all older persons are capable of or desire to make such a change of mode.

Emotion

There is a debate as to whether emotion is an experience or a behavior, and this debate has led to the difficulty in precisely defining emotion. With humans, the more common usage treats experience as the essence of emotion, but it also includes behavior (facial features like eyebrow and mouth movements).

Emotions used to be considered subject to the regulations of cognition, but more recently two perspectives have emerged. One perspective is that emotions are fixed and biologically wired, thus showing universal manifestations irrespective of context, experience, or developmental stage. For example, the emotions of happiness, surprise, sadness, fear, anger, and disgust are universally expressed (Ekman, Friesen, O'Sullivan, Chan, Diacoyanni-Tarlatzis, et al., 1987), but contempt distinguished from disgust appear to be also universally shared (Ekman & Friesen, 1986; Ekman & Heider, 1988; see also Izard & Haynes, 1988).

The other perspective suggests that cognition acts as a filter (Eyetsemitan & Eggleston, 2002; Gross, 1998; Lazarus, 1991) leading sometimes to new and complex emotions, which may not be universally shared.

There are arguments suggesting that both cognition and emotions are linked (Fischer & Ayoub, 1994), but they could also be separate. In the context of these two arguments, how does the development of emotions then proceed across the life span? The emotions that are separate from cognitive influences would remain invariant throughout the life span, but those emotions that are influenced by cognition are likely to change across the life span because of cognitive changes. However, if biologically wired emotions do not change across the life span, the intensity of their expressions do (Lawton, 1996; also see Levenson, Carstensen, Friesen, & Ekman, 1991). But this decrease in emotional intensity is not quite clear, as it may be due either to physiological declines or to learning.

The effect of learning on emotions takes a variety of forms throughout the life span. For example, as new roles are acquired and different activities are engaged in at different stages of the life span, new emotions are developed (spirituality or religiosity, which, if accentuated in later life, can lead to the development of peace and serenity). Also generational differences in socialization patterns that occur can account for differences in emotional expressions, with the older generation more likely to have stricter control over their emotions. Apart from socialization, intelligence is also linked to emotional expression (Labouvie-Vief, 1998). More resourceful individuals display more control over their emotions. For instance, an aspect of intelligence called "crystallized intelligence" (Baltes, 1993) increases over the life span and involves accumulated knowledge through formal and informal education and from life experiences. Thus with an increase in "crystallized intelligence" over the life span, older adults are better equipped to appeal to general norms and principles, to reinterpret situations, and to accept negative events in their emotional expressions than younger adults (Blanchard-Fields, 1998; Labouvie-Vief, 1998).

Whereas "crystallized intelligence" is an example of a resource that increases over the life span, time is an example of a resource that decreases. Time is not to the advantage of older people. Therefore, older people tend to gradually narrow the span of people with whom they interact or share emotional ties. Older people restrict their emotional involvement to family and close friends, and trade quantity for quality (Carstensen, 1992).

Cognition

Cognitive changes not only affect emotions across the life span, they also affect learning, memory, reasoning, and response speed. Age-related cognitive declines involve processing efficiency or effectiveness at the time of assessment. Typically, they are in the areas of fluid intelligence (Baltes, 1993), learning, memory, reasoning, and spatial abilities (Salthouse, 1999). Cognitive gains assessed by tests of general knowledge and acquired information are typically in crystallized intelligence and wisdom. There appears to be more interest, however, in cognitive declines as a result of aging, and most theories that relate cognitive changes to aging fall under two categories: 1) Remote and 2) Immediate.

The Remote theories evaluate factors in the individual's earlier life that now affect performance (cohort effects and sociocultural factors). These theories generally consider contextual factors in accounting for cognitive changes, as against processes that are inherent in the individual. For example, people born at different times (cohort effects) perform differently on cognitive tests because of differences in their sociocultural environments (Flynn, 1987; Schaie, 1996; also see Tuddenham, 1948). For example, Tuddenham (1948) gave a test of general intelligence to a sample of soldiers in 1943, and, comparing their results to those of another sample from 1918 to 1919, found the average score of the

1943 sample was at the 83rd percentile of the 1918 to 1919 sample. He concluded that the different environments and cultures in which the soldiers lived accounted for the results. Perhaps a better demonstration of the power of the environment on cognition is called the "Flynn effect" (Flynn, 1987, 1994; also see Neisser, 1998), a phenomenon that showed an increase in IQ in successive generations in 30 years around the world, due to environmental changes.

Because cohort effects alone do not explain cognitive differences in performance, researchers have investigated the "disuse hypothesis" as a plausible explanation for age-related declines. In this regard, different approaches have been adopted, including considering past disuse, recent disuse, and the effects of training. The "disuse hypothesis" has not been generally confirmed when people with different amounts of experience in spatial tasks, including architects, are compared (Salthouse, Babcock, Skovronek, Mitchell & Palmon, 1990; Salthouse & Mitchell, 1990); and people with different amounts of musical experience are compared (Meinz & Salthouse, 1998). While there are exceptions (Morrow, Leirer, & Altieri, 1992), the general tendency is to find, irrespective of the amount of experience, similarity in age decline; and even when training to remediate disuse is provided, there is no significant change. For example, given the same amount and extent of training, older adults do not perform as well as young adults, and, in some cases, training even led to increases rather than decreases in age-related differences (Kliegl, Smith, & Baltes, 1989).

Whereas contextual factors are important, they are not the only factors that help to explain age-related declines in cognitive functioning. As mentioned earlier, the other category of theories that helps to explain changes is the "Immediate" theories. The "Immediate" theories emphasize process; they look for factors that operate in influencing cognitive functioning at the time of assessment. One set of "Immediate" theories explains that cognitive declines arise from poor strategy in carrying out cognitive operations. Poor strategy can emanate either from a suboptimal use of strategy (i.e., older people compared to younger individuals use strategy inefficiently due to ability differences) or from a specific deficit inherent in the information-processing stages or components. For example, some studies suggest that older persons experience declines in mental energies or "attentional resources" (Craik & Jennings, 1992; Smith, 1996) whereas others suggest that they experience declines in the speed to encode and decode information, attributable to the slowing of the central nervous system (Salthouse, 1993, 1994). Approximately 2% of the neurons in the hippocampus region of the brain are lost after the age of 50 years (Selkoe, 1997).

Another set of "Immediate" theories and perhaps the most promising perspective, suggests that cognitive declines result from age-related declines in "cognitive primitives" or "processing resources." This is similar to the specific-deficit approach explained earlier, except that it has a broader implication. Declines in "cognitive primitives" have implications in areas such as attention, working memory, and processing speed; and because of its broad implications evidenced from findings in a variety of cognitive tasks of age differences, the "cognitive primitives" approach is more popular than the other approaches (Salthouse, 1996).

Although not necessarily age-related, the health status of the elderly also accounts for cognitive declines. For example, cardiovascular diseases and severe cases of hypertension are implicated in poor intelligence test scores (Hultsch, Hammer, & Small, 1993). Also, nutritional deficiency impairs cognitive functioning of older persons (Larue, Koehler, Wayne, Chiulli, Haaland, & Garry, 1997), as do depression (Rabbitt, Donlan, Watson, McInnes, & Bent, 1995), and sensory loss of vision and hearing (Lindenberger & Baltes, 1994).

Wisdom, like "crystallized intelligence," is one area where age-related gains occur in cognitive functioning. Wisdom is defined as the ability to transcend the basic needs of health, income, and housing (Orwell & Achenbaum, 1993), and it requires factual and procedural knowledge, life-span contextualism, value relativism, and uncertainty (Baltes, Staudinger, Maercker, & Smith, 1995). Traits associated with wisdom are linked to experiences that are not necessarily age-related. They come about as a result of an individual's peculiar life experiences, especially the difficult ones, but some level of intelligence is required to interpret the experiences and to understand the world in a deeper way (Eyet-semitan, 1991). But how much of wisdom is affected by the age-related declines in cognitive abilities discussed earlier is not fully known.

THE DEVELOPING WORLD

In this section, we examine each of the major concepts discussed above, but within the context of the developing world. In other words, we will present research findings that show either similar processes within the developing world or point to the mediating role of the ecocultural context.

PERSONALITY THEORIES

In an extensive review of the cross-cultural literature on personality, Church and Lonner (1998) noted the limited cross-cultural applications of some existing personality theories. Among others, they pointed to the lack of cross-cultural support for Erikson's (1959) personality stages (particularly the higher level ones) but noted that in contrast, McCrae and Costa's (1990) Big-Five personality model enjoys a good measure of cross-cultural success.

However, there are still questions about the suitability of the Big-Five personality trait measure in developing societies, which are largely collectivistic. According to Markus and Kitayama (1998), the Asian culture has a construction of personality as an interdependent entity, which is embedded in, and not separate from, a context. This view of personality is also common in much of South America and Africa (Markus & Kitayama, 1991; Marsella, DeVos & Hsu,

1985). Therefore, an interdependent model of personality will not describe personality in terms of traits within the individual but rather in terms of how the individual interfaces with social structures and interpersonal frameworks like family, work groups, social roles, position, and other relationships (Markus & Kitayama, 1998).

In addition, when using personality traits, the nuances of various societies should be taken into consideration in order to understand the extent of their applicability (Church & Lonner, 1998). For example, the dimension of Openness (one of the Big-Five personality traits), which includes openness to feelings, actions, ideas, and values should be understood in terms of "private openness" and "public openness," at least in developing societies. We propose that "private openness" will occur at the small group level with family (in-group) and "public openness" will occur at the large group level outside the family (out-group). We further propose that in developing societies there will be a low tendency toward "public openness" as a result of loyalty toward the in-group. For example, it will be unusual for in-group members to publicly disagree with each other as it is sometimes seen on American talk show television among family members. In a cross-cultural study of self-disclosure among Americans and Chinese, Chen (1995) reported that Americans had more self-disclosure than their Chinese counterparts on issues of opinion, interest, work, finance, personality, and body, and they also showed more self-disclosure even to strangers. Also, Americans were less likely to feel shame for their behaviors that would bring shame to their family members (Stipek, 1998). Furthermore, because of a restraining political environment that restrains freedom of expression (Bronfenbrenner, 1979), "public openness" will not be encouraged in developing societies. However, given their cross-cultural environmental context (Eyetsemitan, 2002a), the influence of the developed world cannot be ignored. There would be individuals, especially young adults who are more exposed to Westernization influences, whose personality traits would reflect those described by McCrae and Costa (1990).

The Self

There has been much cross-cultural interest in the study of the self, and this growing interest is not unconnected to Hofstede's (1980) work that described Western societies as individualistic and non-Western societies as collectivistic. The interest in how the self is expressed in both Western and non-Western societies has formed the basis for making differential projections in areas like motivation, emotion, learning, and cognition (Markus & Kitayama, 1991). The effect of self-expression has also been linked to societal development. In other words, it is suggested that Western societies are developed because of the nature of self-expression in those societies, while non-Western societies are not so developed because of the nature of the self-expression of people in those societies. Therefore, in making the connection between individualism (a trait found in Western societies) with societal development perhaps requires people in non-Western societies to have a different self-construal first, before their societies can develop. This assumption is not entirely correct as demonstrated by Japan and up-and-coming non-Western societies like Korea, Taiwan, Hong Kong, and Singapore (Kagitcibasi, 1996b).

People in developing societies do demonstrate a self that is separate from others. For example, there is a strong belief in the spirit world, and destructive evil forces that could be wished upon someone, even by a fellow in-group member, as a result of jealousy or competition (Markus & Kitayama, 1998). Ironically, the fear of evil forces triggers an autonomous self that is separate from others, including members of the in-group. Such fears could lead to self-protection measures that include the use of special charms and amulets and regulation of self-disclosure. Therefore, the autonomous self and the relational self are separate dimensions rather than one continuous entity (Gabrielidis, Stephan, Ybarra, Pearson, & Villareal, 1997) with each dimension being triggered separately by the cross-cultural environment.

In fact, the nature of selfhood in developing societies is complex and can be expressed in more than one way. For example, Markus and Kitayama (1998) note that a manager can be compassionate, strict, or both, and a father can be kind and enthusiastic or negligent (Kagiticibasi, 1996a: "autonomous-relational self;" J. B. P. Sinha, 1980: "nurturant-task leader;" and Kwan, Bond, & Singelis, 1997: "relationship harmony"). These self-expressions are not consistent across various contexts but are rooted in roles, statuses, and in-group membership (Markus & Kitayama, 1998). For example, using a "collectivist language" increases cognitive accessibility of the collectivist self more than when an "individualist language" is used (Trafimow, Silverman, Fan, & Law, 1997).

Although the self is a social construction, it is also a social constructor. It adjusts to changes, and at least two areas where changes occur, are from aging and the environment. As most people in developing societies become older, they become dependent on their children for support (Kagitcibasi, 1996b), while others (including their children) depend on their leadership roles in the community. The change that comes from the environment is mainly due to acculturation influences or modernization. We propose that elderly people will adjust to their cross-cultural environment based on a *supply* and *demand* dynamic. For example, they can exercise the option to accept Western medical treatment (developed world dimension), or combine Western treatment with native medicine (developed and developing world dimensions), or subscribe to only native medicine (developing world dimension). The cross-cultural environment offers an even more flexible option for the development of the self. While such flexibility can be equated with "waffling" in the developed world (Markus & Kitayama, 1998), it calls for a different way of understanding and measuring the self in the context of developing societies.

Emotion

There is a relationship between the self and emotional expression. The emotions associated with an "autonomous-relational self" will be different from those of an "autonomous self." Nonetheless, the basic emotions of happiness, surprise, sadness, fear, anger, disgust, and contempt are shared universally (Ekman, Friesen, O'Sullivan, Chan, Diacoyanni-Tarlatzis, et al., 1987; Izard & Haynes, 1988) because people in different cultures can recognize them. But the degree to which each of these emotions is displayed in different cultures is a different matter, and there might be cultural differences in the recognition of emotions, especially sadness and fear (Schimmack, 1996). However, knowing the degree to which each of these emotions is displayed in a particular culture (happiness), the forces that shape emotions in each culture can then be identified (Mesquita, Frijda, & Scherer, 1997). Such cultural forces may be universal or unique to a particular culture.

With the componential approach, it is easier to evaluate the impact of either biology or culture on the different components of the emotion process, rather than just assuming a biological universal of emotions. Generally, the componential approach includes the following: a) antecedent event, b) emotional experience, c) appraisal, d) physiological change, e) change in readiness, f) change in action readiness, g) behavior, h) change in cognitive functioning and beliefs, and i) regulatory processes (Lazarus, 1991).

Biologically wired emotions will not be influenced by culture and are expected to persist throughout the life span, but perhaps with diminished intensity in expression in old age. The diminished intensity in expression may be attributable either to biology or to culture. If attributable to culture, then we propose that the effect of culture will be manifested in generational differences (older people are more likely to be conservative than the younger generation), and in "crystallized intelligence," which increases over the life span and enables older adults to appeal to general norms and principles, to reinterpret situations, and to accept negative events in their emotional expressions (Blanchard-Fields, 1998; Labouvie-Vief, 1998). We also propose that because self-expression is tied to roles, status, and position (Markus & Kitayama, 1998), emotional expression will be affected differently across the life span.

In Carstensen's (1992) social selectivity model, influenced by the disengagement theory, older people restrict their emotional involvement to family and close friends and trade quantity for quality because time is the essence. We propose that in developing societies (which are mostly collectivistic), restricting emotional involvement to only family members and close friends is not normative at any age. However, this is not to suggest that some elderly persons would behave in ways not considered "normative." For example, in a study among 75-plus-aged individuals in Delhi, India, van Willigen and colleagues (van Willigen, Chadha, & Kedia, 1995) reported a substantial reduction in the network size (about 25 persons) of these individuals, but this was influenced by gender, household resource control, and health status, and not because their lives were coming to an end. However, because of the cross-cultural environment of developing societies (Eyetsemitan, 2002a), we propose that the emotional expressions of those individuals with beliefs and values reflecting the "developed world" will be different from those with beliefs and values reflecting either the "developing world" or the "developed and developing worlds."

Cognition

It is plausible that there will be age-related cognitive declines in the areas of learning, memory, reasoning, and spatial abilities and in "fluid intelligence" and age-related gains in "crystallized intelligence" (Baltes, 1993). However, the aspect of intelligence most likely to be influenced by culture is "crystallized intelligence" or "pragmatics of intelligence," but this is not to suggest that the biologically wired "fluid intelligence" will not be influenced by culture, for example, nutrition and training.

Certainly the cultural meaning of intelligence, which is different in developing societies, will also affect how cognitive declines and gains are evaluated. For example, Dasen (1984) pointed to the relevance of culture in the conception of intelligence, whether from a Piagetian or from any other perspective. In a study of the Baoule culture of Ivory Coast, Dasen (1984) found that there is a strong social component to the concept of intelligence, for example, usefulness, obedience, and respect. Although technological skills, such as attention, memory, and manual dexterity, are also important these skills are useful only as long as they are of service to the social group. In another study comparing Australian and Malay students on the elements of intellectual competence, Gill and Keats (1980) found that whereas the Australians rated academic skills, speaking, reading, and writing more highly, the Malays placed more emphasis on social and practical skills. Zebian and Denny (2001) in their own study reported differences in thinking patterns; they reported higher levels of differentiation thinking among people of European origin and higher levels of integrative thinking among people of Middle Eastern origin.

Other studies comparing Europeans and Asians show that whereas Europeans process information in an analytical way, Asians perceive and reason in a holistic manner (see Morris & Peng, 1994; Morris, Nisbett, & Peng, 1995). Even in reading strategy, similar differences have been noted, with Westerners focusing on word features, and Asians paying more attention to whole sentences (Chan, 1996). It is no surprise, therefore, that because of culture, people are biased in what information to pay attention to and remember (Park, Nisbett, & Hedden, 1999). In reviewing cognitive test scores published between 1973 and 1994, van de Vijver (1997) noted that reports on performance differences between Western and non-Westerners were larger on common Western tasks than on locally produced non-Western cognitive tasks, and most of the studies were done on primary-school-age children.

However, the cross-cultural environment of the developing world would account for generational differences in cognition, and should also influence how cognition is assessed. Because younger people are more exposed to Western formal education system, urbanization, and industrialization, their cognition may be influenced by either the "developed world dimension" or the "developed and developing worlds dimensions." For example, bicultural Hong Kong citizens demonstrated the ability to reason in both American and Chinese contexts when primed with Mickey Mouse and cowboy cues and with dragons and temple cues (Hong, Wong, & Lee, 1996).

Being biologically wired, "fluid intelligence" is expected to demonstrate cultural universality. It is interesting, however, that there is confounding evidence for this assertion. For example, Asian superiority in mathematical reasoning has been attributed to hard work, to higher motivation, and to superior education (Stevenson & Stigler, 1992). Cohort influence is also implicated (Geary, Salthouse, Chen, & Fan, 1996) because mathematics education has been emphasized more to the younger generation of Asians as a way to a better life than to the older generation. But reports from cross-cultural studies between older Americans and older Chinese point to either a biological or a cultural convergence. Geary and colleagues (1996) found that old Chinese and old Americans were no different on tests for mathematical skills. Although these findings could suggest the universality of "fluid intelligence" as a biologically wired phenomenon, the cultural convergence that occurs in late adulthood stage can also be a function of cohort effects, especially if both old Americans and old Chinese share similar cultural experiences such as conservatism.

Gender disparities in opportunities, which are marked in developing societies, also contribute to cognitive declines. Males have more opportunities than females, including for formal education. In a study by Shanan and Sagiv (1982) of 220 Israelis, aged 46 to 65 years, divided by age, level of education, and cultural origin, men performed better than women, but culture played important roles. They were tested on using information, comprehension, block design, digit symbol substitution, and digit span sub-tests of the Wechsler-Bellevue Intelligence.

We are proposing that the following cultural factors seem to be relevant to cognitive development in developing societies and perhaps in the following order:

1. Collectivism: this is the development of skills and abilities relevant to the group (usefulness, respect, and obedience).
2. Maleness: although this is more associated with men, it is related to opportunities for leadership roles.
3. Knowledge: this includes knowledge acquired either formally or informally.

We further propose that the group (collectivism) comes first, followed by gender (maleness), and then by education and experience (knowledge). If this order is true, then a female who is useful to the group is likely to be evaluated as more intelligent than a male who is not. Furthermore, maleness is more important for decision making than knowledge, which comes last; however, there may be a correlation between maleness and the acquisition of formal education.

We expect that medical conditions such as cardiovascular diseases, severe cases of hypertension, depression, nutritional deficiencies, and sensory losses of hearing and vision will be associated with cognitive declines. However, the role assumed and the position occupied within the collectives may attenuate the social implication of this decline.

One of the cognitive gains associated with aging is wisdom. Elderly people in developing societies are believed to be wise just like their counterparts in developed societies but no systematic study of wisdom has been carried out in the developing world that we are aware of. The wisdom ascribed to the elderly usually stems from their age, position, roles, experience, and knowledge (including both temporal and spiritual).

However, the difference between the elderly in the developed and developing worlds, we suggest, lies in the opportunities available to them in exercising their wise attribute. Developed societies provide less opportunity to the elderly than developing societies. In developed societies, emphasis is placed on professionalism and the orientation is to seek counsel from service providers with credentials and formal training. Moreover, service providers are forced to be bonded or to take up third-party insurance policies in case an unsatisfied client sues them. In developing societies, on the other hand, the opportunity for elderly people to provide wise counsel to others, especially to young people, is rife and is reinforced by a pervasive belief in the spirit world. Elderly people occupy a niche as those closer to the spirit world.

This chapter has reviewed the topics of personality, the self, emotions, and cognition. In the next chapter how these characteristics of the individual interface with those of others and society in a more explicit way will be the subject of discussion.

SUMMARY

Western theories and perspectives on personality, the self, emotion, and cognition were reviewed. Under the section of the Developing world these topics were discussed, based on available literature, drawing attention to similarities and differences with the developed world, with proposals made for areas where studies need to be carried out.

Personality is that unique way a person thinks or acts and is relatively enduring. It develops in stages or by the acquisition of traits. In both cases heredity and environment are implicated. In the developing world, the stage approach is yet to be validated unlike the trait approach. Even with the trait approach, there is need for caution. For example, the lexical meaning of words in a particular culture needs to be taken into consideration as does the conceptualization of personality, which is rooted in interdependence as against independence.

The self, an aspect of personality, is the unique way an individual characterizes himself or herself in the world he or she lives in. It is a response to the question "Who am I?" The self is rooted in physical and personality attributes and is more or less perceived to be constant across contexts. In the developing world, however, the self is rooted in roles, statuses, and in-group membership. It is multifaceted and is not constant across contexts.

Emotion is both an experience and a behavior. It is both biologically wired (happiness, sadness, fear, anger, disgust, and contempt) and learned. The biologically wired emotions are universal whereas the learned ones are not and are unique to a particular culture. But culture still attenuates the biologically wired emotions, and how it does requires significant empirical investigation in the developing world.

There are both declines and gains associated with cognitive changes. While declines are measured in the areas of learning, memory, reasoning, and spatial abilities, gains are tested through general knowledge and acquired information. There are two perspectives to declines: Remote and Immediate. The Remote perspective evaluates factors in the individual's earlier life that affect current performance (sociocultural factors and cohort effects). The Immediate perspective, on the contrary, emphasizes factors that operate in influencing cognitive functioning at the point of assessment (poor strategy). Studies from the developing world point to the importance of the role of culture in the conceptualization of cognition and its measurement.

Wisdom, one of the cognitive gains associated with aging, is the ability to transcend basic needs, and it requires the acquisition of factual and procedural knowledge, life-span contextualism, value relativism, uncertainty, and difficult life experiences. Although there appears to be an intuitive understanding of what wisdom is in the developing world, there is still a need for empirical studies that take into consideration its conceptualization and practice.

In the conceptualization and measurement of psychological concepts, the cross-cultural context of the developing world needs to be taken into consideration. The developing world environment is not monolithic and would influence aging and development differently.

5

Social Aspects of Aging and Adult Development

This chapter will focus on how aging and development are influenced by the interactions between the individual and societal structures, leading to activities and roles that typify the different adulthood stages. For example, marriage, parenthood, intergenerational relationships, career, and retirement would be typical activities and roles that span various stages of adulthood. Through cultural practices, every society transmits norms and expectations about social activities and roles and the nature of interactions that are expected at every stage in the life course. Culture's role, therefore, fits under three major models (Fry 1999).

GENERATIONAL SYSTEMS

Generation is determined by time relativity, for example, junior versus senior. While generation may correlate with chronological age, it does not necessarily have to. For example, a stepmother may be younger than a stepson or a stepdaughter or an uncle may be younger than a nephew. Usually generational systems are most functional within families and are made up of three classes: seniors, such as parents and uncles, equals, such as siblings and cousins, and juniors, such as children, nieces, and nephews.

AGE CLASS SYSTEMS

Age class systems are the extension of generational systems into the larger society (Fortes, 1984). Here, age is used to stratify the life course, serving as a criterion or set of expectations or norms for entering or leaving certain roles, and for access into certain resources, for example, money, power, and prestige. Age class systems are used to frame the "three boxes": education for the young, work and family for the middle aged, and retirement or leisure for the old (Riley, Foner, & Riley, 1999).

STAGED LIFE COURSE

Based on both generational systems and age class systems, the life course is then divided into stages. Thus education for the young becomes a stage of preparation, work and family becomes the stage of participation, and retirement becomes the stage of disengagement from society.

Some of the activities associated with both age and life course stages are reinforced by legal norms: age to vote, to have a driver's license, to work, and to retire. Even in the face of postmodernism, the influence of age norm continues to show considerable stability in the American society (Settersten & Hagestad, 1996a, 1996b), and in most other societies.

The three models of culture, especially the Age Class Systems and the Staged Life Course discussed above, are exemplified by such popular theories as Role Theory, Activity Theory, Disengagement Theory, Continuity Theory, Age Stratification Theory, Labeling Theory, and the Aging as a Subculture perspective. Due to space consideration each of these theories will be briefly described and then followed by a discussion of the roles and activities that typify the different stages of adulthood: marriage, parenthood, intergenerational relationship, career, and retirement.

Role Theory

This theory explains how an individual adjusts to the changes that occur with aging. It contends that changes from aging bring about different abilities and opportunities, but they generally apply to a cohort, that is, the group of individuals aging together, rather than to the individual. Therefore, to age well is to ascribe to the roles assigned to the cohort. For example, the use of terms such as "act your age" are reserved for those individuals whose behaviors are not in conformity with the expected behavior of their cohorts. In other words, people are socialized to follow norms (Neugarten, Moore, & Lowe, 1965; Rosow, 1974), and norms are learned and internalized.

Chronological age usually is the basis for role determination. Therefore role expectations become age norms, which are formal or informal, resulting in social clocks, against which individuals then assess their aging and developmental trajectory. For example, if in a particular culture the social clock for females to marry is in the 20s, then both the individual and society can assess whether marriage was "early" or "late" for a particular individual. Social clocks regulate behavior by reminding the individual what should be done at a particular time in life. But social clocks can be changed. Nowadays with women delaying marriage in preference for education and careers, there is a shift in the social clock and, by implications, the age norm for marriage.

Age Stratification Theory

The Age Stratification Theory by Riley (1971) is similar to the Role Theory. This theory suggests that different cohorts (or age groups) are stratified as "young," "middle aged," or "old." Even in the "old" group, people are further classified as "young-old," "old-old," and "oldest-old." The people in each stratum are expected to think and behave in the same way. For example, whereas the "young" are expected to be liberal in their attitudes toward sex, the "old" are expected to be conservative. This assumption is partly based on the value systems that characterize the historical times associated with each cohort. Because one cohort differs from the other, their aging and development are therefore expected to be different.

A "structural lag," however, occurs when there are changes in aging and development as a result of historical times, but no corresponding changes in the existing social structures in the society. For example, as a result of increased active life expectancy, mandatory retirement at 65 years should also change. The corollary also occurs when society modernizes and the values and behaviors of elderly people do not change accordingly. This creates what we call an "elderly lag."

It should be noted that both "structural lag" and "elderly lag" provide an opportunity for human agency. For example, in the United States, through the American Association of Retired Persons (AARP), elderly people have been able to influence policy issues and social norms that affect them.

Activity Theory

Proponents of the Activity Theory (Maddox, 1964) argue that remaining active is the best way to age, especially in those activities associated with middle age. It leads to a better adjustment and to a positive self-concept (Bengtson, 1969). But in deciding to maintain the roles and activities that are consistent with middle aged, the value placed on being active (and the types of activity) would be influenced by the age norms and social clock in the society, and also by the individual's own value systems.

Disengagement Theory

With disengagement theory, the way to adapt to aging is to relinquish roles gradually, and then concentrate on the inner self. This way, both the individual and society will adapt to changes, allowing roles, power, and resources to shift from one generation to another in an orderly fashion (see Cumming & Henry, 1961 for details).

Although this theory contradicts the activity theory, which advocates that remaining active leads to a better adjustment, it bears some resemblance to both role and age stratification theories that advocate appropriate roles for different age groups. In spite of being heavily criticized, disengagement theory continues to be given credence.

Continuity Theory

This theory suggests that an older person will experience life satisfaction if there is a match between that individual's current lifestyle and his previous one. In order to accomplish continuity therefore, the individual will have to replace lost roles with almost similar ones. Thus, successful aging only occurs when a mature, integrated personality is maintained through role continuity. However, this theory assumes that the individual must take the initiative in seeking similar roles, and that there are opportunities for roles similar to the ones dropped.

Labeling Theory

This theory posits that the labels we give to people will affect their self-perception and the reactions of others. For example, negative stereotypes about the elderly like "grumpy" and "senile" are likely to influence young people's tendency not to help the elderly, while positive labels like "wise" and "experienced" are likely to influence young people's tendency to help them (Eyet-semitan, 2002b).

Aging as a Subculture

This perspective proposes that elderly persons interact more with each other than with other members of the society, because they share common experiences, interests, and background. But, also, they are forced to interact with each other because of the out-migration of young people from rural to urban centers.

From participating in their own subculture, therefore, elderly persons maintain their self-worth and self-concept (Rose, 1965). Belonging to a subculture is something positive, but it could also be negative. While it constitutes a platform for fighting for and protecting shared interests, it also provides an opportunity for others to stereotype and segregate the group.

Although discussed discretely, these theories are interrelated. For example, labeling elderly people could result from a subculture of the elderly; it could also just as easily result from the activities and roles associated with the elderly. Based on the foregoing discussions, we will now turn to the following typical adult roles and activities that these theories and perspectives help to explain.

Marriage

Early adulthood is the typical stage for marriage and for the formation of new attachments (Erikson, 1959). It involves emotional emancipation from parents, while still being engaged as a son or a daughter (Nydegger, 1991). With a secure attachment to parents, it becomes easier to make the attachment transition from parent to spouse. In addition, the new roles that are assumed in marriage (the man assumes the role of a provider) help to delineate a new stage in the individual's life span.

Parenthood

Becoming a parent is also one of the typical experiences of early adulthood stage (see Baltes, Staudinger, & Lindenberger, 1999, for details on discussion on senescence). Parenthood is tied to a greater sense of purpose. Usually for the man it is to provide physical support and protection, while for the woman it is to provide emotional support. These gender roles seem natural, but they are also intensified as a result of parenthood (Gutmann 1975).

Although parenthood brings a greater sense of self-worth and purpose, it also puts demands on time, including the time spent with a spouse (Belsky, Lang, & Rovine, 1985). With external influences like work (Bronfenbrenner, 1979), parenthood could be stressful, making the individual feel inadequate as a parent.

Parents usually adopt different styles in performing their roles. Baumrind (1983) identifies the following parenting and discipline styles:

1. authoritarian parent: gives strict rules with little or no room for discussions of the reasons behind the rules;
2. authoritative parent: provides rules with explanation for them. The child is free to participate in discussions of those rules; and
3. permissive parent: parent provides few rules and hardly punishes misbehaviors by the child.

Research shows that the authoritative style works best for middle-class white American families (Baumrind, 1983), and is linked to higher levels of prosocial behavior and to internalization (Dekovic & Janssens, 1992; Grolnick & Ryan, 1989). Authoritarian style, on the other hand, promotes lower prosocial behavior, lower self-esteem, and poor feelings of empowerment; and children perceive it to be less fair and are less likely to internalize parental values through this style (Grolnick & Ryan, 198). But authoritarian style can be positive. However, there are contrary findings from the authoritarian parenting style. For example, among African American girls, greater assertiveness is associated with an authoritarian style (Baumrind, 1972) thus suggesting that cultural differences may account for the perception of, and the efficacy of, parenting and discipline styles. Whereas individualism will be more in tune with an authoritative style, collectivism will be more in tune with an authoritarian style (Markus & Kitayama, 1991).

Work Career

Choosing a career is also typically associated with the early adulthood stage. Education level not only affects career choices but also predicts movement along the career ladder (Dreher & Bretz, 1991). Because society ascribes roles to different genders, jobs are stereotyped as either a "man's job" or a "woman's job" (Reskin, 1993), and such stereotypes invariably affect the types (and levels) of education men and women seek, as well as the hiring dispositions of potential employers.

Apart from parental influences and stereotypes about "gender appropriate" jobs, Holland (1992) suggests that personality dispositions do affect career choice. For example, an individual with an aggressive, strong personality, but with low interpersonal skills, will choose practical (realistic) jobs like mechanic, electrician, or surveyor. Although Holland's preposition has been cross-culturally validated in both Western and non-Western cultures (Kahn, Alvi, Shaukat, Hussain, & Baig, 1990), people are likely to go with whatever job is available especially when choices are limited.

Women's Work Pattern

Whereas the work career of men during early adulthood stage is more predictable, most women move in and out of work careers mainly for family reasons, for example, children and job-related relocation of spouse. Work and family roles conflict for women, but they seldom do for men. In other words, for women, work and family roles occur concurrently, while for men, they occur simultaneously. For example, women are more likely than men to interrupt work in order to take a sick child to the doctor or to look after a sick parent (Pleck, 1977).

Women who work possess certain advantages over those women who do not work. They have more leverage in marital decision making and household responsibilities, because with more earning power, they get closer to men in equality (Spitze, 1988).

Intergenerational Relationships

Taking on care-giving roles to help elderly parents is common during the middle adulthood stage, with the daughter more likely than the son to provide care when an aging parent needs assistance. However, it depends on the nature of care. Men do provide care in many cases and are more likely to provide financial assistance or instrumental help, like lawn mowing, to elderly parents than women. In return, elderly people serve as baby-sitters to their grandchildren (Lee, Dwyer, & Coward, 1993). But the perception of a parent's need is a major factor in an adult child's caregiving behavior (Cicirelli, 1983), without which caregiving behavior may not be initiated. Even so, caregiving is a dyadic process between the caregiver and the care receiver and the elderly could refuse care if offered (Wolinsky & Johnson, 1991).

Unfortunately, with caregiving sometimes comes loss of opportunities, stress, and physical illness. For example, those who provide care to frail and demented elderly persons have a reduced functioning of their immune system (Hoyert & Seltzer, 1992), but this is moderated by whether the need for care is sudden, such as a stroke, or if it develops gradually, such as chronic illness (Biegel, Sales, & Schulz, 1991). There is more stress on the caregiver if the care need developed suddenly or if the caregiver is ill prepared for the caregiving role (Eyetsemitan, 2000).

Intergenerational Living Arrangements

With a high need for individualism living alone is commonplace in the developed world, even among those elderly people with declining health. In the case of a significant decline, elderly people are forced to live with their children (Worobel & Angel, 1990) but poverty, ethnic values, and the number of female children an elderly person has would also influence the decision to live with children (Choi, 1991). For example, in the United States a three-generation family living arrangement is a higher possibility among Blacks, Hispanic, or Asians than among Whites. Since minority groups are more represented among the poor, it is difficult to know whether a multigenerational living arrangement is based on cultural values, or it's based on poverty with the need to share scarce resources.

Retirement

Retirement will be given more detailed attention in Chapter 8, but here it will only be discussed as a stage that typically occurs in late adulthood, with preparations for it beginning in middle adulthood. As a stage in the life course, retirement is usually age determined. Among various individuals, it can lead to those behaviors espoused by activity, disengagement, and continuity theories. For example, there are individuals who are retired but who still maintain a work regimen either through part-time jobs, volunteer work, or work around the home (activity theory). Others, after retirement, may decide that it is now time to rest from any type of work (disengagement theory), and yet there are others who believe that, after retirement, they have to maintain work similar to the type of work they retired from, in order to have an integrated personality (continuity theory).

The preparation for retirement may begin as early as 15 years before the anticipated date (in middle adulthood), and when this occurs, work gradually becomes less central to the individual. For women who start a work career late, however, their work trajectory will be different. While retirement usually occurs around 65 (this may vary according to occupations), two important factors that are likely to influence retirement timing are financial security and health status.

THE DEVELOPING WORLD

MARRIAGE

In the developing world, marriage as a marker of the early adulthood stage may have different beginning and ending times than the marriages of people living in developed societies because of differences in life expectancies. And, some of the characteristics of marriage are different from marriages in the developed world. For example, married couples may still not completely break their ties with parents. Also, for females, the marriage age may be earlier, especially in cultures dominated by Islam. Furthermore, given the collectivistic nature of most of the developing world (Hofstede, 1980), marriage as an event may occur between two families first, and then the two individuals later, as opposed to an event that occurs between two individuals who may or may not bring two families together. For example Harry Gardiner, in Gardiner, Mutter, & Kosmitzki (1998), narrated the marriage perspective of a female Indian graduate student in his cross-cultural course in the United States. This Indian student said she trusted her parents to make a wise decision on her future husband back in India because they knew her, and also knew her future husband and his family. She received admonitions from her fellow classmates not to marry someone she didn't know. Levine and others (Levine, Sato, Hashimoto, & Verma, 1995) carried out a multinational study on the role of love in marriage decisions among university students from India, Pakistan, Thailand, Mexico, Brazil, Japan, Hong Kong, the Philippines, Australia, England, and the United States. They found that students from individualistic cultures (Western) assigned greater importance to love in their marriage decisions than students from collectivistic cultures (non-Western).

Because of the way marriage comes about, it is difficult for couples to be emotionally emancipated from their parents and for parents to let go in return. Thus marital problems are taken to parents (or to parent surrogates) to resolve rather than to professionals (marriage counselors), as is often the case in developed societies.

But the physical distance between urban centers (where most young people now migrate to in search of wage employment) and rural areas (mostly inhabited by elderly people) creates a new dimension to marriage. Modernization (a reflection of the "Developed world" environmental dimension) leads to the erosion of the influence elderly persons have over young people (Apt, 1996). This may also affect the area of mate selection. But if modernization influences do not match an individual's *demand* values, modernization influences will not change the person's behavior. The case of the Indian graduate student narrated earlier exemplifies this assertion. Although far away in America (a modern society), she still holds traditional views about marriage ("Developing world" environmental dimension).

We also propose that although marriage signifies emotional emancipation from families in developed societies, it does, however, represent a time for expanding emotional relationships in developing societies to members of the in-group or the collectives that now include another family. Also, whereas it is a time for learning new roles as husbands and wives, it is also a time for learning to expand one's responsibilities toward the spouse's family. Hui and Triandis' (1986) assertions about the beliefs and behavior that characterize collectivism strengthen these propositions. They include the following:

1. people are concerned about how the decisions they make affect others in their in-group; people have the need to share material resources;
2. people share nonmaterial resources like time, affection, fun, or sacrificing some interesting activities for a member of the collective; and
3. people have feelings of involvement in others' lives.

We suggest that marriage, perhaps more than any event preceding it in the individual's life, provides an opportunity to put into practice those beliefs and behaviors that characterize collectivism, beyond one's own family group. This practice extends to not just the spouse's family but also to the spouse's ethnic group or nationality (if the spouse belongs to a different ethnic group or nationality). Thus marriage represents not just the expansion of the collectives. It leads to the assumption of new roles and responsibilities within the expanded collectives.

PARENTHOOD

Parenthood and marriage typically occur during early adulthood stage (see Baltes, Staudinger, & Lindenberger, 1999 for details on discussion on senescence), and are almost inseparable. Becoming a parent may not be contingent upon marriage, but when marriage occurs parenthood is highly expected. Denga (1982) studied childlessness and marital adjustment in northern Nigeria and concluded that there is a higher level of marital adjustment among mothers than among involuntarily childless women. In other words, married couples cannot voluntarily choose to be childless, as is the case in Western societies. And when couples have children, there is a special preference for male children over female children. For example, in a survey of 3,006 men, aged 20-plus years, in western Sierra Leone, Campbell (1991) reported that over 70% of his sample, made of up 80% urban and 20% rural dwellers, considered male children as more important. Sex preference for males was significantly stronger among the male respondents. This is because male children keep the family name and remain members of the in-group, whereas female children are "lost" to the out-group after marriage. In China, for example, a married woman only becomes a full member of her husband's family when she gives birth to a male heir. And when financial resources are inadequate to send all the children to school, sons are given preference even if the academic records of the girls are better (Yu & Carpenter, 1991). In Turkmenistan and Azerbaijan, there are also studies that report Turkoman men and women as well as Azerbaijani desiring more sons than daughters (Hortacsu, Bastug, & Muhammetberdiev, 2001).

But with the influence of the "Developed world dimension" of the cross-cultural environment of developing societies (Eyetsemitan, 2002a), the preference for males over females is not always the case. For example, Gardner and Gardner (1991) report that parents in Thailand prefer neither males nor females, and in Turkmenistan and Azerbaijan, urbanization and the status of women are associated with gender preference (Hortacsu, Bastug, & Muhammetberdiev, 2001).

Studies on parenting and discipline styles suggest that the authoritarian style is more of a reflection of the collectivistic culture. Because self-assertion is discouraged and self-restraint is encouraged in such a culture, the authoritarian style is more effective and desirable than the authoritative style. For example, Chao (1994) suggests that Chinese parents pursue authoritarian style for the purpose of promoting family harmony; in other words, getting everyone "in line." However, such a parental child-rearing style should not be mistaken for a demonstration of a lack of love or for a maladaptive and inflexible manner of processing information (Duane & Grusec, 2001).

But, again, the "developed world dimension" of the cross-cultural environment as reflected by Western education and urbanization can promote an authoritative parenting style, which may be adaptive in urban settings. However, the same cross-cultural environment can also promote the coexistence of authoritative and authoritarian styles (a reflection of the developed and developing world dimensions) similar to J. B. P. Sinha's (1980) organizational "nurturant-task" leader and to Kagitcibasi's (1996a) "autonomous-relational self." When such occurs, each environmental dimension is likely to trigger the appropriate parental style. For example, while on a visit with relatives in the rural areas from the city, an authoritative parent might become authoritarian with his children because that is the norm and expected way of child rearing in his new environment.

WORK CAREER

Work career for most people in developing societies, and developed societies, typically begins during early adulthood stage. This is largely due to the influence that governments in almost all societies have in ordering the stages of human development into a tripartite life scheme of education, work, and retirement (Kohli, 1986). In other words, the educational phase precedes work. But what happens in developing societies where there is a high rate of illiteracy? We suggest that a shrinking span of the educational phase may allow for working careers to begin relatively early (resulting in some cases to what the developed world refers to as child labor) and to an early onset of early adulthood stage.

FEMALE WORK PATTERN

There are a number of factors that would interfere with the onset of work career for females, including a lack of formal Western education and early marriage. In a study of parental attitudes toward female education in northern Nigeria, Niles (1989) reports that rural parents had unfavorable attitudes toward Western-style schooling for girls, despite the government's efforts to universalize primary education. In other words, there is a low *demand* for Western-style education even though there is a high *supply* of Western education. But to not embrace Western-style education in an Islamic culture (northern Nigeria is predominantly Islamic) does not necessarily mean that children are not exposed to other types of schooling. For example, children are sent to Arabic and Koranic schools that emphasize religious training. Because many Western-style schools in the developing world are run by Christian organizations like Catholic, Methodist, and Anglican, they emphasize the Christian religion (a reflection of the Developed world environmental dimension) over Islamic or traditional religion (a reflection of the "Developing world" environmental dimension). Therefore, for some, this results in a low *demand* for Western-style schooling because of a low *demand* for Christian religion (or the Developed world environmental dimension) of their cross-cultural environment.

Apart from education, marriage also could interfere with the onset of a work career. Marriage for females can occur as early as between 12 and 14 years in the case of the Tharu tribal women of India (Singhal & Mrinal, 1991) or as late as 20 years, the age of first marriage for women in Samoa (Muse, 1991). Whatever the age of marriage, Gardiner and Gardiner (1991) assert that marriage is an important event for women in Asia with only a small percentage opting to not marry. Apparently marriage takes precedence over work and career. Even parental expectations for daughters place marriage above work and career, and these expectations are inculcated in the children from early childhood, and they are conveyed in parental preference of boys over girls for Western-style education (Yu & Carpenter, 1991).

But formal Western education could be beneficial to women in marriage. Women with social skills and training have leverage in winning over their husbands and in-laws (Kumar, 1991). For example, a survey of Egyptian husbands found that 58% of them described working wives as more mature, more stable, and more adjusted in marriage (Abd el-Fattah, 1984). But to some men, Western-style education for women could be threatening. Miller (1984) examined interview data on men's attitudes toward extended-family authority and women's right. She collected data from about 6,000 male factory workers (aged 18 to 32 years) in India, Bangladesh, Israel, Nigeria, Argentina, and Chile, and concluded that, across cultures, higher levels of education and improved standards of living led to belief of female independence from the extended family (members of the collectives).

INTERGENERATIONAL RELATIONS

Helping dependent parents occurs mainly in middle adulthood stage, but also in early adulthood stage, especially in countries that fall under the United Nations' Human Development Index low category for life expectancy. There is, however, a psychosocial aspect to dependency that is not tied to physical frailty, but to a psychosocial contract between parent and child. This contract is reinforced through socialization practices beginning from early childhood. The child is the parent's "walking stick" and "social security" (Kagitcibasi, 1996b; Nsamenang, 1992), and this notion is a shared knowledge between the parent and the child on the one hand, and between both of them and the larger society on the other. For example, among the Ju/'hoansi tribe of Botswana, care is a right, and the elderly do not negotiate it as a favor. In fact, parents boast in the community about the help they receive from their children (Rosenberg, 1997). However, modernization (a reflection of the Developed world environmental dimension), could be a threat to adult children's parental caregiving behavior. The migration by young people from rural to urban areas in search of wage employment, coupled with other Western cultural opportunities in the urban centers, could reduce the status of (and support for) the elderly (Apt, 1996; Cowgill & Holmes, 1972).

Older people value maintaining regular interactions with children, siblings, friends, grandchildren, and other members of the collectives, even if they are far away. But the extent of their interactions is likely to be influenced more by physical proximity—being a member of the household or living close-by. With poor access to telephones and means of transportation, the frequency of interactions that elderly people might want to maintain with their family members and friends in faraway places would be limited. Therefore, frequency of interaction with distant family members and friends would be out of elderly people's control, and would depend largely on how loved ones in distant places frequently correspond with and/or visit them. In her study of the Ghanaian elderly, Apt (1996) observed that: "Elderly people themselves rarely visit their children in far away places due, perhaps, to long distance of travel involved and immobility of the elderly" (p.76). But elderly people are not so helpless. They can exercise human agency in getting distant children to visit, even when the children are not prepared to. For example, from studying the Dobe Ju/'hoansi elderly of Botswana, Rosenberg (1997) noted that, although materially poor by North American standards, the elderly are "equipped with rich cultural resources for articulating their concerns, fears, and anxieties and for ensuring support" (p.50).

Dependency, coupled with the influence of modernization, seems to portray elderly people as disengaged from their society (Disengagement theory), or as having lost their traditional status and roles. This is not entirely correct. While it is expected that some roles will be lost as a result of senescence (Baltes, Staudinger, & Lindenberger, 1999), others will be retained (Continuity theory) with young people simply joining their ranks and taking on roles alongside the elderly. When young people assume status and roles that are usually identified with the elderly, it does not necessarily mean that elderly people have lost their status and roles. For example, the Akan tribe of Ghana (and the Ibos of eastern Nigeria) have a proverb that says, "When children learn to wash their hands, they may eat with the elders" (Apt 1988, p. 25). This implies that as young people distinguish themselves, they are honored and admitted into the community of elders. Eyetsemitan (1997) notes that because some young individuals "age" faster than their roles and are so recognized does not necessarily mean that elderly roles are usurped or that the prestige (or content) of those roles are diminished. Furthermore, the belief in the spirit world helps to maintain the roles and prestige of the elderly. Cohen (1994) suggests that no matter how Westernized or urbanized people become, they still believe in the powers of the dead to do harm when disobeyed or angered. Elderly people are believed to be close to the dead, and therefore serve as intermediaries between the living and the dead, interpreting the wishes of the dead. This intermediary role is age-related and may not be shared with even deserving young individuals. Another age-related role is the role to pronounce blessings or curses.

Age-related roles (a reflection of the Labeling theory) usually are resistant to modernization influences (the Developed world environmental dimension), and the activities required in an age-related role such as ancestral consultation, blessings, and curse span the different societal layers (Bronfrenbrenner, 1979). For example, blessings or prayers are sought for marriage and for a child (representing the *microsystem*), for promotion at work, and for rains in order to ensure a fruitful harvest (representing the *mesosystem*), and during dedication ceremonies for government projects (representing the *exosystem*).

As long as there is a *demand* for the spiritual services offered by elderly people, the elderly will continue to maintain their age-related spiritual role in the society. Singhal and Mrinal (1991) noted that the elderly in India are not only experts in herbal medicine, but there is always a need for them because families are large corporate bodies with common social and religious obligations.

INTERGENERATIONAL LIVING ARRANGEMENTS

It is uncommon for elderly persons to live alone, and even when they do, it is usually not by choice. Unlike in developed societies where living alone signifies independence, self-sufficiency, and a lack of dependency, all of which are highly valued, in developing societies there is a negative perception to living alone. Independent living in the developing world, connotes a different meaning. It includes a coresidency arrangement with an elderly person as the head of the household (Apt, 1996). For example, in Ghana the common living arrangement is where the elderly live with relations, but with the majority of them as heads of household. Although children and grandchildren most often live with the elderly, other relations who live with the elderly in ranking order, include sisters and brothers, nieces and nephews, and occasionally cousins (Apt, 1996).

But there is also a coresidency arrangement where the elderly are not the head of household. For example, living with a married son is the ideal living arrangement for elderly parents in Taiwan, but here the strongest motive is poor health (Lee, Lin, & Chang, 1995). Even so, there is still a strong expectation that adult children should care for and support their elderly parents, and a strong sense that at least one child coresides or lives in close proximity to them. In Latin America, unmarried elderly persons are more likely to live in extended households (de Vos, 1990), sometimes, but not always, as heads of household. In the Philippines most elderly people prefer coresidency with children (Domingo & Asis, 1995), and in Singapore the normative patterns of obligation that children have toward parents are important for coresidency, although government housing policies, modern lifestyles, and rural-urban migration patterns of young people are also important factors (Mehta, Osman, & Alexander, 1995). In a survey of seven developing countries Hashimoto (1991) concluded that the elderly still maintain coresidency with children, despite changing socioeconomic and demographic conditions.

Usually, a coresidency arrangement with an adult child is most likely to occur in urban centers because of the job opportunities that cities provide to young people. Cities may not be ideal for elderly people who are psychologically attached to their "soil of origin" back in the villages. In addition, with relatively few elderly persons living in cities, urban centers may not help to promote an elderly subculture. The government of Singapore developed a measure to encourage families to take care of their elderly parents. This measure encourages married children and their parents to apply for adjoining public apartments and it gives them priority in the allocation process. The thinking is that elderly parents who reside close to their adult children would enjoy care and support and interactions with their grandchildren. But the psychological effects of displacing elderly people from their "soils of origin" and of not having the opportunities of a subculture should be given equal consideration by policymakers. In Chapter 8, we shall discuss more on the importance of housing with regard to retirement, in addition to other social policies for the elderly.

RETIREMENT

For those on wage employment, retirement will typically occur in late adulthood stage (see Baltes, Staudinger, & Lindenberger, 1999 for details on discussion on senescence), but determined largely by retirement policies, health status, and financial security. Financial security sources would include pension, but it would also include the amount of financial support received from adult children and relatives (Rosenberg, 1997). As their parents' "walking stick" or "social security" (Kagitcibasi, 1996b; Nsamenang, 1995), adult children would be instrumental in determining retirement timing. Retirement may not necessarily lead to disengagement from society, especially if elderly people are still sought in leadership roles by family members and by their communities (Singhal & Mrinal, 1991). It may lead to role continuity or even to the adoption of new roles. Again, in Chapter 8, more attention will be given to retirement in addition to other social policies.

In this chapter we have discussed the influence of culture in influencing the roles and activities that the individual engages in during the different stages of adulthood. This is further illustrated in the next chapter through the presentation and discussion of primary data collected from seven developing countries from around the world.

SUMMARY

In this chapter the influence of the life course by three models of culture are discussed. The three models are Generational Systems, Age Class Systems, and Staged Life Course, and they are exemplified by popular theories like role, age stratification, activity, disengagement, continuity, labeling, and aging as a subculture. These theories help to explain activities and roles, like marriage, parenthood, intergenerational relationships, work career, and retirement, that typify various stages of adulthood.

Marriage is a stage that is typically associated with the early adulthood in both developed and developing societies, although the onset may occur earlier in developing societies. In both developed and developing societies new roles and responsibilities are assumed as a result of marriage, and they include parenting and discipline.

Intergenerational relationship includes the support young people provide to their elderly parents. There are similarities and differences in the nature of support that young people provide to elderly parents in developed and developing societies. In both developed and developing societies, support includes physical assistance and coresidency arrangement. But whereas support for elderly parents in developed societies is more likely to be based on need, support for elderly parents in developing societies is more likely to be based on expectations.

Work career typically begins in the early adulthood stage, the onset of which varies between developed and developing societies. Because of the high rate of illiteracy in most developing societies, work career, like marriage, is likely to start relatively early if formal Western education period is short. But, in both developed and developing societies, it is the woman's work career that is more likely to be interrupted than the man's work career—usually by family matters.

Although retirement is a stage that typically occurs in late adulthood, it is likely to be influenced by retirement policies of employers, health, and financial security. As their parents' "walking sticks" and "social security," adult children also are likely to influence retirement timing in developing societies. In retirement it is expected that certain roles would be lost, while others are continued and new ones added.

6

A Seven-Country Study of Aging and Adult Development in the Developing World

Our theme throughout this book has been that processes in adult development and aging are influenced by interactions between the person and his or her environment. If person-environment interactions were not important, all aspects of the aging process and adult development would be the same across the globe. In reviewing several theoretical positions relating to aging and development, we have tried to evaluate these theories in terms of how applicable they are to the developing world. In order to empirically establish the role of sociocultural variables in aging and development in the developing world, we conducted a seven-country study. First, we wanted to establish the age boundaries along which people from the developing world placed the three stages of early adulthood, middle adulthood, and late adulthood. However, age is not the only criterion that defines the three stages of adulthood; these stages are also demarcated by the roles that are typical of the different stages. Therefore, we obtained data in terms of those roles that were typical for early adulthood, middle adulthood, and late adulthood stages.

The countries selected for the study were developing nations from different regions of the world—Botswana and Nigeria (Africa), Bangladesh and Indonesia (Asia), Brazil and Chile (South America), and Bahrain (Middle East and Mediterranean). These countries have many things in common. In many respects, they were exposed to modernization influences through contacts with the countries that colonized them. These countries also have fairly young and predominantly rural populations that are involved mainly in agricultural production. But they also differ in several dimensions, including their rankings on the United Nation's Human Development Index (HDI). Bahrain, Brazil, and Chile are high on the HDI, Botswana and Indonesia have a medium rating, while Bangladesh and Nigeria are low on the HDI. In addition, these countries have different climates, political structures, and religions. Based on the factors that they have in common, we expected that there would be similarities in some variables that affect aging processes and adult development in these countries, and perhaps throughout the developing world. However, the differences might help to shed some light on those variables that are specific to each country or a subset of countries examined in this study. In order to highlight both similarities and differences, we provide a brief overview of each of the seven countries. Most of the information used in these summaries was obtained from Encyclopedia Britannica Online (1994–1999). Afterward we shall present the results from our study.

HIGH HDI COUNTRIES

Bahrain

The State of Bahrain, as this country is officially called, consists of Bahrain Island and approximately 30 other smaller islands along the Arabian Peninsula in the Persian Gulf. Most of the country's 546,000 people (1993 population estimates) live on the main island, which is also the center of economic activity. Bahrain was in many ways a colony of Britain, which gained extensive control of Bahrain from 1820 to 1968 when it decided to withdraw all its forces from the Persian Gulf. In August 1971, Sulman al Khalifa officially proclaimed Bahrain an independent state. To this day, the Khalifa family still runs the constitutional monarchy of Bahrain.

The climate of Bahrain is mostly warm all year round—winter temperatures (November to February) average below 19° C (67° F); it is within this period that all of the country's three inches or so annual rainfall occurs. Humidity is high throughout the year, particularly in the summer months (May to October) when temperatures rise to about 88° F (31° C).

The majority of the country's population is Arab, about two-thirds of these are native-born. Islam is the predominant religion consisting of two main sects: the Shi'ites, who are in the majority, and the Sunnites. Although Arabic is the official language, English is widely spoken as well (reflecting the "Developed and Developing worlds" environment described in Chapter 2). Approximately one third of the country's population is aged 15 years or less. Males outnumber females significantly, owing in part to the large number of male temporary workers. Relatively high birth rates in the face of low death rates have resulted in a high rate of population growth. Bahrain is one of the most urbanized countries in our study—an estimated four-fifths of the population is urban, a characteristic of the "Developed world" environment.

Bahrain is a developing economy with a mixture of state- and privately owned enterprises. The main sources of wealth are petroleum and natural gas. These have given Bahrain a gross national product (GNP) per capita that is similar to that of the developed world. Because only 3% of the country's land is arable, agriculture is of minimal economic importance. The little that is produced is from the springs north of Bahrain Island and consists mainly of dates, bananas, mangoes, tomatoes, and other vegetables.

The government is giving increasing importance to manufacturing due to dwindling petroleum reserves; however, the impact of this new emphasis is yet to be felt. Manufacturing and utilities together still account for only 10% of the labor force. The major nonpetroleum industrial products include aluminum, plastics, asphalt, tiles and cement blocks, wheat flour, and soft drinks. Bahrain also has about 60 offshore banks and started a stock exchange in 1989. Combined with efficient and elaborate telecommunications facilities and a computer services company, Bahrain has become the preeminent financial center in the Persian Gulf.

Bahrain operates a constitutional monarchy. The 1973 constitution vested most of the powers in the emir who makes most of the government's major decisions. A once popularly elected legislature was disbanded in 1975 by the emir who accused many members of engaging in subversive activities. Political parties are not allowed; public representation is through the traditional Arab and Islamic system of a *majilis*, through which citizens and residents present petitions to the emir.

Perhaps owing to its size, the mass media in Bahrain is not elaborate; whatever little of it that exists is privately owned, however. Though not officially censored, the press seldom criticizes the ruling family and its policies.

Bahrain runs an elaborate social services system. The state offers free and comprehensive medical care to all citizens and expatriates—a reflection of a "social democratic" approach to public policy except that benefits are also extended to foreigners. The state also provides free education and has benefits programs for the old and the disabled. Consequently, health conditions in the country have improved greatly since independence in 1971. Most tropical diseases have been eradicated, which has resulted in the life expectancy of Bahrain rising to 71 years for men and 76 years for women, the highest in the Middle East.

Brazil

With a land area of 3,300,171 square miles, Brazil is the fifth largest country in the world and makes up about half of the South American continent. Brazil also has the largest population in South America, though its population density is still relatively low, mainly due to the vast land area. The several ethnic groups, the early Portuguese, Indians, and people of African ancestry, have intermixed considerably over the years to such an extent that it is rare to find unmixed ethnic elements. A former colony of Portugal, Brazilians speak Portuguese, the only country in South America to do so, although the Portuguese version spoken in Brazil has been transformed and enriched by Indian and African influences. Almost all Brazilians are Christians—Roman Catholics—which makes Brazil the largest Roman Catholic country in the world, a reflection of "Developed world" environmental dimension. The population of Brazil has witnessed rapid growth, although family planning programs have been introduced to reduce growth rate. However, the death rate has declined progressively. Brazil has a very young population; about 50% of Brazilians are 20 years of age or under. There has been so much rural-urban migration that the urban centers now make up approximately 75% of the population.

Brazil operates a market economy that consists largely of manufacturing, financial services, agriculture, and trade. Brazil's per capita GNP is higher than the average for the countries in South America. Although agriculture accounts for about 10% of the gross domestic product (GDP), it employs approximately 20% of the labor force. Corn, rice, and wheat are the staple crops and occupy one-third of the arable land. In terms of agricultural exports, Brazil is the world's leading producer of coffee, sugarcane, soybeans, papayas, oranges, and cassava. Livestock raising is a major activity, with Brazil among the world leaders in cattle and pig stocks. Brazil also has a well-developed lumber industry.

Manufacturing makes up one quarter of the GDP and, together with mining, employs nearly 20% of the workforce. The various products produced by this sector include petroleum products, steel ingots, fertilizers, machinery, aircraft, electrical goods, textiles, and automobiles. Even though Brazil runs an essentially free-enterprise economy, government holds a monopoly in petroleum and natural gas exploration, production, and refining.

Health conditions vary widely in Brazil, from excellent to poor, depending on income and remoteness of region; health conditions are worst among the poor and those in the rural areas where there is a severe shortage of qualified health personnel. The most serious health problems are diseases of circulatory system, malaria, communicable diseases such as influenza and tuberculosis, and malnutrition. The life expectancy in Brazil is 66 years, lower than that of Argentina and Venezuela. The continuing rural-urban migration has created a shortage in housing, resulting in urban shantytowns known as *favelas*.

Government provides free primary and secondary education, which is compulsory between ages 7 and 14. Nearly all school-age children can read and write, although approximately 25% of adults are still illiterate. Brazil has many universities, about half of which are operated by the government. After several encounters with repressive regimes, Brazil enacted a new constitution in 1988 that abolished the president's power to rule by decree. The same constitution has ensured freedom of the press from government censorship. The country has several print and broadcast media that operate mainly in the major cities of Sao Paulo and Rio de Janeiro.

Chile

The Republic of Chile, a former colony of Spain, is located along the western seaboard of South America and extends nearly 2,700 miles from its boundary with Peru to the tip of South America at Cape Horn, a point only 400 miles north of Antarctica. Chile is a long, narrow country with an average width of only about 110 miles. It shares borders with Peru and Bolivia to the north, with Argentina on the long eastern border, and is bounded on the west by the

Pacific Ocean. Chile exercises sovereignty over a number of offshore islands such as Easter Island and Juan Fernández. The landscape of Chile is for the most part mountainous, dominated by the Andes range. Because of its extreme length, Chile's climate varies widely from the coastal desert beginning in the tropical north to the low temperatures in its sub-Antarctic southern tip. Severe winter storms and flash floods alternate with serious summer droughts.

Pre-Spanish indigenes of Chile included the Diaguita, Picunche, Mapuche, and Cunco Indians. However, a relatively homogeneous, mainly mestizo population, has developed, with a strong sense of cultural unity. The only significant minority is the Mapuche. A majority of Chileans are Christians, mostly Roman Catholics, a reflection of the "Developed world" environmental dimension. Chile's population is growing at a moderate rate, due primarily to a relatively high birth rate and a low death rate, although its growth rate is the lowest in South America. Like most countries in the developing world, Chile has a young population—nearly one-third of the population is under 15 years of age. About 75% of the population is urban, with the national metropolis, Santiago, dwarfing all the other cities, another reflection of the "Developed world" environmental dimension.

Chile has a partially developed free-market economy that is operated by both state and private enterprises and is based mainly on services, mining, and manufacturing. The GNP is growing rapidly, and per capita-wise, is higher than average in South America. The GNP originates primarily from finance, real estate, defense, wholesale and retail, mining and manufacturing. Agricultural production is limited due to the small amount of arable land. Therefore, Chile does not produce enough food to feed its population. Aside from producing significant amounts of petroleum, natural gas, and iron ore, Chile is the largest producer of copper in the world, and one of the world's leaders in the production of molybdenum and iodine. Other minerals extracted in Chile include gold, silver, manganese, lead, limestone, and hydraulic lime.

After a spate of political instability from military coups and dictatorships, Chile has been governed by an elected president since 1990. The country has a bicameral National Congress that consists of a 120-member lower house that is elected to four-year terms. The 47-member upper house has a complex composition: 37 members are popularly elected to eight-year terms, 5 members are appointed by the president and the Supreme Court, and 4 are commanders in chief of the four branches of the armed forces.

Chile runs a fairly elaborate social security system that provides benefits for old age, maternity, disability, and sickness, and has been expanding steadily. In 1981, government transferred the management of social security to the private sector. Government has increased per capita spending on health and reorganized the National Health Service to provide decentralized, local health units. The resultant improvements in health conditions have raised the life expectancy to 68 years for men and 75 years for women, the highest level in South America. In addition, the infant mortality rate has dropped sharply to the lowest levels in Latin America. However, there is a serious housing shortage in Chile, particularly in the urban centers. This has contributed to the development of squatter villages called *callampas* located at the outskirts of the major cities.

With an adult literacy rate of 95%, Chile is clearly one of the most literate countries in the world (representing the "Global world" environmental dimension). Primary education is free, and education in general is compulsory for all children between the ages of 6 and 13 years. The news media in Chile were monitored and regulated during the military era; the return to democracy has led to a much freer press, however.

MEDIUM HDI COUNTRIES

Botswana

Known initially as the British Bechuanaland Protectorate since 1885, Botswana obtained independence and became the Republic of Botswana on September 30, 1966. Botswana is a landlocked country in the center of southern Africa with a population of 1,448,00 (1994 estimate). The entire population is characterized as Botswana regardless of ethnic origin, even though more than half the population may not be ethnic Tswana. Other major ethnic groups include the Khalagari, Ngwato, Tswapong, Birwa, and Kalanga. English is the official language, but the national language is Setswana, a reflection of the "Developing and Developed worlds" environmental dimensions.

Due to the arid nature of the land, water is scarce. As a result, the country is sparsely populated. The eastern part of the country is the most densely populated; the west-central and southwest are the least populated. A majority of the population is Christian, a reflection of the "Developed world" environmental dimension, even though a sizeable proportion adheres to African traditional beliefs, a reflection of the "Developing world" environmental dimension. Botswana's population is mainly rural, with only about 25% living in urban areas. Approximately half of Botswana's population is 15 years of age or less. Life expectancy is 57 years for males and 63 years for females. Declines in birth rate have been attributed mainly to improved life expectancy, making Botswana the first African country in which such a change has been documented.

Both public and private sectors participate in the Botswana economy, which is largely dependent on raising livestock (mostly cattle) and the mining of diamonds, copper, and nickel. The country's GNP has grown rapidly and per capita-wise, though still relatively low, is one of the highest in southern Africa. Drought-resistant sorghum, corn (maize), millet, vegetables, and melons are produced through subsistence-level cultivation, but this output usually is not able to meet domestic demands due to unpredictable rainfall and poor soils. Even though agriculture accounts for a very small percentage of the GDP, it still employs about 75% of the labor force. Mining accounts for more than 40% of the GDP but employs only a small percentage of the labor force. Skilled labor is in short supply and thousands of Botswana workers are employed in South African mines.

Botswana practices a multiparty democracy with a parliamentary government. Legislative power is vested in the unicameral National Assembly, 40 members of whom are directly elected for a five-year term, 4 who are indirectly elected, and 2 ex officio members, the president and the attorney general.

Although Botswana does not have a social security system, government provides free health services. A majority of these health services are provided through mobile clinics; however, there is still a shortage of hospitals and health care personnel. The most common serious illnesses are gastrointestinal and respiratory. More recently, problems from cardiovascular diseases as well as HIV/AIDS have been on the increase. Nearly 75% of the population of Botswana is literate. Free primary education was introduced in 1980. Although 90% of school-age children are enrolled in primary school, only 25% attend secondary school. Tertiary education is available at the University of Botswana in the capital city of Gaborone.

Indonesia

Indonesia is the largest country in Southeast Asia with approximately 752,400 square miles, consisting of about 13,670 islands, at least 7,000 of which are not inhabited. It is an archipelago (an island group) that lies across the equator for more than 12% of the Earth's circumference. The country is located off the coast of the Southeast Asian mainland in the Indian and Pacific Oceans. Approximately 75% of the country's area is contained in the three largest islands of Borneo, Sumatra, and the Irian Jaya portion of New Guinea. Adding Celebes, Java, and the Moluccas accounts for almost the entire land area. The densely populated island of Java alone accounts for more than half of the estimated population of approximately 200 million people. Indonesia has about 220 active volcanoes. The country has a tropical climate that is usually hot and humid; average temperatures range from 74° to 88° F. Precipitation occurs all year round, usually in the form of thunderstorms that result mainly from the monsoon. Tropical rain forests occupy approximately two-thirds of the land area.

Indonesia used to be initially called the Dutch (Netherlands) East Indies and was first named Indonesia in 1884. After a brief period of occupation by the Japanese (1942–1945), Indonesia declared independence from the Netherlands in 1945, though the struggle for independence continued until 1949. Indonesia has more than 300 different ethnic groups that speak 250 distinct languages. However, a majority of the country's population is of Malay ancestry, speaks languages with a Malayo-Polynesian base, and professes Islam as a religion. The Javanese form the largest subgroup and have the most dominant language.

The nonindigenous group is the Chinese, who have lived in Indonesia for several generations. Bahasa Indonesia is the country's official language.

Although Indonesia's population almost doubled between 1960 and 1990, the country's growth rate has declined due to late marriages, birth-control methods and other family planning programs. Infant and child mortality rates have also declined, mainly due to improved health care and overall standard of living. Nearly 40% of the population is 15 years of age or less. Life expectancy is about 56 years for males and 59 years for females.

Indonesia has a developing economy that is based mainly on agriculture and manufacturing. The GNP per capita is low, but steadily rising. Although agriculture accounts for only 20% of the GDP, it employs more than 50% of the labor force. Independent peasant farmers account for most of the country's agricultural production. The country's staple food is rice, though natural rubber (Indonesia a major supplier), coffee, tea, tobacco, and oil palm products are produced for export. However, the timber industry along with petroleum and natural gas products are the major export items. Indonesia is among the world's leaders in tin production. The government owns most of the large industries; however, private firms control the manufacturing of consumer goods. A commercial sector, largely dominated by the Chinese community, has been formed and is well developed.

The political system is based on the 1945 constitution that vests executive power in the president who is elected after every five years by the People's Consultative Assembly. President since 1967, Suharto managed to assert firm control over the People's Consultative Assembly, making his reelection a mere routine. Suharto was forced to step down only in 1998 after several weeks of mass demonstration demanding his resignation. There is also a House of People's Representatives; 80% of this 500-member body is popularly elected while the remaining 20% is appointed by the government.

Health care services have improved in Indonesia but there is still a severe shortage of medical personnel. Malnutrition remains a serious problem, especially among children. Government provides compulsory primary education for six years. This is usually followed by three years each of junior and senior secondary school, although these are not compulsory. Approximately 75% of the population is literate. Indonesia has several print and broadcast media; radio and television are mostly government-owned, though there is some local, private ownership even in this segment of the media.

LOW HDI COUNTRIES

Bangladesh

Bangladesh, formerly known as East Bengal, was also a British colony. By the time the British departed in 1947, it became part of East Pakistan. However, nationalist sentiments championed by the political party, Aswani League, campaigned vigorously for Bengali autonomy. The Pakistani government resisted this agitation for statehood and a civil war ensued. With India joining on its side, East Bengal prevailed and the independent nation of Bangladesh was born on December 16, 1971, and continues to be an independent republic within the British Commonwealth.

Located mainly in the confluence of the Ganges, the Brahmaputra and the Meghna River systems that empty into the Bay of Bengal, Bangladesh makes up the eastern two thirds of the Ganges-Brahmaputra deltaic plain. It has a generally low terrain with few elevations greater than 30 feet above sea level. Therefore, lakes, marshes, and swamps form an important aspect of the landscape. Consequently, several hundred square miles of land are flooded during the monsoon season. The country's climate is drastically affected by the monsoon season, June to October; three-quarters of the precipitation occur within this period. The temperature fluctuates between 70° F in the winter and 95° F in the summer. More than 65% of Bangladesh's land consisting mainly of the lowland area is arable; about 20% of it is often irrigated.

The Bengalis, who speak Sanskrit, form a majority of the country's population. More than 80% of the population is Muslim, principally of the Sunnite sect; and about 10% are Hindus. The population of Bangladesh is predominantly rural, only about 25% of the population lives in urban areas, suggesting an environmental context that reflects more of the "developing world." Bangladesh is one of the most densely populated countries in the world. The highest densities, however, occur around Dhaka, the capital city. Bangladesh has a high rate of population growth, with almost half of the population 15 years of age or under. The country still has rather high birth and death rates, both above world averages; life expectancy for both males and females is about 56 years. Bangladesh runs a democracy that has its legislative powers vested in the parliament, whose members are popularly elected to five-year terms. However, democracy has had little opportunity to flourish due to incessant interruptions by the military through military coups.

Bangladesh's economy is mainly agriculture based—more than 40% of the country's GDP comes from agriculture. Natural gas is the country's richest mineral resource, but it is still minor in scale. Thus, most petrochemical products and metals must be imported. Next to agriculture are services, transportation and communication. The GNP is growing more rapidly than the population, though GNP per capita is still one of the lowest in the world. Two thirds of the workforce is employed in agriculture, followed by manufacturing, trade, and services.

The general health condition of the majority of Bangladesh's population is poor. This is partly due to overcrowding, inadequate nutrition, and poor sanitary conditions. A sizeable proportion of the population suffers from infectious diseases such as malaria, cholera, and tuberculosis. Efforts by government to improve health conditions have failed, principally due to shortage of physicians and modern medical facilities as well as the existing poor sanitation.

In the area of education, government offers free, but not compulsory, primary education for five years. The literacy rate in Bangladesh is still relatively low, and only two-thirds of the children attend primary school. The country has general universities, a few specialized universities for agriculture, engineering, and technology, and an Islamic university. While Bangladesh's print media are mostly privately owned and relatively free, the broadcasting media are owned by the government.

Nigeria

The Federal Republic of Nigeria is located on the western coast of Africa. Its neighbors include Niger to the north, Chad to the northeast, Cameroon to the east, and Benin to the west. Present-day Nigeria came into existence in 1914 when the British joined the Northern and Southern protectorates. Nigeria obtained independence from Britain on October 1, 1960, and became a republic in 1963 but has elected to remain a member of the British Commonwealth. With an estimated population of more than 103 million, Nigeria has the largest population in Africa; indeed, it has the largest Black population in the world. It is often said that if you were to pick Black people at random, every fifth person chosen would be a Nigerian.

Nigeria has a great diversity of peoples and cultures, largely due to its location at the meeting point of transcontinental migration routes. There are more than 250 distinct ethnic groups, each with its customs and language. Of these, ten groups—the Hausa, Yoruba, Igbo (Ibo), Fulani, Ibibio, Kanuri, Edo, Tiv, Ijaw, and Nupe—account for more than 90% of the total population. The most dominant three groups are the Hausa in the north, the Yoruba in the west, and the Igbo in the east. English is the official language but is used mainly in the cities, a reflection of the "Developed world" environmental dimension. An indigenous version of English, called pidgin English, is spoken widely especially in the south. Hausa is by far the most widely spoken language in Nigeria and is used by groups in the northern parts of several West African countries; it is also one of the 40 languages in which the British Broadcasting Corporation (BBC) makes news broadcasts. Nearly half of Nigerians are Muslims, about a similar number are Christians, and the remaining number practice the various traditional religions.

Nigeria has both high birth and death rates, although the latter has witnessed considerable declines, especially infant mortality rates, mainly due to the success of the UNICEF-supported Expanded Program on Immunization (EPI), a reflection of the influence of the "Global" environmental dimension. As a consequence, Nigeria's natural rate of population growth is among the highest in the world. Like most other developing nations, Nigeria has a very young population—more than 45% of the population is 15 years of age or less. Life expectancy at birth is comparatively low at 51 years for men and 59 years for women. Nigeria's population is also predominantly rural with almost 60% of the people living in rural areas, a reflection of the "Developing world" environmental dimension.

Nigeria has a mixed economy that relies mainly on petroleum and agriculture. Rapid economic expansion has slowed considerably since the mid-1980s when prices of crude oil fell sharply. Owing in part to this decline, Nigeria's GNP is lower than most other western African countries. Agriculture accounts for about 40% of the GDP but employs almost half the labor force. Nigeria is self-sufficient in meat products but has to resort to imports to supplement most of its staple crops such as corn, sorghum, yams, cassava, and rice. With significant declines in peanuts (groundnuts) and palm products, cocoa and rubber are the only significant export crops.

Industry and mining account for about 20% of the GDP but employ only a small percentage of the labor force, usually in the petroleum industry. Manufacturing remains predominantly small-scale and underdeveloped. The textile industry is one of the leading nonpetroleum industries but is in stiff competition with smuggled goods. Trade, services, and transportation make up one-third of the GDP and employ about 40% of the workforce.

Nigeria is currently a democracy but has had several interruptions from the military in terms of coups. In fact, the military has ruled Nigeria for more than half the years of its existence. The democracy is based on the United States model and has a president, the National Assembly that consists of the House of Representatives, and the Senate. The president can be elected to a maximum of two four-year terms. The constitution allows for multiple parties, which in the past have tended to be based on ethnic, regional, or religious lines.

Health conditions in Nigeria are generally poor. The government has claimed responsibility for medical and health services, but there is a serious shortage of medical personnel, equipment, and prescription drugs. Major health problems include malaria, water-borne gastrointestinal diseases, cerebrospinal meningitis, cholera, and other preventable diseases. HIV/AIDS has become one of the increasing threats to health in Nigeria.

The first six years of school are officially compulsory and even though government has responsibility for payment, many people resort to sending their children to fee-paying private schools due to the poor conditions in most public primary schools. Enrollment into secondary schools is still not very high, but this sector is expanding. Nigeria's literacy rate is very low—only about 57% (1995 estimates) of the population is literate. Even though Nigeria has many universities and other tertiary institutions, these cannot cope with the increasing demand for higher education. Nigeria has both print and electronic media, the latter owned mainly by the government. Past military governments' attempt to censor the press have been largely unsuccessful. Therefore, Nigeria's press is relatively free.

As can be seen from the brief summaries of these countries, these nations are different in a number of dimensions, but have several things in common. For instance, all the nations in this study share the experience of having been colonized by western nations. They also have very young populations—a sizeable proportion of their population is less than 20 years of age. However, there are differences among various nations or combination of nations in terms of climate, ethnic composition, religion, forms of government, and other indexes of development. Given the importance we place on the interaction between the ecocultural environment and the person, we expected a number of similarities as well as differences among participants from these nations in the experience of aging and adult development.

THE SEVEN-COUNTRY STUDY IN GREATER DETAIL

Throughout this text, we have argued that certain aging and adult development theories and processes may not be suitably transferred to the developing world without appropriate modifications. We have already seen from the brief summaries of the seven countries that, on the average, key indexes such as life expectancy, literacy, urbanization, health conditions, and social security services are much lower in these countries than most countries in the developed world. Similarly, the way in which people in the developing world may experience and perceive aging may be quite different. For example, elderly status may empower people in non-Western societies to perform certain roles such as presiding over marriage and burial ceremonies, and settling family and communal disputes, but the same age status may lead to the loss of relevance by elderly people in the developed world.

We set out to empirically test this notion by designing an instrument that would measure key aspects of this general assumption. Specifically, we expected that the lower life expectancy in the developing world would yield fairly lower age demarcations marking the beginning and the end-points for early adulthood, middle adulthood, and late adulthood stages. Second, given the fact that stages can also be defined by roles as well as by activities, we expected that certain roles and activities would be typical for some stages. In addition, because the environment of the developing world is cross-cultural in nature, we reasoned that the global, developed, and developing world dimensions would influence the roles and activities required of adults. For example, marriage and having children should be characteristics of early adulthood, partly as a result of the effect of senescence, which is global and favors the early adulthood stage more than the other stages. For the same reason, we assumed that retirement from wage employment and grandparenthood would be typical of the late adulthood stage, also partly as a consequence of senescence (see Baltes, Staudinger, & Lindenberger, 1999 for details).

We expected that taking care of the financial needs of family members would be more a typical middle adulthood role because of cultural expectations. Furthermore, we expected that if our postulation of a greater value and sense of purpose accorded the elderly in the developing world holds true, the elderly should be seen in a more positive light in terms of how they are thought of and the functions they are assigned. Thus, they should be seen as being wise, they should be requested to preside over important family and cultural events, and they should be asked to intervene in disputes.

Our study is somewhat similar to the one conducted by Best and Williams (1996) titled "Anticipation of Aging: A Cross-Cultural Examination of Young Adults' Views of Growing Old," but is different in two respects. The two studies are similar in the sense that both used undergraduate participants, who are literate and are able to respond to the same questionnaire, thus providing roughly comparable respondents across countries. Unlike our study, Best and Williams asked young adults about their anticipation of what their conditions would be like in old age. While anticipating old age appears to be a way of evaluating *possible self* (Hooker & Kaus, 1992), it may lead to *unrealistic optimism* (Harris, 1996; Regan, Snyder, & Kassin, 1995). We were more interested in how young people perceived the *current* situation of aging and adult development in their respective societies.

The Participants and the Research Instrument

All 1,015 participants were male and female undergraduates enrolled at various universities in Bahrain, Bangladesh, Botswana, Brazil, Chile, Indonesia, and Nigeria. Average age for the entire sample was 21.3 years. However, Indonesia had the youngest mean age (19.2 years) while Nigeria had the oldest mean age (25. 8 years). Participation was voluntary; students were recruited with the assistance of the cooperating researchers in the various countries.

Three categories of information were obtained through the research instrument (a questionnaire). They were demographic information (age and sex), typical age boundaries for the beginning and end-points for the three stages of adulthood, and specific questions about roles. The item for the beginning ages for the three stages read: In my society this stage typically begins at (please check/tick the appropriate age). Ages 15 through 25 were provided for early adulthood stage; 30 through 40 for middle adulthood stage, and 45 through 55 for late adulthood stage. There were provisions for respondents to indicate the appropriate ages if different from the ages in the age ranges provided for the different stages, and also if there were gender differences in age.

The items for the ending ages for the three stages read: In my society, this stage typically ends at (please check/tick the appropriate age). Ages 30 through 40 were provided for early adulthood stage; 40 through 50 for middle adulthood stage, and 55 through 65 for late adulthood stage. Also, there were provisions for respondents to indicate the appropriate ages if different from the age ranges provided for the different stages, and also if there were gender differences in age.

There were 18 items relating to the various roles and activities that people typically perform in adulthood. These items were derived based on literature review on both the developed and developing worlds. The same items were repeated for each stage, that is, early, middle, and late adulthood, in order to determine if certain roles and activities were typical for more than one stage or for only one stage. The items were framed in the Likert-Scale format.

Respondents were asked to indicate whether they strongly disagreed, disagreed, were uncertain, agreed, or strongly agreed with each statement. They also had the option to indicate if the item was not applicable. The following were the 18 items repeated for the early, middle, and late adulthood stages:

1. In my society, men typically get married at this stage;
2. In my society, women typically get married at this stage;
3. In my society, men typically start to have children at this stage;
4. In my society, women typically start to have children at this stage;
5. In my society, men typically start having a job (paid employment) at this stage;
6. In my society, women typically start having a job (paid employment) at this stage;
7. In my society, most people at this stage are physically strong;
8. In my society, most people at this stage look old;
9. In my society, most people at this stage are retired from their jobs;
10. In my society, most people have grandchildren at this stage;
11. In my society, most people start to provide for the needs (financial, etc.) of their parents at this stage;
12. In my society, most people start to provide for the needs (financial, etc.) of their siblings at this stage;
13. In my society, most people are recognized as leaders in their communities at this stage;
14. In my society, most people are recognized as spiritual leaders in their communities at this stage;
15. In my society, the advice of people at this stage is usually sought by others in cases of family disputes;
16. In my society, the advice of people at this stage is usually sought by others in cases of community disputes;
17. In my society, most people at this stage play leadership roles at ceremonies; and
18. In my society, most people at this stage are believed to be wise.

The instrument was administered in English to participants in countries where English is used as the official language or the main medium of instruction. The questionnaire was translated into other languages as needed (for example, into Arabic and Portuguese) by the cooperating researchers and their graduate students or other qualified personnel.

THE MAJOR FINDINGS

The scores on each item ranged from a minimum of 1 (strongly disagree) to a maximum of 5 (strongly agree). We subjected the data to both descriptive and inferential statistics including correlation coefficients and Analysis of Variance (ANOVA). Given the nature of the text, we will not go into details of such analyses here. For the purposes of our discussion, we decided that since 3 is the midpoint of the scale, a mean score of 3.5 or greater would be regarded as an indication that the function or role in question is deemed typical for that stage. However, any mean score of 2.5 or less on a function would be interpreted as not being characteristic of the given stage. We should add that for the data of this size, any comparisons yielding a mean difference of .92 or higher between groups would be statistically significant at the 95% confidence level.

Age Demarcations for the Three Stages of Adulthood

Table 6.1 (A, B, & C) contains the mean ages for the beginning and end-points for early adulthood, middle adulthood, and late adulthood stages for males and females for each country. There is also a mean total for all seven groups.

As Table 6.1A indicates, early adulthood is said to begin at a relatively early age for both males and females, but especially for females. The start age for all the countries in the study combined was 19.75 years for males and 18.66 years for females. The youngest starting ages were found in Bangladesh, which had 17.53 for males and a very low 15.85 years for females. The mean end-point (overall) for early adulthood was 32.74 years for males and 31.09 years for females. Middle adulthood stage (Table 6.1B) was estimated to begin at 32.58 years for males and 31.19 years for females. The mean end-point (overall) for the middle adulthood was 46.70 years for males and 45.05 years for females. Late adulthood (Table 6.1C) also was viewed as starting at a relatively early age, a mean of 49.79 years overall for males and 48.08 years for females, but as low as 46.71 (males) and 43.42 (females) among participants from Bangladesh.

In all participating countries, respondents indicated each stage as starting earlier for females than for males. It is worth noting that even though the life expectancy for females in each country in this study was higher than for males, there is no significant difference between males and females in the end-point for the late adulthood stage. This disparity in the starting point for males and females for all three stages has some implications for role expectations for the different stages that we will discuss next.

Characteristics and Roles Typical of the Stages

Statements relating to the characteristics or roles and functions typical of the three stages of adulthood were assessed. The mean responses are presented in Table 6.2. Using a mean score of 3.5 or greater as a cutoff point, we can see that marriage and having children are perceived to be typical for females in the early adulthood stage but not for males. While this may be cultural, it may

Table 6.1
Age Distributions for the Three Stages of Adulthood

6-1A: Early Adulthood Stage

| Country | Early Adulthood | | | |
| | Begins | | Ends | |
	Male	Female	Male	Female
Bahrain	19.99	19.55	32.41	31.98
Bangladesh	17.53	15.85	30.61	27.79
Botswana	21.51	20.63	34.44	33.46
Brazil	20.04	19.28	31.55	31.11
Chile	20.49	19.49	34.14	32.25
Indonesia	19.48	17.72	31.44	29.67
Nigeria	19.20	18.11	34.56	31.34
Total	**19.75**	**18.66**	**32.74**	**31.09**

6-1B: Middle Adulthood Stage

| Country | Middle Adulthood | | | |
| | Begins | | Ends | |
	Male	Female	Male	Female
Bahrain	31.79	31.42	43.67	43.12
Bangladesh	31.05	28.34	44.30	41.76
Botswana	34.23	33.32	49.95	49.18
Brazil	32.10	31.76	48.04	47.48
Chile	32.53	32.30	47.61	47.31
Indonesia	32.52	29.58	46.54	42.91
Nigeria	33.86	31.62	46.77	43.61
Total	**32.58**	**31.19**	**46.70**	**45.05**

6-1C: Late Adulthood Stage

| Country | Late Adulthood | | | |
| | Begins | | Ends | |
	Male	Female	Male	Female
Bahrain	47.03	46.26	63.93	63.33
Bangladesh	46.71	43.42	58.90	56.59
Botswana	52.97	52.53	72.43	72.56
Brazil	49.76	49.44	64.78	64.64
Chile	49.42	49.17	63.70	63.42
Indonesia	52.21	47.79	68.43	68.96
Nigeria	50.45	47.98	67.96	67.38
Total	**49.79**	**48.08**	**65.73**	**65.27**

Table 6.2
Function and Role Characteristics for the Three Stages of Adulthood

Role/Function	Early Adulthood	Middle Adulthood	Late Adulthood
Marriage (men)	3.31	3.36	1.91
Marriage (women)	3.76	2.80	1.75
Have children (men)	3.13	3.45	2.04
Have children (women)	3.63	3.07	1.72
Start jobs (men)	3.77	3.01	1.78
Start jobs (women)	3.50	2.91	1.73
Physically strong	3.79	3.50	2.24
Look old	1.87	2.57	3.83
Retired from jobs	1.60	2.64	4.02
Have grandchildren	1.62	2.96	4.21
Provide for needs of parents	3.11	3.62	2.72
Provide for needs of relatives	3.02	3.56	2.91
Recognized as community leaders	2.79	3.88	3.83
Recognized as spiritual leaders	2.50	3.57	4.00
Advice on family disputes	2.83	3.76	3.90
Advice on community disputes	2.76	3.68	3.87
Leaders at ceremonies	2.94	3.91	3.88
Believed to be wise	2.73	3.68	4.18

Scores range between 1 (strongly disagree) to 5 (strongly agree). Thus, a score of 4 on "recognized as spiritual leaders" under the Late Adulthood Stage indicates that the participants viewed this role as characteristic of this stage of adulthood.

also be due to the genetic imperative that highly favors reproduction for females, especially at this stage (Baltes, Staudinger, & Lindenberger, 1999). Although people at this stage were expected to be physically strong, the respondents perceived that starting a job was characteristic of males at the early adulthood stage but not of females.

These results may indicate a pattern of cultural influences typical in many developing nations where females marry at a very early age because formal education for females is not as important as it is for males. The fact that females are not seen as starting jobs at this stage may reflect the traditional belief that males are the major breadwinners, that women are not to engage in wage employment, or that many females are settling into their traditional role (wife).

Being a wife is most times a full-time job, leaving the woman with very little time for wage-earning employment outside the home.

In the middle adulthood stage, people are still expected to be physically strong, which is not surprising, given the relatively low age boundaries for this stage. However, they also begin to take on more demanding responsibilities. People at this stage are expected to take care of the financial needs of their parents as well as their siblings and other relatives. This is in line with the role responsibilities of adult children especially in the developing world, where the expectation is to help parents even when the parents seem to not have any need for such assistance. For example, among the Gusii of rural western Kenya, Cattell (1997) reported the case of a certain man whose children requested him to give up his job so that they could care for him. They made this request because they were concerned that others in the community might get the impression that they were incapable of living up to their expectations—taking care of their father. It also validates the notion that children serve as their parents' "walking stick" or "social security" in societies where social security systems are poor (Nsamanang, 1992, 1995).

The other responsibilities people are perceived to take on in the middle adulthood stage include serving as community leaders, spiritual leaders, and being called upon to advise family and community members in the resolution of disputes. People during this stage also perform leadership roles at ceremonies that may occur in the community, and are somewhat perceived to be wise.

Certain roles are viewed to be most typical in late adulthood, however. Here people are expected to look old, to retire, and to be grandparents. The issue of retirement is interesting in the sense that the starting age for this stage is relatively low; the overall mean is 49.24 years. This may be related to the low life expectancy in most of these countries. Until recently, one could retire from government service in Nigeria at any age after putting in at least 15 years of service. However, one could not begin to receive his or her pension until one reached 45 years of age. This is especially low when you consider that discussions are underway in the United States to shift retirement years upwards from 65 years.

There seems to be evidence of "role continuity" in the sense that certain roles are believed to be typical of both the middle and late adulthood stages. For example, community and spiritual leadership roles, advising on family and community disputes, leadership roles at ceremonies, and being looked upon as wise seem to begin in middle adulthood and persist into late adulthood. Middle adulthood roles appear to persist into the late adulthood stage. This may partly explain why there does not seem to be empirical verification of loss of status among many studies of aging conducted in the developing world.

There are, however, roles or characteristics that are perceived as not being typical of the early, middle, and late adulthood stages. The mean scores on these items for the early and late stages are less than 2.5. For the early adulthood stage, people are not expected to look old, retire from their jobs, nor have grandchildren. On the other hand, people in late adulthood are not expected to marry, have children, hold jobs, look strong, and take care of the financial needs of their parents and relatives. Although cultural factors seem to be at play here, this sequencing of aging and development appear to be influenced more by senescence (a reflection of the "Global environmental" dimension). The other functions for all three stages appear to be gray areas where individual circumstances (Valsiner, 1989) may dictate whether or not a person may perform such roles.

HIGH VERSUS HDI COUNTRIES

Even countries in the developing world are not uniform in terms of many indexes of development. As we presented from our overview of the seven countries, Bahrain, Brazil, and Chile are high on the United Nations' HDI, Botswana and Indonesia have a medium rating while Nigeria and Bangladesh are low on the HDI. We decided to make comparisons between countries to see if there might be any consistent similarities or differences based on HDI rankings. We found that for the most part, differences or similarities did not occur along HDI status with the exception of one variable—whether or not women begin to engage in jobs at the early adulthood stage.

As may be recalled from the discussion of the early adulthood results, we indicated that it was considered typical for males to hold jobs at this stage, but not women. A further examination along this line indicated that this was more so for medium and low HDI countries than it was for high HDI countries. In other words, participants from high HDI countries were more likely to agree that it was typical for females to engage in paid employment during the early adulthood stage. There was a little twist in the results, though. Participants from Chile, Brazil (both high HDI), and Indonesia (medium HDI) endorsed this statement. Here Bahrain (high HDI) swapped places with Indonesia (medium HDI). Participants from Botswana (medium HDI), Nigeria, and Bangladesh (low HDI) did not endorse this position.

We interpret this to be a case of an interaction between HDI status and religion. Bahrain is a Muslim country where women, especially that early in life, may not have as many opportunities to engage in paid employment outside the home. It is true that Indonesia has a very large Muslim population, but it very often "is strongly influenced by Hinduism, Buddhism, and other older, animistic beliefs" (Encyclopedia Britannica Online 1994–1999). Thus, the influences from other religions, as well as other local sociocultural variables, may affect the time frame in which females are expected to start paid employment in Indonesia. In the case of Bahrain, one such sociocultural variable may be the male-female ratio. Males outnumber females by a significant margin in Bahrain. Thus, from a horde of prospective husbands, there could be a greater pressure on females to marry at a relatively younger age. A further exploration of this variable in future research needs to be done before any strong statements can be made in this regard.

CONCLUDING COMMENTS FROM THE SEVEN-COUNTRY STUDY

Erikson's (1950, 1959) stage theory of personality, developed in the developed world, has been described as lacking empirical cross-cultural support, particularly the higher level ones (Church & Lonner, 1998). The result from the seven-country study somewhat validates this assertion. Erikson's early adulthood stage called "Intimacy versus Isolation" is from 17 to 45; the middle adulthood stage called "Generativity versus Stagnation" is from 40 to 65, and the late adulthood stage called "Integrity versus Despair" is from 65 years on.

The focus in Erikson's early adulthood stage is on establishing intimacy or affiliation with one or more others, for example marriage, while the focus in the middle adulthood stage is on establishing and guiding the next generation. In guiding the next generation, the adult, propelled by the desire to do something before death occurs (McAdams & de St. Aubin, 1992), also generates life products and outcomes that benefit both the social system and the next generation. In late adulthood stage, however, the focus is on establishing a sense of meaning in one's life, rather than feeling despair or bitterness that life was wasted. Generally, it is expected that the roles and activities that people will typically engage in will reflect the focus of their life stage. However, it is not unlikely to find young people who engage in generative activities, but more fulfillment for such activities have been identified with the later stage of life (Ackerman, Zuroff, & Moskowitz, 2000).

In the seven-country study, we set to test the proposition that different mechanisms are at work in the developing world, and therefore patterns and experiences of aging and adult development may differ from those of the developed world. We expected that the ages at which many of these adulthood stages would be demarcated would be much earlier than the markers used in the developed world (Erikson, 1959). Furthermore, we hypothesized that there may be differences in the functions and role expectation for people at the early, middle, and late adulthood stages.

For the most part, most of these assumptions were supported by empirical data obtained, supporting the assertion made by Church and Lonner (1998). For example, the middle adulthood stage was reported to begin around 32 while the late adulthood was perceived to begin at less than 50 years of age, as low as under 44 years in a number of countries. These are much lower ages than those typically used in the developed world. These kinds of differences may help explain some of the disputes that can arise in international interactions between developed and developing nations. When, for instance, the developed world complains about child labor, assuming this definition involves females under 16 years of age, their counterparts from Bangladesh might also agree with the use of the term, but could be using different age markers of childhood. Should the same standards be used by every nation? This is a difficult question to answer because of the different aging and developmental trajectories in the various countries.

In terms of roles, our study found that the advice of people at the late adulthood stage is typically sought in family and community disputes. Old people also preside over important social and spiritual functions and are perceived to be wise. While these roles and activities keep the elderly active—a good way to age, according to the "Activity" theory—they seem to reflect Erikson's middle adulthood stage of "Generativity versus Stagnation" more than the late adulthood stage of "Ego integrity versus Despair." According to Erikson, "Generativity versus Stagnation" involves establishing care and concern for the future generation while "Ego Integrity versus Despair" is focusing on finding meaning to life, through a life review, rather than feeling despair or bitterness. This stage suggests a shift in attention from other to self. While this may appear appropriate in individualistic societies, this kind of shift from others to self may not be appropriate in collectivistic cultures. This is one example that also calls for a cross-cultural validation of Carstensen's (1992) socioemotional selectivity theory, which is developed from a Western sample and based on the Disengagement paradigm.

In the move toward modernization by developing nations, we suggest that developing countries adopt only those aspects of the "developed world" environmental dimension that are beneficial to their elderly, for example, Western medical care. Based on the results from our seven-nation study, people from developing nations are better served to keep their positive attitudes and roles for their adults. In other words, a *careful* combination of positive attributes of the Global, Developed, and Developing dimensions of their cross-cultural environment should be encouraged.

SUMMARY

This study surveyed undergraduates in seven developing countries that fit into the high, medium, and low categories of the United Nations Human Development Index. They are Bahrain, Brazil, and Chile (high); Botswana and Indonesia (medium); and Bangladesh and Nigeria (low). Although these countries are different in climate, political structure, and religion, they share certain similarities that include exposure to Westernization influences.

Questions were asked respondents about age boundaries and the typical roles that characterize the early, middle, and late adulthood stages in their respective societies. The results show that certain roles are typical for each stage while others are not. It also shows that there is role continuity from the middle to the late adult stages for some roles. The differences among the countries are minimal.

7

Physical and Mental Health

Physical and mental health problems are important aspects of the aging process. In this chapter, we will discuss some of the common physical and mental health conditions that accompany senescence. Since getting older does not automatically result in health problems, we will also discuss some of the health promotion behavior that modulates the relationship between aging and health. As in the previous chapters, we will first examine the prevailing conditions in the developed world. Following that, we will address parallel processes in the developing world. In this way, the sociocultural dimensions of aging and health will be more clearly illuminated.

The physical, psychological, and social changes associated with senescence that we discussed in the previous chapters can negatively affect our health status. As mentioned, some theories, such as the autoimmune theory, suggest that biological aging causes the immune system to attack friendly cells, resulting in illnesses. In addition, decrements in overall functioning that arise from cognitive or physical changes, or that are due to losses of important roles, like that of a spouse, could cause depression. Certainly, the sociocultural context contributes to our health status and life satisfaction, just as the normal aging process does.

Lifestyle is another major contributor to our health status. There are people who make comments like: "My grandmother lived to be 96 and my mother is close to 90, therefore I hope to live to be at least 90 years old because it is just in my genes." While this may be true, we may ask if this individual has the same lifestyle as his forebears. A stressful lifestyle, cigarette smoking, and being overweight have been associated with cancer, cardiovascular disease, and hypertension (Fant, Pickworth, & Henningfield, 1999; Kawachi, 1999).

Health conditions can be classified based on their duration, which vary from short- to long-term duration with diverse implications for care management.

ACUTE AND CHRONIC PHYSICAL HEALTH CONDITIONS

Two types of health conditions are identified based on duration: acute condition is short-term while chronic condition is long-term. The flu is a good example of an acute condition while arthritis is an example of a chronic condition. However, ecocultural adaptation of individuals to a disease can influence whether that disease will be acute or chronic. This reason may inform why travelers to a foreign culture are advised to take requisite immunization shots against certain diseases endemic in those societies, whereas the natives might not have had those same immunization shots.

Acute diseases are more debilitating to older adults than they are to young adults and can restrict the activities of older adults (NCHS, 1995). Chronic diseases, unlike acute diseases, are long-term, permanent conditions that require management and care rather than cure. They may not necessarily impair Activities of Daily Living (ADL), which include bathing, dressing, using the toilet, and getting in and out of bed. However, the frustration that results from chronic conditions such as arthritis and heart conditions could lead to stress and depression, and in some cases to physical pain.

There is evidence to suggest that chronic conditions among the elderly are related to sociocultural factors. Endemic factors in the society like social class differences, racial and gender biases, and government welfare policies can sustain unhealthy health patterns in individuals and groups. In the United States, for example, severe chronic conditions occur earlier among ethnic minority groups and are also associated with low education and low socioeconomic status and with non-farming rural communities (Cantor, 1991).

The top ten chronic diseases for both men and women are arthritis, hypertension, hearing impairment, heart disease, sinusitis, orthopedic impairment, cataracts, diabetes, visual impairment, and tinnitus (NCHS, 1995). But most elderly adults over the age of 65 in the developed world die from heart disease, cancer, and stroke (Van Nostrand, Furner, & Suzman, 1993). Would an individual's self-concept influence his or her health status? Yes, there is a relationship between self-concept and health status.

THE SELF AND HEALTH STATUS

The way people conceive of themselves is important. But perhaps more important in influencing health conditions is the way people perceive of their future selves, or their projected selves. How people want to be in the future may affect both their developmental trajectory and the choices they make now. Therefore there is a relationship between "possible self" and an individual's health status. The "possible self" perspective includes that aspect of the self one hopes to achieve and is incorporated into the current self system. The aspect of the self one fears to attain is therefore avoided. Among older adults, health status is often reported as both a hoped-for and feared aspect of the self to come. Older adults for whom health is an important hope-for or feared-self issue engage in better health behavior (Hooker & Kaus, 1992, 1994).

Another aspect of a person's self-concept is how much perceived control an individual has over his life's situations. It is important to have a sense of control over the events that happen in our lives. When people believe that they are in control of events in their lives, they are more likely to positively influence the environment or their actions. However, when they feel they lack control, this leads to poor physical and mental health. A sense of control or a lack of it is known severally. Bandura (1986) calls it "self-efficacy," Rotter (1966) describes it as "internal and external locus of control," and Seligman (1991) as "optimism and helplessness." The link between control and health among the elderly has been extensively investigated by Rodin and associates (Haidt & Rodin, 1999; Langer, 1983; Langer & Rodin, 1976; Rodin & Langer, 1977). In one of these studies, Langer and Rodin (1976) encouraged elderly convalescent-home residents to take greater control on a number of day-to-day events. Assessments immediately following intervention and an 18-month follow-up showed the control-enhanced group to be more alert and active and happier than their counterparts who were encouraged to feel that the staff would satisfy their needs. Compared to a 25% mortality rate in that particular nursing home prior to intervention, only 15% of the participants in the control-enhanced group died whereas 30% of the participants in the comparison group died (Rodin & Langer, 1977).

Research also shows that the benefits of control among the elderly are not limited to physical health. For example, Langer, Rodin, Beck, Weinman, and Spitzer (1979) found that enhanced control led to improvements in memory and satisfaction. But control has positive effects only when it is attributed to personal and stable sources, and when the opportunities are there to exhibit one's competence.

BELIEFS ON DISEASE CAUSATION

The beliefs people have about disease causation may affect their health-seeking behavior, assuming health care is affordable. For example, as people grow older it is common to confuse poor health with the normal aging process. Thus, aches and pains are associated with the normal process of growing old instead of seeking health care for them.

We will now discuss physical and mental health and how the self-concept and beliefs about disease causation affect these conditions. This will be followed by an examination of how health promotion can enhance physical and mental health.

Physical Health

The rate of *chronic* (long-term) illnesses is lower in the early adulthood stage. However, sociocultural factors such as level of formal education and economic means would make a difference. Life stresses such as financial troubles are especially associated with lower socioeconomic class, and they are associated with poor health. On the other hand, higher income and better education are associated with longer life expectancy and better health even among ethnic minority groups in the United States. (Guralnik, Land, Blazer, Fillenbaum, & Branch, 1993).

Although chronic illnesses are less common at the early adult stage, current lifestyles set the stage for such illnesses in middle or late adult stages. For example, severe hearing impairment or lung disease in middle or late adulthood stages may be the result of a long-term exposure to noise or smoking started in early adulthood or even before then.

The rate of *acute* illnesses such as colds, the flu, and other infections is higher among young adults, but elderly people suffer less from acute illnesses because they are more likely to take precautions. Taking precautions helps to avoid contracting diseases. For example, a lack of precaution is partly responsible for the high rate of drug, alcohol abuse, and sexually transmitted diseases (STD) in early adulthood stage (especially in men) than at any other adulthood stage (Anthony & Aboraya, 1992). Furthermore, high-risk behaviors are more prevalent among young people. Sexually transmitted diseases are associated with such high-risk behaviors as having multiple sex partners, frequent drug or alcohol use, and having unprotected sex.

Health begins to decline in middle adulthood, with chronic diseases becoming more manifest. The leading causes of death in middle adulthood in the developed world are heart disease and cancer, with heart disease as the leading cause for men and cancer for women. However, men are more likely to contract both diseases earlier than women, which partly explains why women live longer than men—because these are quick-acting diseases. Certain lifestyle risk factors like smoking, overweight, and diet have been associated with one or both of these diseases. During middle adulthood stage, the relationship between social class and education on the one hand and aging and adult development on the other become more pronounced as health begins to decline. Thus, availability of funds to manage and care for chronic health needs, and the knowledge of health issues in particular, place those in the lower socioeconomic class at a disadvantage.

But the incremental effects of an unhealthy lifestyle from early adulthood resulting in chronic diseases such as arthritis can lead to disability in old age. Disability among elderly people is reflected in the limitations in carrying out the Activities of Daily Living (ADL), which include bathing, eating, use of toilet, getting out of bed or a chair. After age 65, more men suffer from heart disease, while more women suffer from arthritis and hypertension. Heart disease, arthritis, and hypertension are two or three times more likely to disable the sufferers (Verbrugge, Lepkowski, & Konkol, 1991).

Mental Health

There is a rise in depression during the early adulthood stage (Kessler, Foster, Webster, & House, 1992). This incidence of emotional disturbances may be related to poor adjustment to the multiple roles of being a spouse, a parent, and a worker. Stephens and her colleagues (Stephens, Franks, & Atienza, 1997) suggested that negative "spillover" in roles, in this case between parent care role and employment role, has a detrimental effect on people's mental health. But "spillover" from one role could have a positive effect on another. Nonetheless, in addition to the multiple roles, the financial burdens such as college loans, car loans, mortgage loans faced by most young couples starting their lives together could be overwhelming and could result in depression.

The big mental health issue in middle adulthood is "midlife crisis," which is based on the idea that there are a series of adjustments to be made, including readjustment of dreams, of roles, and of lifestyles from the early adulthood stage. Studies suggest that "midlife crisis" occurs at about age 40, and is characterized by feelings of turmoil, an acute awareness of aging, and the finiteness of time (Gould, 1980; Levinson, 1986). But middle adulthood could also be a time of better adjustment, marked by declines in rates of suicide and mental health admissions (Chiriboga, 1989). For example, there are women who perceive menopause as freedom from pregnancy (Neugarten, Wood, Kraines, & Loomis, 1963; Newman, 1982). There are also those who perceive the "empty nest syndrome," a time after the last child is launched, as providing a new sense of freedom and an opportunity to pursue dreams hitherto put away in order to raise children (Reinke, Holmes, & Harris, 1985). Therefore the mental health status of people in their middle adulthood is controversial.

Depression is also one mental health condition frequently associated with older people. It seems obvious that the biological changes from aging that may prevent an elderly person from performing certain physical or mental tasks hitherto enjoyed can lead to frustration. The loss of roles, and the prospects of losing other roles coupled with the loss of friends and family and with modernization influences, can all be traumatic experiences to the elderly. However, it does not necessarily mean that elderly people are paralyzed by these changes and cannot carry out their daily functions. Thus, there is a need to make a distinction between clinical depression, which is of a long duration and has a paralyzing effect on normal activities, and depressed mood, which is of a shorter duration. Clinical depression is more common among younger adults and less common among the elderly (Gatz, Kasl-Godley, & Karel, 1996). However, fatigue, complaints about memory loss, difficulties with sleep, and thoughts about death have been reported by depressed older adults (Reifler, 1994), and depression is a risk factor for suicide, especially among white males (Conwell, 1995).

Perhaps the most feared and by far the most devastating disorders in late adulthood are dementing illnesses. There are other disorders in the general class known as dementia, frontal lobe degeneration and Pick's disease, but Alzheimer's disease tends to receive greater prominence. The symptoms of dementia include progressive memory impairment and deterioration of habits and personality (Zarit & Zarit, 1998). Dementia is a syndrome, not a disease, in the sense that it consists of symptoms that can be caused by many different illnesses. Consequently, it is difficult to estimate prevalence because there are no definitive markers for diagnosis for dementing illnesses such as Alzheimer's. Diagnosis often involves multiple criteria including behavioral, neurological, and medical data. In light of the problems involved in diagnosis, there seems to be reasonable agreement regarding prevalence rates of moderate and severe dementia but not mild cases. Many studies estimate prevalence rates of moderate and severe dementia in North America and Europe at 4% to 7% of the population over age 65 (Anthony & Aboraya, 1992; Canadian Study of Health and Aging Workshop Group, 1994; Kay, 1995). A few studies have reported much higher rates. For example, one U.S. study reported prevalence rates of Alzheimer's alone at 10% of those aged 65 and 45% among those 85 years and older (Evans, Funkenstein, Albert, Scherr, Cook, et al., 1989). Although prevalence estimates vary from study to study, what is not in dispute is that rates of dementia increase with age. Prevalence rates among those in their 60s is 1%; this increases to about 7% for adults in their 70s and rises dramatically to between 20% and 30% of those aged 80 years and over (Johansson & Zarit, 1995; Kay, 1995; Zarit & Zarit, 1998).

Dementia is more prevalent among women than men at all ages. This may be due largely to the longevity among women (Kay, 1995). More women than men survive to ages at which the risk of dementia is greatest. This same pattern of longevity would suggest that rates of dementia would be much higher in the developed world where life expectancy is considerably higher than much of the developing world.

HEALTH PROMOTION

The health choices that people make during early adulthood affect their health status later in life. Unfortunately, poor health behavior is highest among young people. They are more likely to skip breakfast, drink excessively, and smoke (U.S. Bureau of the Census, 1989). But to make a connection between current behavior and health status three decades later is a challenge to young people. The reason may be because 30 years is a very long time to wait for one's reward. Therefore, short-term rewards may be necessary for sustainable healthy behavior among young people. Since most young people work, employers may have to play a major role in promoting short-term health rewards. For example, employers can single out nonsmokers and workers who have quit smoking for special recognition and rewards. This is a win-win situation. The employer keeps the health costs of its employees down while the employee is healthy. An increasing number of business organizations are beginning to realize the connection between good health and good business (Ilgen, 1990).

HEALTH PROMOTION AND SOCIOCULTURAL SENSITIVITY

Health promotion has to be sensitive to sociocultural factors in the society. For example, the reason why young people skip breakfast, drink excessively, and smoke may relate to poor adjustment strategies to the multiple roles of being a parent, a provider, and a spouse.

We suggest *stress prevention* through a rearrangement of their ecocultural environment. Whereas *stress reduction* is a post-hoc action, that is, after stress has occurred, *stress prevention*, which we shall emphasize, involves taking action before stress occurs.

Since work and family are two major life events in the early adulthood stage, we suggest that both the workplace and the home are important ecocultural environments to the young adult. There are a number of existing policies in the workplace that could help prevent stress. They include flexible work hours and job sharing. Another is the Family and Medical Leave Act of 1993 in the United States, which requires employers with 50 or more employees to provide 12 weeks of unpaid leave to workers in the case of the birth or adoption of a child. The leave also covers instances in which a child, spouse, parent or the employee is seriously ill. There are debates about whether or not this "family friendly" law should be a paid leave period so that more people can take advantage of it than is currently the case.

Helping the young adult to make the transition into the multiple roles in the home environment is important. For example, incentives for young couples to attend marriage seminars before marrying are important and should be encouraged. However the most important resource should be the family, and the validation of the young couple by other family members who are ready and able to provide support is important. Social support can go a long way in not only preventing stress but also in preventing divorce, which for many couples, seems to be a way of coping with stress. The availability of adequate social support reduces the risk of death, diseases, and depression among adults (Cohen, 1991). But such support has to be subjectively evaluated as adequate (Feld & George, 1994) because the number of people in an individual's support network does not automatically translate into social support.

The lack of social support has been implicated in family breakdown in a multifaceted way in the United States. According to Kilbride and Kilbride (1997): "Support for extended family structures, along the lines of traditional African society, would serve to improve the quality of life of many children in America, children who now, in increasing numbers, suffer from such problems as abuse and neglect, homelessness, and adolescent suicide, to name but a few" (pp. 219–220). But how much social support is acceptable in a society that values individualism? If the extended family is willing to provide support, will young couples accept their support? Also, how much support is too much support? These are questions that the United States and other developed societies still have to address, even if they embrace the notion of social support as an important health care resource.

Women generally maintain a larger network of social support than their male counterparts. As discussed under the Elderly as a Subculture, in Chapter

5, the out-migration of young people to urban centers may provide an opportunity for men to create new friendships and to deepen existing social support networks among peers.

Currently, a number of health insurance policies cover preventive health care for diseases, including cancer and heart disease, the two leading causes of death during middle adulthood in the developed world. Even though most insurance companies have a preventive health insurance coverage policy, not all adults take advantage of it for a variety of reasons, including health beliefs. However, if insurance companies reward men and women (based on the individual or group *demand* values that may or may not be reduced premiums) who have at least one physical examination each year then the benefits will be to the insurance company, the individual, and the larger society.

Exercise assumes significant importance during middle adulthood even though it should be done throughout the life span. Formal exercise programs should be encouraged in the workplace for those in wage employment and in the community. Due to the cumulative effects of poor lifestyle from young adulthood, exercise promotion will be more effective if started early. Maintaining an exercise regimen has positive effects on physical functioning and longevity even among elderly persons who are 70 and above (Wolinsky, Stump, & Clark, 1995). It should be realized that both physical and mental exercises are especially needed in later life, since physical and mental disuse can contribute to some of the symptoms associated with aging.

THE DEVELOPING WORLD

Because of ecocultural differences between the developed and developing worlds (climate, literacy rate, and biomedical technology), the types and nature of diseases in the developing world, including their prevalence rate, are different. Gochman (1997) suggests that research on health behavior in developing societies has a different focus from that of developed societies for the following reasons:

1. With a youthful population, child health and survival is a pre-eminent public health problem.
2. Infectious and parasitic diseases are more prevalent and more important health problems than individual health behavior.
3. Health behavior research in developed countries center around particular behaviors (smoking, exercise, diet, use of seat belt), but in developing societies it is centered on biomedically defined diseases (malaria, HIV/AIDS, tuberculosis, diarrhea) and the efforts to control them.
4. Governments and families have fewer resources for lifestyle changes and individuals have less choice of, and control over, health related behavior than is typical in developed societies.

Based on the foregoing we will place emphasis on those physical and mental health issues that are more pertinent to the developing world.

PHYSICAL HEALTH

The spread of the HIV/AIDS disease especially in sub-Saharan Africa and Asia has made long-term diseases a concern among young adults. HIV/AIDS is such a potential threat to the early and middle adulthood segments of the population that if its spread is not checked, it will not only reverse the modest gains made in life expectancy, but will literally wipe out the productive segment of the population in Africa. HIV/AIDS is the leading cause of death in Africa (WHO, 1999). According to the most recent report by the Joint United Nations Programme on HIV/AIDS (UNAIDS), 34.4 million people are living with HIV/AIDS worldwide. Of this number 24.5 million are from sub-Saharan Africa, 5.6 million are from south and southeast Asia, 1.3 million from Latin America, and 530,000 from east Asia and the Pacific (UNAIDS, 2000). When you add the number of HIV/AIDS cases from the Caribbean and North Africa and the Middle East, it becomes clear that more than 93% of HIV/AIDS cases are from the developing world. Because there is yet to be a cure for HIV/AIDS and the fact that prevention efforts require education and other resources, HIV/AIDS is arguably the most serious physical health issue in all three stages of adulthood in the developing world. In Africa alone, there are 16 countries in which more than 10% of the adult population aged 15 to 49 is infected with HIV (UNAIDS, 2000).

There are three main modes of transmission of HIV/AIDS. Unprotected sexual intercourse; transmission through blood and blood products, mainly through the use of infected needles, syringes and other piercing instruments; or through blood transfusion and through donated organs and semen. The third mode of HIV/AIDS transmission is from a mother to child during pregnancy, delivery, or breast-feeding. This is termed vertical-transmission, and it accounts for more than 90% of HIV infections among children.

Unprotected sexual intercourse is the primary route of HIV infection. Between 75% and 85% of HIV infections in adults, worldwide, have been through unprotected (not using a condom) anal, oral, or vaginal intercourse. Heterosexual intercourse accounts for approximately 70% of HIV infections while man-to-man intercourse accounts for about 5% to 10%. So far there has been no documented case of transmission between two female sexual partners (Hynie, 1998). Some cultural traditions involving sex with multiple partners, such as polygamous relationships where men, either officially or unofficially, have several female partners, as well as by migrant work practices, are major contributing factors for transmission of the disease (McGrath, Rwabukwali, Schumann, Pearson-Marks, Nakayiwa, et al., 1993; Orubuloye, Caldwell, & Caldwell, 1993). Women's subservient position in society in much of the developing world is also a contributory factor to the spread of HIV/AIDS.

HIV/AIDS has consequences that go much beyond physical health. The premature death of potentially half of the adult population, usually at the ages when they have already started to form their own families and have become economically productive, seriously impacts every aspect of social and economic life. Households suffer a dramatic decrease in income, either because the infected person is no longer able to work, or because most of the family's resources are used to provide treatment.

Increasing mortality from HIV/AIDS has led to a dramatic rise in "AIDS orphans." AIDS has thus far left behind 13.2 million orphans, children who, before the age of 15, have lost either their mother or both parents to AIDS. Most of these children are in the developing nations, especially Africa, where an estimated 95% currently live. Before AIDS, about 2% of all children in developing countries were orphans. By 1997, the proportion of children with one or both parents dead jumped to 7% and in many African countries to as high as 11% (UNAIDS, 2000). Studies in Uganda have shown that the death of one or both parents reduces the chances of an orphan going to school by half; even those who go to school spend less time there than formerly. In addition, orphans face an increased risk of stunted growth and being malnourished (UNAIDS, 2000). The problem of AIDS orphans has further implications for development in the early and middle adulthood stages because given the largely collectivist orientation, surviving relatives of these orphans are often obligated to stretch their resources to cater to these orphaned relatives.

Furthermore, HIV/AIDS tends to result in stigmatization of those infected. People with, or in some instances, even suspected of having HIV/AIDS may be turned away by health care providers, denied jobs and housing, refused insurance and entry to foreign countries, thrown out by their spouse or family, or even murdered. Although studies have not yet been conducted, these responses can lead to or exacerbate psychological conditions such as depression and will definitely have a negative effect on psychological well-being of infected people and their families.

In Africa, HIV/AIDS tops the list of killer diseases, accounting for 19% of the total deaths, followed by acute respiratory diseases like flu or bronchitis at 8.2%, diarrhea-causing complaints at 7.6%, perinatal problems fatal to either mother or baby at 5.5%, and cerebrovascular disease at 4.7% (WHO, 1999). But diseases like malaria and cholera are also common and are equally fatal because of inadequate medical facilities.

In addition to poor medical facilities, both socioeconomic class and level of education will affect people's responses to physical illness. With a largely poor and illiterate population, the funds to care for health needs and the knowledge of health issues are limited. However, the knowledge of certain health issues is based on beliefs that cut across socioeconomic strata; and a person's illness belief will influence the type of treatment sought (Cook, 1994). There is a pervasive belief in the spirit world in developing societies. For example, in

Africa, a spiritual belief for the cause of HIV/AIDS directs help-seeking behavior toward spiritual remedies from herbalists—a reflection of the Developing world environmental dimension. It is not yet known, however, the extent
to which insidious diseases, such as heart disease, liver disease, hypertension,
account for deaths among adults. Such diseases are usually detected through
regular physician visits. Both regular checkups and the medical technology
required are lacking in most developing countries. Furthermore, because diseases can be categorized as either "visible" or "invisible," more attention seems
to have been paid so far to the "visible" ones such as AIDS, cholera, malaria.

While there are accounts of those who die from the "visible" diseases like
AIDS, cholera, and malaria, others who die from cardiovascular diseases, from
liver diseases, and from hypertension are poorly documented because of the
insidious nature of these diseases. Yet these "invisible" diseases may be responsible for more deaths in later life than the "visible" ones. When death
occurs from an "invisible" disease like hypertension, it is usually not expected
unlike when it occurs through "visible" causes. Therefore with no apparent
"cause," attributions to nonmedical causes such as witchcraft, offending the
gods, or a lack of harmony between the individual and nature are reinforced.
Even with the "visible" diseases, causal attributions are also made to nonmedical factors (Ingstad, Bruun, & Tlou, 1997). Among the Kallawaya in La Paz,
Bolivia, for example, the model for understanding health is based on a life that
is in harmony with nature, oneself, and one's community. Sickness is a result
of the disruption of this harmony, and both herbal and spiritual treatments are
used to restore balance (Krippner & Glenney, 1997).

A study comparing Filipino women and American women also found that
Filipino women attributed the causes of physical illnesses to spiritual-social
factors more frequently than the Americans did, but more Western-educated
Filipino women were less likely to do so (Edman & Kameoka, 1997). In one
study of health beliefs and behavior among women in Saudi Arabia, Ide and
Sanli (1992) reported that religious beliefs about disease causation persisted
even though there was a strong awareness of germs as causative factors in
illness; a reflection of the influence of both the Developed and Developing
environmental dimensions of their cross-cultural environment (Eyetsemitan,
2002a).

While beliefs about disease causation could lead to health-seeking behavior,
it could also prevent health-seeking behavior. For example, the elderly in Botswana believe that AIDS is caused by pollution (Meila) and feel relatively safe
from this disease, but they could be agents for intergenerational transmission
of the virus (Ingstad, Bruun, & Tlou, 1997).

In the absence of government support and high costs of health care, the
health care needs of the elderly will not be met (Li & Tracy, 1999), but the
perception that the elderly have about their health is also important for initi-
ating health-seeking behavior. Whereas in developed societies poor health is
mostly associated with poor performance on the Activities of Daily Living, in

developing societies the perception of poor health is perhaps more important; it may be influenced by the inability to perform whatever role is important in that individual's life. For example, the inability to perform prayers standing was a significant determinant of the perception of poor health among advanced aged (75 plus years) Saudi women (Jarallal & Al-Shammari, 1999).

In the context of "visible" and "invisible" diseases, it is possible to understand acute cases, such as cholera, as "visible" and the chronic conditions, such as hypertension, as "invisible." To further compound issues, the "visible" diseases generally manifest physical symptoms while the "invisible" diseases may not, and even when they do, might be confused with the normal aging process, thus preventing health-seeking behavior. As mentioned earlier, a poor knowledge of health issues can confound disease or illness with the normal changes of aging. For example, an individual who attributes his or her aches and pains to old age is less likely to seek medical help.

The Activities of Daily Living (ADL) measure has been found to have a pan-cultural application, including in the developing world. It measures sociobiological functioning such as the ability to take a bath and to use the toilet, but does not distinguish between functioning due to disease and functioning due to the normal changes from aging. ADL measures have particular relevance to developing societies where many homes lack the convenience of indoor plumbing. Ikels (1991), however, cautions against a culture-neutral interpretation of ADL items, because the psychological components of the items may not be invariant from culture to culture. For example, most elderly people do not live alone and they receive help from others whether the help is required or not.

As mentioned earlier, health issues in developing societies do not focus on health behaviors like exercises, smoking, alcohol consumption, tobacco usage, and diet. But most of these behaviors are within the individual's control, involving little or no financial burden to the individual, for example, exercises, smoking abstinence, and reduced alcohol consumption. In some cases, the individual saves money. Unfortunately, governments in developing societies and researchers have not identified lifestyle changes to be as important as controlling some biomedically defined diseases. Where efforts are made in lifestyle changes, they are usually in the promotion of health practices that help to prevent those biomedical diseases that are "visible"—AIDS, cholera, malaria, and diarrhea. But little or no effort is made at changing people's lifestyles relating to the "invisible" diseases such as cardiovascular disease, lung cancer, liver disease, and hypertension. This should change.

MENTAL HEALTH

The extended family members help young couples to adjust to their multiple roles of spouse, parent, and worker. Having relatives as members of the household (brothers, sisters, cousins, nieces and nephews, grandparents, etc.) helps to ease the burden of childcare, house chores, and of running errands that young couples in developed societies also have to contend with, but with little or no assistance. Yet a large household could also be a source of stress, especially when resources are limited.

However, young couples in developing societies do not have as many lifestyle choices as their counterparts in the developed world, and may not be saddled with as many bills (credit cards, college loans, mortgage, car loans, etc.). But they do have a different kind of pressure, based on their collectivistic values (Hofstede, 1980). It includes the pressure to be financially responsible to members of the extended family and the community, some of whom are members of the young couples' household. There is also the pressure to become their parents' "walking stick" or "social security." Fulfilling these responsibilities could be stressful, especially when inadequate resources have to be balanced between taking care of their own needs and those of the extended family, including new members of the collectives like in-laws. This dilemma could create tension between husbands and wives and between couples and members of the collectives. Furthermore, with the scourge of unemployment and AIDS in developing countries, young people's dream of becoming financially responsible to members of the collective is becoming elusive. Choi (1992) notes that increasingly in Korea, adult children do not provide financially for their elderly parents because of their inability to do so. Being contrary to cultural expectations, this situation could pose a mental health concern to both the young and old.

Yet another mental health concern, especially for females, is the pressure to have male children. Having a male child is a very important way for a woman to establish herself in the marital home. For example, among the Hindus of India, the birth of a female child, even among educated families, is received with subdued feelings (Kumar, 1991), and postpartum depression is much higher after the birth of a female child (Kakar, 1978). Although there is a strong preference for male children in the developing world, it is not the case in all societies. For example, there is no sex preference in Thailand (Gardiner & Gardiner, 1991). Societies like Thailand may be influenced more by the "Developed world" environmental dimension of their cross-cultural environment.

The strong preference for male children may even necessitate the desire of some men to engage in polygamous marriages (having more than one wife) and/or in extramarital affairs or to have children in old age. Unfortunately, married women who are childless or desire to have a male child do not have this kind of flexibility that their male counterparts have. If they do, it would be discrete. This is an added emotional burden.

Middle adulthood stage seems to be a time when women are better adjusted in their marital life, especially after having a male child. For example, the Hindu woman in India feels considerably more self-confident having established herself both in the family and in the community. This self-confidence comes from having raised her children, especially sons (Kumar, 1991). Friedman (1987) reviewed eight studies published between 1980 and 1987 on changes in Israeli women over the life cycle and found that in the later years women were happier, more powerful, and less vulnerable in their marriages than in their earlier years. This shift in women's position in the family during middle adulthood was attributed to both a reduced demand on parental roles and a reduced dependency on husbands. Women during this period now have the time to seek other avenues of support and satisfaction.

But with the high fertility rate in many developing countries, a woman's reaction to menopause could be a viable area for future studies. How is the woman's self-concept affected by the loss of a childbearing role? And how does this role loss affect the mental health status and self-esteem of women? Among Thai women, for example, menopause is considered a health issue. The women take it in good stride with this Thai idiom, *leod cha pai—lom cha ma*, which means, the blood will go and the wind will come. While some look forward to menopause, others nonetheless approach it with some ambivalence (Punyahotra & Dennerstein, 1997), and this ambivalence may be connected to the imminent loss of their childbearing role.

Menopause is a universal defining characteristic of women during middle adulthood—a reflection of the "Global environmental" dimension—but women's reactions to this experience can be evaluated cross-culturally. With men, the case is different. Men have different dreams and aspirations, roles and lifestyles, which vary cross-culturally, therefore an *emic* rather than an *etic* approach to the study of midlife crisis is more appropriate.

Because "midlife crisis," as conceptualized in the developed world, involves the problems individuals have readjusting to their aspirations, roles, and lifestyles from early adulthood, we suggest that this concept needs to be an important aspect on the research agenda in the developing world, especially in those societies undergoing rapid transition. With modernization, high unemployment rate, and the AIDS epidemic, the readjustment of dreams, roles, and lifestyle may even occur before midlife.

Retirement, which usually occurs in late adulthood, may constitute a mental health issue, especially if adequate preparations have not been made beforehand. One area of anxiety is with housing. Most wage earners are government employees. Certain grades of employees are provided with housing and are expected to vacate their houses upon retirement or when no longer in service. Others are in rental accommodation. Therefore, the anxiety associated with making provisions for their own housing in anticipation of retirement, which can occur unexpectedly through forced retirement, can cause mental health problems. This condition is worsened in developing societies where mortgage programs of financial institutions are not well developed. Based on the authors' experiences in Nigeria and other parts of Africa there is a sense of pride and accomplishment that comes from house ownership, especially in one's own village or "soil of origin." Unlike the "mobile home" concept in the United States, a house is seen as a way of relating to nature. It is permanently fixed to the soil of one's choice. Also, it is a symbolic way of maintaining contact with one's root, even if visits to that root are infrequent. Therefore for those who plan to spend their retirement time in urban centers, there is an added pressure of owning at least two homes before retirement: the "city home" and the "village home."

Apart from home ownership, there are other factors associated with retirement anxiety. For example, Madu and Adebayo (1996) examined 200 male and female Nigerian workers aged 50–58 who were about to retire and found that males were more anxious than females. Maybe because males perceive themselves as providers, and those in polygamous marriages were reportedly more anxious than their counterparts in monogamous marriages. However, smaller family size, fewer dependent children, and higher levels of education were related to lower levels of retirement anxiety. The loss of social status associated with retirement is important, but so also is the general economic situation that may limit postretirement opportunities. Peltzer (1989) found that the loss of social status and the economic crisis in Nigeria were related to retirement stress among predominantly male employees.

Still, there are questions whether mental health disorders are expressed in the same ways across cultures. While there are those who believe that the underlying psychopathological experiences are the same across cultures, but are only manifested differently (universalist school), others believe that culture is at the root of any abnormal behavior expression (culturalist school). Both schools of thought will therefore affect the approaches to the study of abnormal behavior (Draguns, 1997). For example, some of the early researches from Africa reported that depression was not prevalent in Africa, but subsequent studies, using different approaches, have reported vegetative symptoms such as loss of enjoyment, appetite, or sleep as constant across cultures (Marsella, 1980; Marsella, Sartorius, Jablensky, & Fenton, 1985). Although symptoms may be universal simply because of the way they are expressed, the attribution of causes may vary across cultures. Field (1960) reported that complaints about depression in Africa were frequently related to witchcraft. This kind of attribution may be common to other developing societies where a strong belief in the spirit world still persists.

There is a need to comprehend the different cultural idioms by which guilt is expressed in order to understand its expression even within the same society. Within the Indian society, for example, Rao (1973) distinguished between two types of guilt expression: the one related to the previous life (karma) and the other to the present life. Guilt is not a core feature of depression across cultures, but it is an important element of depression in Western societies. This notwithstanding, guilt is usually associated with the occurrence of death. Therefore, the question is, since death is a universal phenomenon, is guilt also universal? If so, are the attributions made to death-related guilt also culturally invariant? In developed societies where there is an emphasis on taking responsibility for one's action, blame is expected to be more self-directed than other-directed. But there are suggestions that when death occurs blame is other-directed. For example, blame may be directed at the medical team, at family members, or even at God (see Kübler-Ross' 1969 book *On Death and Dying* for details on her stages of dying). In developing societies with collectivist cultures, however, blame is expected to be other-directed rather than self-directed, but with attributions made to witchcraft or to evil spirits (Field, 1960). While developed and developing societies appear to share a similarity in other-directed blame in the event of death, the difference, however, seems to lie in at whom or to what the blame is directed. We shall discuss more about issues of death and dying in Chapter 9.

While blaming others is ego-protective, can guilt feelings be associated with this action? In other words, do guilt feelings come only from self-blame and not from other-blame? It could come from both. For example, the individual who blames the doctor for his or her child's death may also blame himself or herself for the choice of a doctor, as in the case of the developed world. Another individual may blame self for not taking precautionary measures, such as performing the necessary rituals, if death is attributed to witchcraft or evil forces, as in the case of the developing world.

HEALTH PROMOTION

In recognition of the "Global," "Developed," and "Developing" environmental dimensions, health promotion should encourage visits to both Western-trained physicians and/or to spiritual healers for improved health practices. There should be rewards tied to such visits and for improved health practices. Rewards should be relevant and practical but based on the *demand* values of the individual and/or group. For example, if a villager is told to boil water before drinking, what will be the reward for doing so? Usually the villager is told that the reward for drinking boiled water is that death will not result from disease. Well, first of all, the villager is alive before being asked to change his or her habit. Prior to this new health promotion, this villager didn't die from drinking water that was not boiled, so how come he is now going to die from not doing so? The same argument can be made for other health issues using the "before" versus the "now" debate. Even if deaths had occurred in the past from not drinking boiled water, does the villager attribute those deaths to water pollution or to other reasons such as witchcraft or evil forces? Ide and Sanli (1992), for example, attributed the low education level and/or the deeply ingrained cultural beliefs of Saudi women to an apparent lack of understanding of specific causes of various illnesses or the rationale for preventive measures. In a study that puts the "before" and "now" debate suggested above in perspective, Tayeh, Cairncross, Sandy, and Maude (1996) carried out a health education intervention to reduce dracunculiasis prevalence in three Ghanaian villages during the 1990 dry season. They promoted the use of cloth filters for drinking water and avoidance of water contact by sufferers, then collected a base-line information of potential risk factors for dracunculiasis, followed by a face-to-face discussion with household members. Comparing the 1990 dracunculiasis prevalence rate to the 1991 rate, after the intervention, the researchers reported that their intervention had a limited impact for the following reasons:

1. Many households did not buy the cloth filters.
2. Many households bought too few filters.
3. The filters were not used away from home.
4. Even at home, the filters were not always used.

Since the prevalence of HIV/AIDS has reached epidemic proportions in the developing world, especially in Africa, and given the prominence we gave to its discussion in the physical health section, health promotional approaches specific to HIV/AIDS are required. There is currently no cure for AIDS, therefore preventing HIV infection through behavior change seems to be the most viable and effective way to control its spread. Given the fact that the primary mode of transmission is through sexual intercourse, some have proposed a catchy ABC message for safe sex: A = abstinence, B = be true to your lover, C = condoms (Hynie, 1998). However, lessons from past successes and failures have clarified some issues, the most prominent of which is that a lot of individual and cultural factors need to be taken into consideration (Mann, 1991).

Any health promotional programs must take into account the different roles for men and women in the developing world. For most of the developing world, women hold a subservient position that puts them at a disadvantage where decisions about sexual behavior are made; this situation is exacerbated for those in polygamous relationships. Other variables include social norms for sexual behavior, attitudes toward condom use, sensitivity to frank and open discussions of sex, education, and the difficulty, due to social isolation, in reaching groups that engage in risky behavior.

Finally, adequate preparations for retirement should be given to workers in wage employment in order to ensure good health, housing, financial security, and social involvement in retirement. Detailed discussion on public policy issues will be covered in the next chapter.

SUMMARY

This chapter focused on the physical and mental issues that accompany aging. A distinction was first made between acute health problems, those that are short-term and chronic illnesses, conditions that are long-term and are usually not curable. While the likelihood of getting chronic diseases increases with age, this need not be inevitable and is most times moderated by factors such as an individual's perception of the self, beliefs about disease causation, for example, locus of control and self-efficacy, and the environment within which a person lives.

Although acute illnesses characterize the early adulthood condition and chronic illnesses seem to be typical of late adulthood, some of the lifestyle choices in early adulthood have implications for the nature and time of onset of chronic conditions in later life. In the developed world, the later-life illnesses include arthritis, various heart diseases, and cancers. Major mental health problems include aspects of dementia and depression. In the developing world, HIV/AIDS has become the most dominant disease condition and is the number one killer, although other diseases such as malaria and some infectious diseases are also prevalent. Due mainly to the much lower life expectancy, the major mental health challenge seems to be depression. Several health promotional suggestions of preventing and coping with both physical and mental health conditions have also been presented.

8

Public Policies

Of the many factors that may account for differences in aging and adult development across cultures, public policies enacted by various governments are perhaps the most important. These policies can thus be considered as key sociocultural variables that influence aging and development. There is a difference, though, between public policies and social policies. The latter has to do with policies of all social institutions, both private and public, while the former has to do with only public institutions. But public policies also influence what happens in the private sector and thus cannot be divorced from social policies. However, the problem occurs when both are confused (see Walker 1999 for details). In this chapter, our discussions will highlight public policies because of their pervasive influence.

The environment, including the government, is influential in developing human behavior. This view has been articulated differently by contemporary scholars (Bronfenbrenner, 1979; Valsiner & Lawrence, 1997). The view that person-environment interactions significantly influence behavior, however, owes its origins to Lewin (1936), who suggested that in order to understand a person's behavior, it is imperative to examine the characteristics of that person and the environment in which he or she lives. A number of more specific theories have derived from this more general conceptualization. For example, using a life course perspective, O'Rand (1996) put forward a theory of "cumulative disadvantage" in analyzing economic stratification among elderly people. Here, both institutional arrangements, such as opportunity structures, and the aggregate actions of the individual over the life course affect inequality. Institutional arrangements not only affect individuals, they also affect groups. For example, Riley (1971) notes that because people are grouped on the basis of age, they are allocated resources accordingly. But age is not the only basis for such groupings as proponents of the political economy perspective point out. Social class, gender, and race are other dimensions used for grouping individuals (Dowd, 1987), and the state, through its public programs and tax policies, is implicated in the differential treatment of people (Esping-Anderson, 1990; Quadagno, 1988).

With illustrations, we shall discuss two other theories deriving from Lewin's (1936) co-constructivistic approach that have public policy implications for the elderly. They are Lawton and Nahemow's (1973) Competence and Environmental Press model and Kahana's (1982) Congruence model.

COMPETENCE AND ENVIRONMENTAL PRESS MODEL

This approach was introduced by Lawton and Nahemow (1973) who suggested that any person's behavior is determined by that person's given level of competence operating in an environment of a particular press level. They defined competence as the highest level of functioning at which an individual is capable of performing. According to Lawton and Nahemow, competence consists of five components that are believed not only to be life-long, but are also presumed to underlie all other abilities: biological health, sensory-perceptual functioning, motor skills, cognitive skills, and ego strength. However, it is difficult to measure any of these components independent of environment. For example, a person's cognitive skills are much dependent on the environment in which the person lives. Thus, it is almost meaningless to talk about competence devoid of a specific environment.

Environmental press refers to the different challenges or demands that environments exert on a person. Environments can place three different types of demands: physical, interpersonal or social. These can operate alone or in any combination of these segments. Physical demands relate to such factors as the accessibility of a medical care facility. Interpersonal demands refer to the kinds of difficulties a person may experience in trying to get along with others, such as cultural barriers between a doctor and patient. Social demands have to do with the norms, laws, or customs that may affect a person's life and may end up constituting the *demand* values of the individual or group.

Lawton and Nahemow (1973) contend that the interaction between competence and environment can produce behavior that ranges from positive to negative, usually displayed in two forms: as observable behavior and affect or feelings and emotions. The implication of this theory for public policy for the elderly is obvious. Changes in the physical or mental well-being of the elderly, such as decrements in motor or cognitive skills, can reduce their ability to cope with environmental demands and move them away from their adaptation levels. For the elderly to maintain their required adaptation levels, there would need to be changes that would either reduce their environmental press or that will raise their competence, for example, providing housing and medical care at reduced costs and also adequate retirement income. But as mentioned earlier, environmental press is not only at the physical level, it occurs also at the interpersonal and social levels. Therefore, provisions for medical care, housing, and adequate retirement income will be affected by these other environmental press dimensions. For example, policymakers are likely to realize that living arrangements in developed societies that uphold individualistic values are different from those of developing societies that are mostly collectivistic in values.

THE CONGRUENCE MODEL

Proposed by Kahana (1982), the congruence model posits that we all have needs, but these needs vary widely among people. At the same time, environments also differ in their ability to satisfy the needs of different people. Therefore, people with particular needs, in exercising agency, will seek out the environments that will most adequately cater to their needs. For example, a person who has to frequently travel to distant locations to seek medical care is likely to seek residence in a place that is serviced by efficient air and rail transportation, if he or she does not own a means of transport. When there is congruence between a person's needs and the environment that addresses these needs, the person is happy and contented. When needs and environment are incongruent, however, the person is likely to experience stress and discomfort.

The mismatch between the person's needs and environment becomes more important when the person's or the environment's options are limited. Kahana cites three main factors that can bring about this limitation: (1) if the person's freedom is limited, for example, in terms of housing options; (2) if the characteristics of the environment are restricted, for example, government resources; and (3) if the person believes that he or she has limited freedom. Nursing homes, hospitals, and prisons are typical examples of restricted environments. Limitations on individual freedom include age-related declines in people's competence.

The implication of the congruence model for policy relating to the older adult is that generalized policies aimed at covering everyone may not be suitable for every elderly person. Even if the environmental factors are uniform, such as residence in a retirement facility, people's individual needs may vary considerably. For people who value independence, programs introduced that have their best interests at heart, but which did not receive their inputs, may end up causing more stress for them. This is especially the case for people living in retirement facilities where the management of the facility is likely to believe that it knows what is best for its clients. In the next section, we will discuss the state and public policies and their implicit relationships to these person-environment perspectives.

THE STATE AND PUBLIC POLICIES

The state both generates and distributes wealth. In doing so, it exercises the power to tax, to regulate, and to distribute wealth among its citizens, based on some set eligibility criteria such as age and social class. According to Quadagno and Reid (1999), benefit or welfare programs can be classified as Social Assistance, Social Insurance, and Fiscal Welfare.

Social Assistance

The eligibility criterion for social assistance, which is to relieve poverty, is need. To establish need benefit, applicants are usually required to provide information about assets, income, and even lifestyle. Some people may find this kind of scrutiny humiliating; nonetheless, they still subject themselves to it. In a way, because social assistance benefits are quite low and coupled with the nature of scrutiny to which people are subjected, they are made to discourage all but the truly needy (Marmor, Mashaw, & Harvey, 1990).

From the inception of the Social Security Act of 1935 until 1978, the elderly in the United States were considered as needy. They were treated as one homogenous group, and this compassionate stereotype became the basis for programs such as Medicare and special tax exemptions and credits for those aged 65 and over.

Social Insurance

The eligibility criterion for social insurance is entitlement, which is earned through contributions made to a common pool of funds. Through this pool of funds, risks are shared when loss of income occurs, such as unemployment, or retirement. Even though the individual is entitled to his or her social insurance benefit, age is usually used as a benchmark for drawing on this entitlement.

As the baby boom generation becomes older in the United States, there are concerns about the solvency of this program as well as those under social assistance. According to the Congressional Budget Office (1997), benefit programs including Social Security and Medicare are expected to consume 16% of the gross domestic product (GDP)—nearly twice the current proportion—by the year 2030 when most of the baby boomers will have reached old age. Therefore, raising the Social Security retirement age is proposed as a solution. At present the eligibility for full retirement benefits is 65, but will be 67 in 2027 under current law.

Fiscal Welfare

Eligibility criterion for fiscal welfare is labor market participation. In this regard, tax exemptions are given, for example, in employee contributions to employer-provided pensions, to personal savings for retirement, and in employer-provided health insurance. Although these tax exemptions are discriminatory (see Street, 1996 for details), they help to reduce the number of need-based recipients. A contrary argument, however, suggests that poor people are ill-served by such a system because they cannot take advantage of these tax breaks due to their low wages.

Countries differ on their leanings toward the three benefit programs of social assistance, social insurance, and fiscal welfare. Based on its leaning, a country's administration is classified as either "liberal," "conservative," or "social democratic." A "liberal" administration is more inclined toward means-tested benefit programs such as social assistance in the United States, whereas a "conservative" regime is more inclined toward labor force participation such as fiscal welfare in Germany. However, a "social democratic" administration is more inclined toward providing benefits to all its citizens as an entitlement such as social insurance in Sweden (Quadagno & Reid, 1999). We shall now review retirement income, health care, and housing programs, three popular areas affecting the elderly that have been shaped by public and social policies.

PENSIONS AND OLD-AGE PROGRAMS

Pensions serve as the major source of income for the elderly in many societies, especially in the developed world. With the exception of some European countries whose pension schemes started around the end of the nineteenth century, most pension plans are a fairly new phenomenon, starting mostly after World War II (Kinsella & Gist, 1995). The major aim of most old-age pensions is to provide income to all qualifying people in their retirement that would be: (1) continuous; (2) adequate; (3) relatively stable, in terms of purchasing power; and (4) would enable the retired population to attain acceptable socioeconomic standing relative to the active population (Nektarios, 1982). In other words, to reduce the "environmental press" in old age. Pension plans fall into two main categories: public and private pension systems.

Public Pensions

Although the establishment of public pension schemes proliferated after World War II, this is mainly a feature of the developed world. This may be due to the higher life expectancy in these countries. However, with the projection of the impeding boom in the population of the elderly in the developing world, this issue has to receive urgent attention. Most pension plans are financed through the pay-as-you-go method, a system whereby current beneficiaries are paid with the contributions of those who are yet to qualify for this benefit. Payment is usually through payroll taxes paid by employees and employers. The logic is that by the time the present contributors attain old age, they, in turn, would be paid from contributions by the generation of workers that replaces them. The concern to many governments of late is that the projected boom in the elderly population is so vast that funds now available in the system will be completely used up. Consequently, when those currently paying into the system retire, there may not be sufficient funds left for them to receive their pension benefits.

Health and Medical Care

Access to adequate medical care remains one of the most important needs of older adults. As people grow older, they begin increasingly to suffer from progressive diseases and sensory or structural abnormalities that start in middle adulthood or old age, thus reducing their competence level. Some of the chronic conditions that afflict the elderly include arthritis, Alzheimer's disease, hearing and vision loss, chronic back pain, cancer, and emphysema. The quality of life of the older adult depends, to a great extent, upon his or her ability to afford quality health care that is needed to treat and manage these disease conditions. Using the United States as an example, and although the United States is a "liberal" regime, we will review the health care benefits offered to the elderly in the developed world. Two main health benefit programs that are available to the aged in the United States are Medicare and Medicaid.

Medicare

Partially funded through payroll taxes of 1.45% on all earnings, Medicare has been used to provide universal care for the aged since 1965 (Social Security Administration, 1997), in order to reduce "environmental press." Prior to the program's inception, only 56% of older adults had hospital insurance. By 1992, at least 97% of all older adults had coverage because everyone who qualifies for social security is eligible for Medicare (Meyer & Bellas, 1995). Medicare has two main parts: Part A provides insurance that covers hospital inpatient services and is compulsory. Part B provides supplemental coverage for physician and related services, is available for an additional premium, and is usually deducted directly from a beneficiary's social security income.

Even though the eligibility for Medicare is age based, the coverage itself is not comprehensive. Some estimates indicate that only about 44% of all old-age health costs are borne by Medicare (Holden & Smeeding, 1990). The kinds of services not covered by Medicare include long-term care, preventive care, co-payments, Medicare Part B premiums, and charges that surpass allowable fees. Consequently, up to 75% of older adults obtain at least one supplemental health insurance, often referred to as Medigap (Iglehart, 1992). However, even with this Medicare and Medigap coverage, older adults still pay higher out-of-pocket health care expenses than any other age group (Davis, 1986). It should be noted that other countries such as Canada and Great Britain offer broader coverage with less out-of-pocket expenses by the elderly than the United States.

Medicaid

The United States Congress created the Medicaid program in conjunction with Medicare in order to provide health care to poor people of all ages. However, a disproportionate amount of Medicaid money is spent on the elderly and institutionalized individuals, who apart from children are more vulnerable to "environmental press." People aged 65 and older constitute just over 12% of the U.S. population and yet account for more than 50% of Medicaid expenditures (Meyer & Bellas, 1995). More than 75% of this amount goes to nursing care, even though only about 5% of the older adults reside in nursing homes at any given time.

Eligibility for Medicaid is based on family assets and income (means tested). The type of resources used in the computation of assets include monies that a person has in savings and checking accounts, stocks, bonds, and any form of property that can be converted into cash. Under certain conditions, some assets such as a home, car, funds up to $1,500, and some insurance policies are excluded. For a person to be found eligible, the remaining assets must total less than $2,000 for a single person and $3,000 for an elderly couple (Social Security Administration, 1992). Like other poverty-based welfare programs, reliance on Medicaid is sometimes regarded as stigmatizing and degrading, a humiliation that should be avoided if one has any options (U.S. Senate Select Committee on Aging, 1988). As a result, although Medicaid provides medical coverage to many elderly with few resources, eligibility is sometimes accompanied by discrimination, restricted access to medical care, and lower quality care (Margolis, 1990; Wallace, 1990). The government not only reimburses health care providers at a lower rate, but also at a slower pace than private insurers. Therefore, some health care providers refuse Medicare recipients altogether (Brown, 1984). Despite some of these drawbacks, there exists fairly substantial health coverage for a majority of older adults in the developed world.

HOUSING

A number of housing options have been adopted with a view to enhancing the physical and psychological well-being of the elderly by providing a more flexible environment. Four such approaches will be examined in this section: age-segregated housing, apartment complexes for the elderly, retirement communities, and continuing care retirement communities.

Age-Segregated Housing

A majority of older adults live in communities that are age-integrated, but older people are increasingly opting to live in communities that are designed exclusively for the elderly. Although federally assisted, age-segregated housing started in the United States in 1956, only about 6% of older adults live in age-segregated housing. This percentage is considerably lower than the proportion found in European countries such as Sweden, France, and the Netherlands (Silverman, 1987). The main advantage of age-segregated housing is that it would be designed specifically to attend to some of the needs of the elderly. However, even when these homes are federally assisted, they are offered at some cost. In developed societies where there are well-established old-age income programs, this can constitute a viable option for the elderly.

Other advantages to age-segregated housing arrangements include the development of an elderly subculture. Early research by Rosow (1967) on the elderly in Cleveland found that living among fellow older adults led to higher levels of social contacts and morale, especially among women. Even later research (Lawton, Moss, & Moles, 1984) confirmed this earlier finding, although these authors cautioned that the findings could be due to other factors such as the kind of housing and the specific neighborhood that was studied.

Apartment Complexes for the Elderly

This is similar to age-segregated housing in also creating a subculture of the elderly, except that instead of older adults living in houses, they reside in apartments that are occupied only by people who reach a designated age. A study of 46 low-income elderly residents in San Francisco by Hochschild (1973) observed that the residents celebrated birthdays together; shared information, costs, and shopping; looked in on one another and so forth. According to Hochschild, these roles appeared to be replacements for roles lost in their former communities and helped to protect the residents against loneliness.

Retirement Communities

In contrast to age-segregated housing, not only housing, but the entire community is restricted to people of a given age, and it is designed to cater to the needs of older people. These communities usually have single-story houses, and activities are usually planned with the older adult in mind. In the United States, these communities are found predominantly in the Sun Belt states, notably Arizona and Florida.

Survey studies show that retirement communities tend to have relatively affluent, better educated, healthier, married older adults (Heintz, 1976). These survey studies have found the residents to be highly satisfied, unwilling to leave the community, and fully involved in social activities of the community. In contrast, participant observation studies from at least one such retirement community in California (Jacobs, 1974, 1975) found the typical occupant to be lonely and unhappy, because, according to Kahana's (1982) congruence model, individuals' needs vary. Social participation was also low, with only about 500 of the 6,000 participants fully involved with a club or organization.

It should be noted however, that the well-established pension and old-age income programs in the developed world help to make such expensive living arrangements affordable to some.

Continuing Care Retirement Communities

Another variation of age-segregated housing is the continuing care retire-ment community. This typically offers options ranging from independent housing to full nursing care. Individuals are expected to pay a very high lump sum as they move in and make smaller monthly payments for as long as they live there. The strong point of this arrangement is that payment does not vary with the level of care (Sherwood, Ruchlin, & Sherwood, 1990). As with the retirement communities, continuing care retirement communities are usually expensive, therefore, occupants tend to be wealthier, more educated, unmarried, and childless, compared to the average older person. As expected, funding for living in such communities would be aided by pensions and old-age income programs that are reliable.

According to Thompson (1994), continuing care retirement communities are increasingly being designed to integrate the social, physical, psychological, medical, and operational needs of older adults such that those among them that have fully functional abilities would enjoy a high-quality lifestyle. The design arrangement provides several options in terms of paths from one location to another, user-friendly apartments, single-story construction, and so forth. This provides independence for those who can still enjoy it and also reduces medical and social problems. Very few studies have examined the effect of these com-munities; many people wait until they are in their late 70s before deciding to take residence.

THE CHANGING PERCEPTION OF THE ELDERLY AND PUBLIC POLICIES

Starting from 1978 there began a rethinking about considering all old people in the United States of America as needy. This was precipitated in part by the state of the Social Security system, which has been problematic since going back to the days of President Carter (see Light, 1985 for details). Another reason as documented by both Hudson (1978) and Baugher and Lamison-White (1996) was a change in the perception of the elderly from being poor to being well-off. As a result, as Binstock (1994) notes, beginning in 1983 the government started to make changes in Social Security, Medicare, and the Older American Act, thereby further restricting certain benefits to only rela-tively poor elderly people.

THE DEVELOPING WORLD

In his book, entitled *Social Policies for the Elderly in the Third World*, Tracy (1991) notes that policies for youth, economic development, and primary health care take precedence over policies for the elderly, and this is reflected in researchers' poor attention to this matter. He, however, highlighted some of the challenges that the governments of developing countries face in intervening in elderly people's lives. It is in this light, therefore, that the limitations of the Western models of Social Assistance, Social Insurance, and Fiscal Welfare as applied to developing societies can be better understood. The limitations include the following:

1. Most developing countries lack the administrative infrastructures to support social policies, including the capacity to collect revenue and to dispense benefits.

2. The number of people engaged in full-time, wage-related employment to support programs based on the principles of social insurance (payroll contributions) is limited. Despite urbanization influences, developing countries remain predominantly agricultural and rural.

3. The implementation of a Western model retirement plan is restricted to mostly male workers employed by large industries in urban centers.

4. Social programs are expensive. Therefore, it stands to reason that if developed countries continue to grapple with the financial cost of their social programs, then developing countries with limited resources will have more problems attempting to use Western models. In addition, with a mostly young population, there are competing demands for limited resources.

5. Western models conflict with the traditional values and beliefs that elderly care is the responsibility of the family and community.

Against the backdrop of the limitations listed above, we shall discuss the appropriateness of Western models as they relate to retirement income, health care, and housing programs for the elderly in the developing world. Where applicable, alternative indigenous practices that either we are aware of through personal experiences or are documented will be discussed. In other cases, we shall make suggestions that will require systematic study in the future.

PENSIONS AND OLD-AGE INCOME PROGRAMS

Public pension schemes cover only a very small proportion of the elderly in developing countries because most of them have not participated in wage employment, resulting in "cumulative disadvantage" (O'Rand, 1996). Even when these are tied to labor-force participation, coverage is still quite limited. For example, whereas mandatory old-age pension programs cover 90% of the labor force in most developed countries, even economically viable developing countries such as Hong Kong and Thailand do not have publicly supported comprehensive retirement pension schemes (Domingo, 1995). Where such plans exist, the coverage is usually limited to certain categories of workers such as civil servants, military personnel, and those working in the formal sector (akin to "Fiscal Welfare" in the developed world). Rural workers, especially those involved in the agricultural sector, petty traders, and the self-employed, have little or no pension coverage in the developing world. Figure 8.1 illustrates the

Figure 8.1
Percent of Labor Force Covered by Public Old-Age Pension Program, 1991

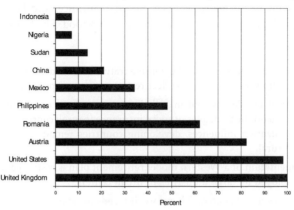

Source: Kinsella & Gist (1995).

wide disparity in percentage of the labor force covered by old-age pensions between the developed and developing countries. At the low end of the spectrum are countries like Nigeria and Indonesia with roughly 7%; the medium range has countries like the Philippines with about 48%; and Romania with roughly 61%. The high end includes the United States with 98% and the United Kingdom with 100% of the labor force covered by old-age pension programs.

Another indicator of rate of coverage for old-age pensions is the expenditure by respective countries as a percentage of their Gross Domestic Product (GDP). Figure 8.2 presents the expenditure on public pensions as a percent of GDP for different regions of the world. As the graph shows, public pensions make up almost 10% of the GDP in Organization for Economic Cooperation and Development (OECD) countries, followed closely at 8% by Eastern European countries. The Middle Eastern countries spend nearly 3% of their GDP on public pensions. Latin America and Asia spend about 2%, while public pensions make up less than 1% of the GDP in Sub-Saharan Africa.

This relatively low expenditure on, and coverage of, old-age pensions in developing countries has been attributed to two main factors: the relatively younger populations and correspondingly smaller elder population resulting mainly from lower life expectancy. However, the reality of a rapidly aging population suggests that it is time to reform and expand the pension programs currently in use.

The implication of this very restricted coverage and low GDP expenditure on old-age pensions is that the bulk of the responsibility of economic and social support for the elderly is passed on to informal sectors, mostly the family, especially in Africa and South Asia. The assumption has been that the well-entrenched extended family systems that operate in most developing countries

Figure 8.2
Public Pension Expenditure as a Percent of GDP, Circa 1990

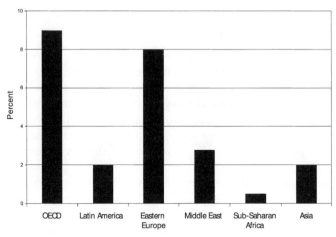

Source: World Bank, 1994.

will continue to provide direct support for a majority of the elderly. In some cases, leaving family members to cater for their elderly is woven into public policy. In other words, it seems that the social demand dimension of Lawton and Nahemow's (1973) "environmental press" (norms, laws, customs) is considered in public policies. For example, under Chinese law, children are required to fulfill care-giving obligations to their parents, failing which the parents can appeal to employers to have part of their children's pay garnished. Even in rural areas replete with nonwage work activities, parents have a legal right to exercise claim over part of their children's grain ration (Petri, 1982). A flagrant noncompliance on the part of the adult child can result in a prison penalty of up to five years (Tout, 1989). However, where there is an established case of the absence of family or that a family is incapable of taking care of their elderly, then the community and local governments step in (Chuanyi, 1989). Here, the community and government act as a safety net, if family care fails.

The importance of the family as the primary source of care for the elderly was also the highlight at a workshop on aging held in Lagos, Nigeria, in 1981. At this workshop, experts from various nations in Africa prepared a document for the African region's participation in the 1982 World Assembly on Aging in Vienna, Austria. This report was also to be used for planning aging policies and services in Nigeria. The overriding theme from this workshop and other documents was to do nothing to jeopardize the role of traditional family support (Tracy, 1991). The Nigerian philosophy, which reflects the philosophy of many African nations, has thus been to enact programs and policies that will foster family and community-based services (Nigeria, 1983). It is not clear, however, if the family approach to elderly care is a convenient excuse to continue a nonchalant approach by government or if there is a genuine belief that government involvement in elder programs on the scale of those employed in developed societies will weaken family systems.

Private and Other Pensions

Public pensions are not the only old-age security systems available to the elderly. Private old-age security programs serve to complement and, in some cases, replace those operated by the public sector and are severally referred to as occupational pensions, supplementary pensions, or private pensions (Kinsella & Gist, 1995). Ironically, it is those countries that already have well-established public pensions that also tend to operate extensive private pension programs. These private pensions usually target specific industrial sectors or private companies.

In the developing world, these private pension programs operate in the form of provident funds. A provident fund is a form of compulsory contribution program in which regular specified portions of an employee's wages are withheld and invested for later payment. Employers are usually required to match or exceed employee contributions, similar to the "Fiscal Welfare" programs in developed societies. With the exception of countries from Latin America, a majority of these countries were former British colonies. This difference in colonial history may also account for why employer contributions are not required in the Latin countries that operate provident funds. See Table 8.1 for a representative list of countries and proportion of employee and employer contributions. Even though provident funds tend to cover private-sector workers, they are managed publicly (Kinsella & Gist, 1995).

Payments from provident funds are usually in the form of a lump sum at retirement equal to the total contributions plus interest. In some cases, benefits can be payable at any age if the worker is permanently disabled or dies. The performance of provident funds has been very erratic. In some developing countries, such as Sri Lanka, inflation and worsening economic conditions have lessened the value of fund contributions to the extent that the real annual return rate for the Provident Fund often has been negative (ILO, 1993). Consequently, several countries have abandoned provident programs in favor of defined-benefit pension plans.

An encouraging example, and perhaps a possible model, for the developing world is Chile, which first enacted a public pension scheme in 1911. However, by the late 1970s, the pension system had stagnated to a point where it was no longer able to meet current obligations. Therefore, Chile abandoned its public system in 1980 and instituted a compulsory savings plan administered by private sector companies. All salary earners are required to contribute 10% of their earnings to a privately run retirement fund. In providing more environmental flexibility, contributors themselves choose from competing investment companies and have the freedom to switch their accounts. They also have many options for withdrawal and annuities upon retirement. To minimize the

Table 8.1
Payroll Tax Rate for Provident Fund Schemes, 1991

Country	Employees	Employers
Africa		
The Gambia	5	10
Ghana	5	12.5
Kenya	5	5
Nigeria	6	6
Swaziland	5	5
Tanzania	10	10
Uganda	5	10
Zambia	5	5
Asia		
Fiji	7	7
India	10	10
Indonesia	1	2
Kiribati	5	5
Malaysia	9	11
Nepal	10	10
Singapore	7-30	10
Solomon Islands	5	7.5
Sri Lanka	8	12
Western Samoa	5	5
Latin America		
Argentina (1994)	11	0
Chile	13	0
Colombia (1994)	2.9	8.6
Peru (1993)	13.3	0

Source: Kinsella & Gist, 1995.

risk of mismanagement, the government maintains a tight supervisory and regulatory role (Schulz, 1993). The results have been very satisfactory for over a decade, with annual returns on contributions in excess of 12%. Due to the success in Chile, many countries in Latin America as well as some in eastern Europe and Africa have adopted or are giving serious consideration to adopting aspects of the Chilean plan (Harteneck & Carey, 1994). But as laudable as the Chilean plan is, it will be difficult for relatively poor developing countries that lack the necessary infrastructure to implement such a plan.

It should be noted that provident funds in the developing world cover a fairly narrow range of people. Even the Chilean plan applies only to salary and wage earners. Unfortunately, most people in the developing countries are employed in the informal, usually agricultural sector and live primarily in rural areas where old-age coverage is limited. In the absence of a comprehensive public pension scheme, the earning capacity of the elderly is seriously compromised. This financial inadequacy has important and far-reaching implications for the well-being of the elderly. However, elderly people can and do exercise agency in trying to create a balance with their environmental press. This is exemplified in the indigenous funding schemes, which we shall describe next.

Indigenous Funding Schemes

As indicated, income programs and even private, or formal, pension programs in the developing world cover principally those employed in the organized work environment. Consequently, a majority of informal sector and self-employed people are left to fend for themselves. As a way of meeting some crucial financial needs, and as a way of exercising agency, some communities in the developing world that the authors are personally aware of have developed some innovative ways of solving short- and mid-term financial problems. For example, some communities in Nigeria operate two types of programs that have some semblance with formalized social insurance or banking systems, synonymous with the "Social Insurance" model of the developed world. One such program is called *adashi* in certain parts of Nigeria and *esusu* in other regions. Essentially, a number of people get together and make monetary contributions, the amount of which has been agreed upon beforehand. The contributors then take turns as recipients of the total contributions. The time cycle could be monthly or bimonthly. If you have ten people each making a contribution of $500, the amount that each recipient receives is $5,000. There are several variations of how this *adashi* is run, one of which is especially noteworthy. In this case, the person who is the last to receive in a given round is usually the first to receive in the following round. This means that the person who received $5,000 the previous month might again receive $5,000 the following month in the start of the next round. This is an amount that could be used to execute a lot of essential projects but which would otherwise be unavailable. This resembles an insurance concept in the sense that the contributions can be viewed as premiums.

The second system resembles operations in a regular bank and is indeed called *bam*, a Tiv word for bank. In this system, people come together and decide on dates on which they would meet to discuss the affairs of the bank. There is usually a token minimum contribution or deposit that every member must deposit at every meeting; however, there is no maximum amount, so some members make much higher deposits than others. Anyone who fails to make a minimum deposit is charged a small fee. The bank usually has a leader, a position akin to chairman; a secretary; and a treasurer. Any member can borrow money from the bank, at a predetermined fixed interest rate, up to that person's deposits at that time. A person can borrow more than his or her deposit if that person has a guarantor or surety, but the amount cannot be more than the combined deposits of the borrower and his or her guarantor. If the borrower fails to pay off the loan, all his or her deposits are taken to cover the loan. If these are insufficient, then the guarantor's deposits are used up to the remaining unpaid balance.

At the end of the year, usually around Christmas, each person gets back all the deposits that he or she made. Most people use these savings to do their Christmas shopping as well as execute other important projects. The proceeds from the interests on loans, fees, and services are used to buy cows or goats to be slaughtered and shared. The quantity of meat a person gets is usually commensurate with his or her contributions. As a reward for their services, the officials of the bank are also given extra shares of meat, in addition to the shares they got on the basis of their contributions. People who wish to continue with this process the following year decide on dates and officials for the next cycle. Thus organized, these events serve several functions. They enable people to save money for important projects, provide lending facilities that are otherwise unattainable through the more formalized banking systems, and serve as avenues where people socialize and bond with each other. It is not uncommon for other community-wide issues to be discussed at these venues. Similar to the African example, in Asia, Help Age International (a non-profit organization) sponsored a project that helped elderly people in a village in Cambodia to start up rice banks. Participants borrow rice for food and sowing from the bank, then repay with rice after harvest time with interest. The bank afterward distributes some of its "profits" to frail elderly people in the village free of charge (UNESCO Courier, 1999).

While such programs are empowering, some of them (like the *esusu*) however, require participants who are nonwage earners to have a regular supply of income from other sources. A highly possible source of income for the elderly is monetary gifts by adult children and relatives, but if these gifts are not regular then the future of these programs can be in jeopardy. To complement self-help projects like those described above, governments in the developing world should provide seed money or start-up resources to foster and expand on existing indigenous schemes, especially in the rural areas.

HEALTH CARE

It is not easy to provide a general view of available health care benefits in the developing world since each country has its own system and laws that are mostly determined by such variables as social structure, history, political and economic systems, and constitution. However, from a comparative viewpoint, and just like in the areas of old-age income and housing programs, the legal framework for the policies enacted by these nations is strikingly similar. This may be due in part to the fact that most of the countries of the developing world were under the rule of few colonial powers—a reflection of the Developed world environmental dimension. The colonial influence is still evident in social legislation especially in Africa and Asia and to a lesser extent in Latin America (Fuchs, 1988). Furthermore, international conventions and the activities of international organizations may have contributed to the prevailing similarity of the overall approach to health coverage resulting in Global or Developed environmental dimensions. Consequently, it is possible to provide a brief description of the basic health care system.

Usually administered by the ministry of health, the bulk of health care services in the developing world is run by state agencies, and tend to provide preventive and treatment services at local, regional, and state levels. These general hospitals and dispensaries, as they are often called, are intended to offer free treatment to all patients, although in some countries wealthier people are required to pay just a modest fee. These services are synonymous with a "Social democratic" administration. Unlike in developed societies, there are no specialized health care programs for the elderly. Medical care for the elderly usually is contained under a general health care program for the society. A number of reasons may be responsible for this, including lack of resources (Tracy, 1991) and the low life expectancy in most developing countries.

On the surface, the free medical care offered to most people may give the semblance of access to health care to a wide segment of the population, including older adults. However, as this example from Egypt would indicate, this is often not the case. In a study cited by Azer (1988), local authorities on the outskirts of Cairo sited a hospital that was five kilometers away from the community in a place to which no transportation was readily available, thereby creating what Lawton and Nahemow (1973) refer to as a physical environmental press. In addition, the operating room and in-patient ward were not usable, the hospital lacked basic supplies, and medicine was often unavailable. This gloomy picture unfortunately characterizes the state of public hospitals and health clinics in much of the developing world.

In Latin America, health insurance programs are very common, but are almost nonexistent in most of Africa and Asia. Under schemes such as found in Latin America, benefits are delivered directly or indirectly (Fulcher, 1982). Under the direct method, the health insurance institution administers medical care directly to participants. They sometimes develop their own health infrastructure that consists of a wide range of medical equipment and medical staff including physicians and nurses. Another variation of the direct method is whereby the health insurance institution sends its clients to public health institutions for treatment, then pays the Ministry of Health a regular subsidy as a form of reimbursement for medical services provided to the insured (Fuchs, 1983).

Under the indirect service model, an insured person may be required to first pay for the services himself or herself, then is later reimbursed for the total or partial sum expended. Alternatively, the administering health insurance agency may pay the medical service providers directly based upon previously estab-lished conventions and agreements between the establishments.

Against the background of public health institutions not being well-staffed and located, and lacking in essential medications and services, and coupled with the absence of health insurance programs in much of the developing world, the result is limited access to quality care by the elderly. In other words, in terms of health, the environment provides limited options (Kahana, 1982). The scenario is the same even in Latin America where health insurance programs exist because the insured are required to pay some premiums. Unfortunately, a majority of older adults lack the resources to pay for adequate health insur-ance packages due to the paucity of old-age income programs. As Lawton and Nahemow (1973) would suggest in their Competence and Environmental Press model, governments in the developing world should either improve the quality of services available at public health institutions or enhance the earnings of the elderly to enable them to participate in quality care offered by the private sector.

HOUSING

From the standpoint of the elderly in the developing world, housing options are limited because of coresidency arrangements (Choi, 1992) and income re-strictions.

In the developing world, very few, if any, age-segregated communities exist. The major reason is that the family has traditionally taken care of housing needs for the elderly. Proposals to change things, such as having different hous-ing arrangements, threatens to undermine customs and practices that individ-uals expect to be in place in their old age. For example, Baihua (1987) reports that the emphasis in China on family and community resources has hindered the development of long-term facilities, which primarily are for elderly people without family or income. Consequently, it is common to find up to three generations of families residing within the same household pattern. In addition, since a majority of the elderly in the developing world live in rural areas, such age-segregated housing arrangements become less practicable. However, they happen by default, because young people continue to migrate from rural areas to urban centers in search of wage employment, leaving the rural areas to be heavily populated by old people.

Another major obstacle to age-segregated housing is affordability. Due to less established old-age income programs, a majority of elderly people could not afford these housing options even if they were available. Moreover, the severe shortages of income, food, and health care for the general population, especially children, is such that special programs of this nature aimed mainly for the elderly are viewed as superfluous indulgence (Tracy, 1991). The end result is that older people in the developing world have limited housing options. With collectivistic values, however, it is not clear how limited housing options impact on their physical and psychological well-being.

Because of financial considerations also, retirement and continuing care communities are not yet large-scale options. Where continuing care facilities exist they are usually meant for the poor, and for those without families (see Adi, 1982, for details).

However, there are a few features that would make a variant of this arrangement acceptable. Even though families in the developing world typically keep their elderly, it is also a fact that the elderly increasingly require medical services that the families are unequipped to provide. Policy planners could work to bring health care closer to the elderly. Governments would have to contribute in terms of building the physical and medical infrastructure and structuring reliable old-age pension and income programs that would enable the elderly to pay their way, if necessary. But design and implementation must be done in such a way that it provides a good fit between the person and the environment. One environmental consideration should be location. There appears to be a strong attachment to the "soil of origin," which partly explains why most elderly people live in rural areas and not in urban settings.

ADMINISTRATIONS AND PUBLIC POLICY

Most administrations in developing societies appear to be "social democratic" in their public policy perspective. Understandably, it is hard for them to be "liberal" as the United States is because most people in the developing world are poor. It will be inappropriate to rely heavily on a means-test as the basis for providing services. Also inappropriate will be to have a "Fiscal Welfare" orientation that only serves the relatively few people who are engaged in the wage economy.

But having a "social democratic" perspective may be more of an intent than a practice, because, while governments are "social democratic" in their constitutions, they do not have the resources to implement their goals. For example, based on the social security conference held in Chile in 1942, the Conference of Chapultepec in 1945, the Inter-American Conference on Social Security in 1947, and the Declaration of Human Rights in 1948, social security is a firmly ideological goal for governments in Latin America. But social security has remained more of an objective than a reality in many Latin American countries because of insufficient resources (Tamburi, 1985).

Furthermore, apart from resource constraint, there is overreliance by developing world governments on the traditional family structure for both formal and informal support. In some cases, as in China, such support is incorporated into policy while in other cases, as in Turkey, family support is expected because it is consistent with the social, cultural, and religious mores of the society (Tracy, 1991). The emphasis on family support for the elderly by governments of the developing world points to the interface between public policies and social policies, which, as mentioned earlier, could be confusing.

CHANGING PERCEPTION OF THE ELDERLY AND PUBLIC POLICIES

Concerns have begun to emerge regarding this usually formidable bastion of support for the elderly—the family. Industrialization and modernization have combined to produce migration from rural to urban areas and have changed traditional family structures (Apt, 1992; Kinsella, 1988). Consequently, there are fewer people left behind to cater to the elderly and more people who are unwilling to perform their hitherto traditional roles of providing elder support. These factors threaten to create a marginalized class of older citizens in many developing countries and understandably have created economic insecurity among the elderly (Apt, 1992; Choi, 1992). Commenting on the Korean elderly, Choi (1992) noted that: "An increasing number of elderly Koreans suffer from financial difficulties because of their children's avoidance of, or inability to provide, economic support. This is one of the emerging aspects of the aging problem in Korea" (Choi, 1992; p. 151). While many researchers and commentators have realized this trend, governments in developing countries are yet to develop a coherent and comprehensive policy that would help families cater to the needs of their elderly without compromising traditional values. Some governments have taken measures to ensure continuity of familial support through legislation, but they should do more than instituting punitive measures for a lack of elderly support.

SUMMARY

Public policies that affect the elderly fall under Social Assistance, Social Insurance, and Fiscal Welfare programs. These policies appear to be based on person-environment interaction perspectives. The essence of Social Assistance programs is to relieve poverty based on means-testing. In Social Insurance programs individuals make contributions to a common pool of funds and only the contributors are entitled to benefits, for example, in the case of unemployment or a loss of income. With Fiscal Welfare programs benefits are tied to wage employment participation with tax breaks provided for those who participate, for example, in employer-provided pensions and employer-provided health insurance. These benefit programs affect retirement income, health care, and housing benefits, three areas important to the welfare of elderly people, and each country's administration differs on its leanings toward any of these programs. According to its leaning, a country is "liberal" if it is more inclined toward Social Assistance such as in the United States; it is "conservative" if it is more inclined toward Fiscal Welfare such as in Bismarck's Germany; and it is "social democratic" if it is more inclined toward Social Insurance as an entitlement to all citizens such as in Sweden.

Using Western models of Social Assistance, Social Insurance, and Fiscal Welfare in developing societies is fraught with problems. Some of these problems include the lack of resources and infrastructure to tax and disburse benefits, the relatively low percentage of people engaged in wage employment, and the reliance on family and the community for the traditional support for the elderly. Most governments in the developing world appear to be "social democratic" in intent but in practice they fall short because of problems with resource and infrastructure to implement their programs, as well as their desire to retain the traditional values of family and community support for the elderly. The traditional family support for the elderly is being eroded and governments in the developing world need to develop programs that strengthen the family support base.

9

Death and Dying

Literally every adult knows something about death, and as one ages it becomes difficult not to think about it. Each one of us has at least read or heard about people dying, and in some cases, death hits close to home when a family member or a friend dies. Like most common phenomena, it is easy to talk about death but not that simple to define it. One of the many common definitions of death one will find in dictionaries is that death represents a cessation or end of life. But exactly when does life end, and what are the characteristics that signal this end? We will first present the medical and legal definitions of death, which for the most part, represent the Western perspective. We will then examine the main causes of death, discuss where people die, the anxiety people express about dying, the dying process itself, and the issues of grief and bereavement.

MEDICAL AND LEGAL DEFINITIONS OF DEATH

Many people are usually surprised to learn that even medical experts do not have a unanimous, clear-cut, definition of death. Rather, these experts have tended to present a set of criteria that are then adopted by different societies as they deem fit. For many years the most singularly used criterion has been the absence of heartbeat and respiration, otherwise known as clinical death. However, Jeffko (1979) suggests that the most commonly used definition of late is *brain death,* which encompasses the following eight criteria:

1. complete lack of responsiveness to the most painful stimuli;
2. absence of spontaneous response or movement to all stimuli;
3. no pupil responses, blinking or eye movements;
4. lark of spontaneous respiration for one hour or more;
5. no motor reflexes;
6. a flat electroencephalogram (EEG) for a duration of at least 10 minutes;
7. no yawning, swallowing, vocalizing, and postural activity;

8. there is no change in the above criteria when tested again within a 24-hour time period.

In addition to these eight criteria, conditions such as hypothermia, coma, and an overdose of chemical substances, which may be capable of mimicking death, must also be ruled out.

A major point of contention within this approach is the distinction between general brain death and cortical death. The cortex is that part of the brain that performs higher level functions such as planning, thinking, and language. The brain stem (lower brain) on the other hand, performs some of the basic life-sustaining functions such as breathing and heart rate. Sometimes a person's cortical functions may cease but his or her brain stem may continue to function. The person can remain in this vegetative state—some have survived in this state for several years—never to regain any of the higher level functions that make us meaningfully human. Would it be appropriate to classify a person who has lost cortical functioning as dead even though his brain stem processes are still active? Advocates of the cortical death definition argue that when a person loses cortical functions, that person ceases to exist in the real sense of the word. This position has many adherents but not many countries have adopted the definition of cortical death to define when life ends. The debate continues.

THE DEMOGRAPHY OF DEATH

Advances in medical treatment and health prevention measures have not stopped people from dying—an estimated 53, 929,000 people worldwide died in 1998 (World Health Organization, 1999). These developments have changed what we are likely to die from, at what age we will die, and where we are likely to die, however.

Causes of Death

The World Health Organization (WHO) publishes mortality rates as well as the causes of death, classified by gender, age, and region of the world. Recently, categorization of the burden of disease, the human cost of living with a disease, has also been computed.

Chronic versus Acute Causes of Death

The top ten causes of death are presented in Table 9.1; these are further categorized and ranked by each health region based on the World Health Organization's categorization. The picture that clearly emerges is that there is a significant change in the manner in which we are dying. People are now dying more from noncommunicable *chronic* diseases as opposed to the communicable

Table 9.1
Leading Causes of Mortality in All Member States and Their Ranks in Some WHO Regions

Causes of Deaths	All Member States		Africa		The Americas		Europe		South-East Asia	
	Rank	% of Total	Rank	% of Total	Rank	% of Total	Rank	% of Total	Rank	% of Total
Ischaemic heart disease	1	13.7	9	2.9	1	17.9	1	25.5	1	13.8
Cerebrovascular disease	2	9.5	7	4.7	2	10.3	2	13.7	4	6.5
Acute lower respiratory infections	3	6.4	3	8.2	3	4.2	4	3.6	2	9.3
HIV/AIDS	4	4.2	1	19.0	13	1.8	42	0.2	8	2.2
Chronic obstructive pulmonary disease	5	4.2	14	1.1	6	2.8	5	2.7	11	1.6
Diarrhoeal diseases	6	4.1	4	7.6	10	2.0	22	0.7	3	6.6
Perinaral conditions	7	4.0	5	5.5	7	2.6	13	1.2	5	6.0
Tuberculosis	8	2.8	11	2.2	19	1.0	23	0.6	6	5.1
Trachea/bronchus/lung	9	2.3	38	0.3	4	3.2	3	4.2	15	1.2
Road traffic accidents	10	2.2	12	1.8	5	3.1	8	1.9	7	2.5

Source: The World Health Report (1999).

acute diseases. Among the top three killers are ischemic heart disease, cerebro-vascular disease, and acute lower respiratory infections. These are basically chronic diseases. Among the top ten causes of death, only HIV/AIDS (fourth) and road traffic accidents (tenth) appear to result from acute causes, although even in the case of HIV, more people are living longer with HIV-related ill-nesses, thanks to new advances in treatment. This implies that fewer people are dying at an early age and that for most people, dying is likely going to be a drawn-out process. Consequently, there will be a considerable increase in the demands that will be placed on family and friends, making issues of dying of major importance to the study of aging and adult development. Given this change in what people die from, we will examine, in the next section, whether this has any impact on where people are likely to die.

WHERE DO WE DIE?

In Western countries, at least 80% of people die in institutional settings such as hospitals and nursing homes even though most people would rather die at home in the company of family and friends (McCue, 1995). One of the con-sequences of people dying in these settings is that professional health personnel are increasingly required to play a very influential role in this very important aspect of the dying person's life. This also tends to exert some emotional toll on these health care professionals ranging from doctors to nurses.

Given the general preference to die at home even among people in the de-veloped nations, Kalish (1984) suggested six factors that determine where a person will die. One of these is the physical condition of the person; if the condition demands specialized care, the person will very likely be in an institution. The individual also has to have the finances to be able to afford the care, the care has to be available, and the institution has to have the competence to provide the service that is required. Age is also an important factor. If a person is so old that he or she is not capable of taking good care of himself or herself, the individual may be taken to the hospital or a nursing home where competent staff may perform this function. Finally, the person may prefer to remain at home or go to an institution. We believe that a seventh factor, culture, may also be a strong determinant of where we die. Most of the countries in the developed world, where autonomy and independence are valued attributes, have an individualistic value system, which may factor into the decision of where a person may die.

Thus, not everyone, especially in the developed countries, prefers to die at home. According to Kalish, people who are concerned that they may be placing an undue burden on their family members or who are apprehensive that some required emergency care may not be available when needed, may choose to stay in a hospital or nursing home. Some have suggested that dying at home is best when a person is still sufficiently alert to interact with family members, or when the condition is so severe that death is imminent (Kalish, 1985).

THE HOSPICE OPTION

With the exception of the few people who fear being a burden to their families, most people who have a choice prefer to die at home. The major factor listed by Kalish (1984) that often negates this wish is the person's physical condition, which often does not give the individuals or their families a choice. The main problem with the hospital and other settings is that these advantages of better and professional care come at some serious costs besides just finance. For instance, the person in a hospital or nursing home tends to have very little, if any, autonomy. These facilities often set fairly rigid visiting hours, decide when their residents should eat, engage in some recreation (where this is possible), when they ought to sleep, and so forth. Do things have to be this way?

One of the innovative approaches regarding where people may die is the *hospice* option. The major goal of a hospice is to assist people to die with dignity and as little pain and discomfort as possible (Koff, 1981). Thus a hospice emphasizes the quality of life and not the prolongation of death. Even though medical care is often available, the role of these professionals is not so much to treat the illness, but to control pain and enable the person to function as regularly as possible. Hospices are thus midway between hospitals and the dying person's home, and, subject to the availability of care, closely approximates the context of dying that is found in many developing countries.

There are two types of hospices: inpatient hospice and outpatient hospice. The former involves the complete care of the patient by the hospice. Outpatient hospices tend to provide services to patients or clients in their own homes, and they are increasing in popularity because more people can be served at a much lower cost. The approach in hospice is significantly different in that the staff work together with clients to determine what they should do. The family and friends of the client are also extensively involved. Hospices often do not have restrictions on visiting hours and usually encourage as much involvement by family members as possible (Miller, 1996). Some researchers found that clients appeared less anxious and less depressed; hospice personnel were also viewed as more accessible. In addition, hospice clients who had come to a hospice from hospital settings showed a significantly stronger preference for the hospice than the hospital (Walsh & Cavanaugh, 1984).

Despite these advantages, hospices may not be for everyone. Some people's illnesses may require specialized treatment that is unavailable at hospices. Also, the notion of hospice may not coincide with a given person's beliefs. People who feel that life should be pushed as far as possible may not share in the concept of, in essence, merely waiting to die. Besides, the needs of clients, their families, or hospice staff may not always coincide and could lead to some problems. Finally, a hospice may not be available to all the people who wish to have it. When demand for hospice is much more than the available spaces, rather stringent conditions may be set for acceptance, denying some people this much needed alternative. Notwithstanding, this approach provides a viable option regarding where people may spend their final days.

THE FEAR OF DEATH: DEATH ANXIETY

Many humans are afraid of death, and this fear or anxiety (both terms are used interchangeably here) is believed by some theorists to be the major motivator of all behavior (Becker, 1973). When death anxiety is excessive or is not handled properly, it can become a destructive force and might even result in abnormal behavior. The same death anxiety if channeled properly can be a motivating force for individuals to engage in phenomenal achievements in order that their achievements would transcend their physical mortality. For example, every president of the United States tries to make a contribution that will be permanently recorded in the history books as an enduring legacy of his administration. Another positive aspect of death anxiety is that people who are afraid of death may do whatever it takes to ensure that they stay alive.

Fear of death can be conceptualized in various ways: fear of death of oneself, fear of death of others, fear of dying of self, and fear of dying of others.

Fear of death of oneself relates to fear of the event of death; this includes what happens to the individual after the experience of death. Such fear could involve anxiety about judgment—heaven, hell; earth burial; cremation; the possibility of donating one's body to science; and what might happen to people and possessions that the individual may leave behind—spouse, children, friends, businesses; and so forth.

Fear of death of others involves the apprehension by an individual of the event of death occurring to significant others in the individual's life, notably family members and friends.

The fear of dying, of self-distinction, here is between the event and the process. Death is an event; dying is a process. Some people are not afraid of death itself, but are extremely anxious of the process of dying. Anxieties here may relate to notions of wasting away, the possible deterioration in one's physical appearance, which may be of greater importance to females than males. Some individuals worry about the possibility of being a burden to others in terms of both time and financial costs.

Fear of dying of others is similar to fear of dying of self, mentioned above, except that the fear is directed at the process of dying of significant others such as one's spouse, parents, children, siblings, and any others for whom the individual perceives some form of commitment or responsibility.

Why do people fear death, and how is this anxiety manifested? There are two broad categories of reasons for death anxiety. One relates to the fear of physical suffering, mentioned above in the fear of dying of self and of others, and the other centers on psychological suffering. It should be noted that these are not mutually exclusive and both have been broken down into several components.

Some of the components listed by Schulz (1978) include the fear of physical suffering or pain, concern over the inability to complete some important goals that people may set for themselves, the negative impact that the death may have on survivors, and fear of isolation and loneliness. Many people are understandably reluctant to stay with a dying person. The prospect that one might contract a protracted illness that would result in isolation may be another reason why people experience death anxiety.

From an adult development and aging perspective, it is important to examine how age is related to death anxiety. Intuitively speaking, one would expect that the elderly should show greater death anxiety than people in the early adulthood stage since they, the elderly, are theoretically closer to their death. However, some studies have shown that while older adults think more about death than the young age categories, they are also less fearful of death and more accepting of this final outcome (Keller, Sherry, & Piotrowski, 1984; Thorson & Powell, 1990).

Kalish (1987) has offered some reasons why older adults consistently display fairly low death anxiety. One reason is that when people get really old, their satisfaction and value of living may be considerably diminished such that death may not be viewed as a very negative event. Second, as we have stated several times in the last chapter, older people begin to develop chronic illnesses over time. As a result, they are aware that the chances of fully recovering from these illnesses are not very high, and death could result at any time. Also, older adults are likely to have seen many friends and family members die already and might expect their own time to come soon. Finally, people in late adulthood stage are not only more likely to have completed most of their life's tasks, but also would have given considerable thought to their own death.

However, more recent research has indicated that death anxiety may be more complex than has been measured in earlier studies. Some researchers have distinguished between overt and covert death anxiety and have found that contrary to previous studies, older adults showed higher levels of overt fear while younger adults evidenced greater covert death anxiety. The authors suggest that the cumulative differential death loss experiences by older adults over the life course probably lessened the need to deny fears of their own death (Galt & Hayslip, 1998). Regardless of the pattern of death anxiety and the differences in its manifestation between older and younger adults, it may be related to beliefs about, and anticipation of, the dying process, a topic that we discuss in the next section.

THE DYING PROCESS: THEORIES OF DYING

Understanding the process of dying is very difficult because no one has ever died and returned to tell us exactly how they proceeded to this last stage of being. What scholars have done, therefore, is to obtain as much information as possible from people who know that death is imminent, either the terminally ill or the very old, in order to discern how people feel about dying. Using mostly in-depth interviews, researchers have developed theories regarding the complex processes that take place as a person approaches death. In this section, we will consider two theories of death: the stage theory and the phase theory of dying.

The Stage Theory of Dying

Based on over 200 interviews with terminally ill people, Elisabeth Kübler-Ross, M.D., noticed a consistent and predictable pattern of thoughts and emotions that a majority of the dying expressed. The insights obtained from these interviews led her to develop one of the most widely known frameworks for understanding the dying process. According to Kübler-Ross (1969, 1981), the process of dying involves a sequence of five identifiable stages, namely: denial, anger, bargaining, depression, and acceptance.

People are initially shocked upon hearing that they have a terminal illness. The most common emotional response accompanying this news characterizes the first stage and it involves *denial*. The person may at first believe that there was a mistake in the diagnosis, or that his or her test results must have been mixed up with someone else's. After much thought, people typically accept the diagnosis, which gives way to a new wave of emotional reactions, mainly anger.

The *anger* stage tends to be very potent as the person may display feelings of hostility, rage, envy, and resentment to almost anyone in sight. Whereas in the denial stage a person might offer an expression such as "This can't be true," this changes in the anger stage to such questions as "Why me?" The person views it as totally unfair that others more "deserving" of the mishap were not the ones affected. Eventually, these feelings diminish, however, and the person proceeds into the bargaining stage.

The *bargaining* stage is marked by attempts by the dying person to postpone the obvious. The person's angry responses do not seem to change his or her condition, so it appears as if this is a way of changing tactics; to see whether a different outcome would be obtained if the person somehow mellows. It is almost as if the person is saying "Okay, God, I reacted angrily and have seen that my situation has not improved, would you acquiesce if I ask you nicely?" Alternatively, the person may request God to grant him or her enough time to get through some important events, such as seeing a son or daughter graduate from college or get married.

In the *depression* stage, the person figures out that his or her condition is real, anger will not help, and the chances of getting an extension on life are slim. This grim reality triggers serious feelings of depression, expressed in the form of guilt, extreme sadness, shame, or sorrow. When the dying person has an opportunity to discuss these feelings with others, it helps the dying person to reach the final stage, acceptance.

The *acceptance* stage is reached when the person now seems to accept the inevitable. There may even be a feeling of being at peace. The person seems to express little pain, and might discuss his or her condition in a somewhat detached manner. The person is getting his or her last rest to prepare for the final journey.

The problem with most stage theories, and Kübler-Ross's is not an exception, is that it is often difficult for everyone to rigidly progress through the stages. In fact, Kübler-Ross (1974) concedes that though the five stages represent the typical process of death for most people, there are considerable individual differences such that some people may follow a different sequence while others may not go through all the stages. People may also simply alternate between different stages, such as between acceptance and denial (Kastenbaum, 1991). Thus, applying the theory rigidly with all categories of dying people may be misleading and harmful. The practical utility of the theory lies in the fact that it can serve as a guide to help people meet death in a manner that best suits their needs.

The Phase of Dying Theory

Somewhat similar to the stage approach is the notion that the dying process involves three main phases: acute, chronic living-dying, and terminal phases (Pattison, 1977; Weisman, 1972). The *acute* phase begins at the time the individual learns that his or her condition has become terminal. The emotional responses said to characterize this phase can involve the feelings described in several of Kübler-Ross's stages, including anxiety, anger, denial, and bargaining. After some time, however, the person may come to terms with his or her condition and then shift to the *chronic living-dying* phase. This phase is marked by contradictory feelings such as anticipation of loss of self-control and identity, fear of the unknown, and loneliness, which could exist simultaneously or interchangeably with feelings of acceptance and hope. The *terminal* phase is the last and shortest phase and is reached when the individual begins to withdraw from others and culminates with the individual's death.

The amount of time that a given person can spend in each of the three phases can vary widely. Therefore, some scholars introduced what is termed a *dying trajectory* that describes both the length and form of a person's dying process. Four dying trajectories, differing in terms of the certainty or uncertainty of death, have been proposed (Glaser & Strauss, 1968; Strauss & Glaser, 1970). The first trajectory refers to cases in which death is certain and is expected within a certain time frame; the individual may be informed that he or she has six months or less left to live. With the second trajectory, death is certain but the time within which it will occur is not; it may range anywhere between six months to six years. In the third trajectory, it is not certain that one will die, but the answer will be known within a certain time; results from a biopsy will be obtained within two weeks and will determine if death is certain. The fourth trajectory combines both uncertainty of death and uncertainty of time. In this situation, a person may have a growth that may or may not become malignant, and it is not certain when this outcome would be fully determined.

In what ways do these trajectories help in determining the amount of time a given person may spend in a particular phase? The first two trajectories seem to yield a fairly short time in the acute phase. However, the uncertainties that mark the third and fourth trajectories tend to result in high levels of anxiety over a long period of time. The implication here is that being certain of an outcome, even such a negative one as one's impending death, is very helpful in enabling one to deal with a difficult situation.

The problems we mentioned with regard to the stage theory are also applicable to the phase theory, even though the phases cover broader segments of the dying process than stages do. Although both the stages and phases frameworks imply qualitative differences between the different stages or phases, they do not explain what causes the transition from one stage or phase to another. People may show the reactions described in the phases in different order or may display simultaneously the behaviors believed to characterize different phases. Alternatively, these stages or phases may be valid but only within certain cultural settings. Our view is that there is no set way to die. Trying to help people across stages or phases that may not exist for them could be counterproductive. The best approach is to make a reasoned and determined effort to assist a dying person meet death in a manner that makes the person most comfortable.

IMPLICATIONS OF THE DYING PROCESS ON ADULT DEVELOPMENT AND AGING

Even though death occurs across all categories, it is easier to conceive of death only in old age. Older people die mostly of diseases such as cancer and heart disease, which incapacitate them before they die, resulting in a longer dying trajectory. Young people die mostly from accidents (Kalish, 1987); consequently, the dying processes of people in late adulthood and younger people differ.

Kalish (1987) suggests that most concerns of dying people are specific to how old they are when death is about to occur. The major difference seems to be in the degree of how cheated a person feels. In this regard, people in the early adulthood stage often feel robbed of the opportunity to live a full life. Older people feel that they are losing what they have while younger people are sad about losing what they might have attained.

One very important aspect of distress for the dying older adults is the view that their deaths are viewed as less tragic by society than the death of younger people (Kastenbaum, 1985). As a result, older adults are less likely to receive certain life-saving treatments, and are not perceived to be worthy of major investments in time, money, and resources. For example, there is an age limit on when a person becomes ineligible for receiving organ donations and transplants. Furthermore, many dying older adults stay in long-term residential facilities where there is reduced contact with family and friends. Thus, in addition to the problems they share with all dying people, older adults are further burdened with feelings of loneliness, loss of status, and increased feelings of worthlessness. At least at this point in time, this may be a more serious problem for the elderly in the developed world than their counterparts in the developing world.

GRIEF AND BEREAVEMENT

The devastating impact of a terminal illness or the dying process does not end with the death of the person in question. Family members and friends of the deceased person have to deal with the painful process of grief and mourning. Worden (1991) makes a distinction between grief and mourning. Whereas grief refers to the personal emotional reactions that follow a loss, such as sadness, anger, and guilt, mourning is the process through which grief is expressed. Mourning thus represents the culturally accepted expression of the personal feelings following a loss. In some cultures, close relatives are expected to shave their heads, wear either white or black clothing, and express grief for a specified minimum period of time. In other cultures, mourning involves a lot of drinking, dancing, and in some cases, a person within a certain kinship position is expected to marry the spouse of the deceased. Because people grieve in remarkably different ways, one of the concerns by researchers has been to examine whether or not grief or mourning involves a specific sequence.

Stages or Phases of Grief

Given the fact that many feelings and behaviors characterize grief, some theorists have found it convenient to view grieving as a process that consists of stages or phases. In our earlier discussion on the dying process, we commented on some of the main problems associated with stage or phase theories. Therefore, when we talk about stages or phases of grief, we should be aware that the goal here is not to suggest that everyone goes through all these phases or that the phases are necessarily sequential. It is more an attempt to organize the grief into major segments the bereaved go through before they recover from their loss. Most of these theorists have divided grief into three phases (Parkes, 1972).

Many of the common feelings people report in the first phase of the grief process are shock, disbelief, and numbness. They often feel confused and empty, and this might last for a few days. These feelings are actually believed to be adaptive in the sense that they protect the person from the severe pain of bereavement. Then the persons get into the second phase where they realize that the deceased is gone, never to return. Three behavior patterns typical of this phase are as follows: First the bereaved may think a lot about the deceased, which is often followed by feelings of guilt. The person wonders whether there is something he or she could have done that would have prevented the death. It is not uncommon for people to report that they are confused, that they feel empty. Second, the bereaved try to find a reason why the person died. Finally, there is a tremendous longing for the deceased, leading the bereaved to search for the deceased; it is common for the survivor to dream about the deceased or even speak to him or her. When these feelings diminish, the bereaved is ready to move into the final phase—recovery.

Recovery comes about due to conscious and concerted efforts by the bereaved who realize that there is no sense in dwelling on the loss and that they have a lot of other responsibilities to take care of. Mourners may now enthusiastically seek out the company of others and socialize actively. We should caution that there is no specified time frame within which a person should stay in one stage or across stages; it depends on a variety of factors that we will discuss later in the chapter. However, experts believe that it takes at least a year, perhaps more, to progress through the first phase through to recovery.

Tasks of Mourning

Worden (1991) prefers to view the grieving process in terms of tasks, not stages or phases, because these two terms imply some passivity on the part of mourners; as if they have no option but must pass through them. In contrast, tasks imply some action on the part of the mourner, and suggest that the grieving process can be subject to external intervention. This tends to provide some hope that there is something the bereaved can actively do about the situation. Worden (1991) suggests four tasks of mourning.

Task 1: Accept the reality of the loss. The first task of the grieving process is to shake off the disbelief and come to terms with the fact that the person is gone, and that earthly re-union is not possible. This can be enhanced by viewing the corpse, attending memorial services, and funerals, and so forth.

Task 2: Work through the pain of grief. The bereaved ought to acknowledge that the death of someone you care about brings pain. According to Parkes (1972), trying to avoid pain or refusing to express the obvious emotional turmoil can prolong the course of mourning and may actually lead to abnormal mourning. Societal influences can present problems at this stage. In some societies, it is deemed inappropriate for men to cry over the death of a loved one. The person may deny the pain or use a lot of drugs or alcohol. This can delay the completion of Task II.

Task 3: Adjust to an environment in which the deceased is missing. This task usually involves a cognitive readjustment. For spouse survivors, this might involve a realization that one will now live alone, or raise the children by oneself.

Task 4: Emotionally relocate the deceased and move on with life. The task here is not to disengage completely one's relationship with the deceased. Rather, it is to find a more suitable place for the deceased in the life of the survivor so that it is not activated with exaggerated intensity so that the mourner can continue to live an effective life (Shuchter & Zisook, 1986).

Normal or Uncomplicated Grief Reactions

Two criteria are typically used to define normality: 1) a clinician may determine a normal mourning behavior; and 2) the preponderance of specific grief reactions among the bereaved in a given society will determine normal grief (Worden, 1991). Much of the current work on normal grief can be traced back to Lindemann (1944) who had extensive interviews with more than 100 family members of the almost 500 people who died in a nightclub inferno in the Boston area in 1942. Based mainly on the commonality of the feelings and behaviors of these people, he characterized normal grief to encompass five major aspects:

1. bodily distress of some kind;

2. hostile reactions;

3. preoccupation with the image of the deceased person;

4. guilt feeling related to the deceased or circumstances surrounding the death; and

5. not being able to function as one had done before the loss.

Expanding on the initial work by Lindemann, Wordon (1991) identified four major categories under which the broad range of reactions to grief can be subsumed, namely, feelings, physical sensations, cognitions, and behaviors.

Feelings: Shortly after the loss, the experience is usually that of shock and numbness. Then there is sadness, which can be marked by crying; this is viewed by some to evoke a sympathetic response and suspends competitive behavior from others (Parkes & Weiss, 1983). Anger is a common feeling and may arise out of frustration that the survivor could do nothing to prevent the death. The bereaved may also experience guilt for certain things the person feels could have been done to save the deceased that were not done.

There are also feelings of anxiety, which can range from a mild insecurity to panic attacks. Anxiety often results from two sources: the fear that the survivor may not be able to take care of himself or herself and the increased awareness or reminder of the survivor's own mortality (Worden, 1976). Bereaved people also tend to experience feelings of fatigue, loneliness, helplessness, and a yearning for the deceased. Finally, the survivors can feel some relief, especially if the deceased battled through a lengthy illness or experienced a lot of pain. They may also feel emancipated if the deceased had so much control over them that it restricted their independence. The feelings of relief and emancipation can sometimes be accompanied by a sense of guilt that the person is somehow happy about the deceased's death.

Physical Sensations: In addition to feelings, physical sensations also characterize normal grief. Some of the sensations identified by Worden (1991) include tightness in the chest and throat, experiencing difficulty breathing, a general lack of energy, dry mouth, and a sense of depersonalization. These physical sensations are often of sufficient concern to the bereaved that he or she may visit a physician to check the problem.

Cognitions: People undergoing grief often express specific kinds of thought patterns. One of the first thoughts, especially when the news is about a death that was sudden and unexpected, is disbelief. Bereaved people may also report feeling very confused, preoccupied, sometimes obsessed, with thoughts about the deceased, and might have difficulty concentrating. Finally, the grieving person may display both auditory and visual hallucinations. These are usually transient illusory experiences that occur within a few days or weeks following the loss, and they tend to disappear shortly thereafter.

Behaviors: A number of specific behaviors are frequently reported after a loss. Fortunately, these typically correct themselves after some time. One of these behaviors is sleep disturbance; the grieving person may either experience difficulty going to sleep, or wake up prematurely, sometimes as early as four or five o'clock every morning. Dreaming, sometimes nightmares, about the dead person are also common. Bereaved people also exhibit eating difficulties. Some people may eat too much or too little, although under-eating occurs with greater frequency.

Abnormal or Complicated Grief Reactions

The responses mentioned under normal grief are termed "normal" because they are very common, but more important, these problems tend to be transient; the person gets over them within a reasonable time and moves on with life. Also severally referred to as pathological grief, unresolved grief, chronic grief, or exaggerated grief, abnormal grief reactions refer to a situation whereby grief responses such as loneliness, sorrow, guilt, and depression may so overwhelm bereaved people that they become the focus of the individual's life. In essence, what distinguishes normal from abnormal grief is not the type of reactions but instead their severity and duration (Schulz, 1985). Some researchers have found that among the elderly, those who underwent abnormal grief had lower self-esteem, were more confused, cried more, and had a greater desire to die than their counterparts who experienced normal grief (Lund, Dimond, Caserta, Johnson, Poulton, & Connelly, 1985–86).

In general, the most common manifestation of abnormal grief reaction is excessive guilt and self-blame. This guilt sometimes results in a disruption of daily routines and reduces the ability of these individuals to function properly. Other manifestations include major psychiatric disorders that develop following a loss, such as severe depression, anxiety states including phobias, extreme identification with the deceased, and Post-Traumatic Stress Disorder (PTSD).

Widowhood

The loss of a spouse to death is one of the most distressing experiences a person can have, especially in later stages of life. Widowhood in late adulthood is more common for women than for men; widows outnumber widowers by a ratio of 5 to 1. It is estimated that among women age 65 and over, 50 to 70% are widowed compared to 12 to 22% among their male counterparts. Furthermore, widowhood occurs sooner for women—the average age of widowhood is 66 years for women and 69 years for men. When this is combined with the higher life expectancy for women, the result is a longer average duration of widowhood for women, 15 years compared to 6 years for men (Martin-Matthews, 1996).

Like other types of bereavement and grief, widowhood first results in experiences of depression, sadness, and loneliness. Fortunately, spousal bereavement is often characterized by resiliency; many of the surviving spouses develop effective coping skills that often result in feelings of confidence and personal self-efficacy. According to some estimates, only 15 to 25% of bereaved spouses have long-term difficulties in coping (Lund, 1993).

The severe impact of spousal bereavement can be moderated by factors such as having adequate social support networks, especially closeness to one's children and the availability of intimate friends, a given individual's typical way of dealing with stress, and religious commitment. Since friendships developed on the basis of marital relationships do not always survive widowhood, the ability to make new friends is sometimes an important predictor of how well an individual would cope with the loss of a spouse (Ducharme & Corin, 1997).

It is difficult to determine whether the stress of bereavement is greater for the young than for the old survivors. Initially at least, the psychological distress is often greater for younger than older widows because the death of the spouse is more likely to be unanticipated. In addition, the bereaved may not have many peers that have experienced or are experiencing similar losses. However, this tendency for more intense grief by younger widows is said to reverse after a period of about 18 months while older spouses tend to show extreme grief reactions. One possible explanation is that older people are more likely to experience other losses simultaneously that may thus intensify and extend their grief (Kastenbaum, 1991).

Another important question in widowhood has centered on whether or not widowhood is more difficult for men or women. Research has found higher income to be associated with better bereavement outcomes (Sanders, 1993). This makes sense since adequate financial resources are needed for the surviving spouse to maintain a sense of self-sufficiency and to continue involvement in meaningful activities. In this regard, older widows are generally worse off than widowers in terms of finances, years of education, and prospects for remarriage. Coping with the loss of a spouse is likely to be most difficult for women who have had few economic and social resources throughout their lives, are in poor health, perceive themselves as dependent, and for whom the loss of the identity of wife is not replaced by other viable roles and lifestyles (O'Bryant & Morgan, 1991).

However, it is not all women that depend on men for economic or social support. In fact, since women tend to have more diverse and extensive friendship networks than men, and because widowhood is more prevalent in later life, older women develop very strong social networks with other widows. These support networks tend to compensate for the loss of a husband's companionship and facilitate the adjustment to living alone. For women over age 70, the married person is in the minority, and such a woman may have fewer friends than the widow in the same age group (Martin-Matthews, 1996).

Because there are a lot more widows than widowers, most research on widowhood has focused on women. Consequently, not much is known about the impact of widowhood on older men. The little that is known suggests that men often complain more of loneliness, have more difficulty expressing their grief and adjusting to the loss, and are slower to recover emotionally than are women. Men have been found to experience more medical problems and to be at greater risk of dying during the six months following their wives' death. Also, most men have inadequate housekeeping and cooking skills and are more likely to experience a double role loss of worker and spouse (Patterson, 1996). It has been suggested that because older men have depended on their wives for emotional support, household maintenance, and social planning, men seem to need remarriage more than women. The higher rates of remarriage among widowers may not be based on need but rather on the fact that men have been socialized to hasten the restructuring of their lives through remarriage.

Despite these differences, many aspects of bereavement that impact older people's mental health are comparable for both men and women (Lund, Caserta, & Dimond, 1993). Widowhood increases social isolation, which tends to give rise to loneliness, a factor that has been identified as a major problem by both men and women. To help address the problem of isolation and loneliness, mutual help groups and bereavement centers have been developed that try to bring bereaved spouses together to share the common experience of widowhood. The concept of a support group of other bereaved people is appealing, but research is needed to evaluate how support-group dynamics affects adjustment outcomes.

Additional Problems in the Grief Process

In addition to the pain resulting from the loss, certain conditions in the environment can contribute to make the already complex burden of the grief process even more complicated. In this section, we discuss the problem of disenfranchised grief and stifled grief, which are brought about mainly by norms in society that attempt to govern and restrict the process of mourning.

Disenfranchised Grief

Doka (1989) used the term disenfranchised grief to refer to a process whereby some bereaved people are not allowed, or are unable, to openly express grief because such expression is not socially sanctioned. Society prescribes who, when, where, for whom, how, and how long people should grieve. The problem is that these rules may not have much bearing on the attachments or the sense of loss of the bereaved. This may apply to situations in which (a) the relationship is not socially sanctioned, such as extramarital affairs, cohabitation, and homosexual relationships; (b) the ties between the deceased and the bereaved may not be recognized as being sufficiently close, such as lovers, neighbors, or friends; and (c) past relationships, such as an ex-spouse or former friend.

Disenfranchised grief tends to exacerbate the grieving process and at the same time removes or minimizes social support. Reactions that typically characterize normal grief such as anger, guilt, depression, and numbness can intensify if grief is disenfranchised. Cohabiting partners may experience problems with inheritance, ownership, and credit (Doka, 1987). Ironically, even though grief is complicated, a lot of the factors that facilitate mourning are absent. For example, the bereaved may not only be excluded from an active role in the dying process but might also not be allowed to attend the funeral. Finally, the survivor may not be able to verbalize the loss, get time off work, or receive the much needed expression of social support from others.

Stifled Grief

Commenting on the work of Doka (1989), Eyetsemitan (1998) argued that Doka's concept might be limited in the sense that even cohabiting or homosexual relationships could be "publicly" shared by like-minded people, especially given the proliferation of support and interest groups available today. Besides, in any given society, sets of norms on grief may vary as function of age group, ethnicity, and socioeconomic status, and the norms may not be static across time. He thus proposed a more encompassing, but equally limiting, concept of stifled grief. Like disenfranchised grief, this concept was also introduced mainly within organizational settings but can be applied across a wide range of settings in society.

Stifled grief, which may encompass disenfranchised grief, refers to any kind of recognized grief that is denied its full course. That is, society—the workplace, friends, one's local community—might put time lines on when an individual should have completed the process of mourning. The organization may set an arbitrary number of days following a loss after which they may expect an employee to resume full-blown participation in the workplace. This is hardly sufficient, since as we saw earlier, a period of up to one year or more is typically the amount of time required for normal grief. Thus, both disenfranchised grief and stifled grief could constitute additional problems to the already complicated process of grief and bereavement.

THE DEVELOPING WORLD

SOCIOCULTURAL DEFINITIONS OF DEATH

Not all societies rely on the medical and legal definitions of death. In fact, some societies have various notions of death. Counts and Counts (1985) report that some cultures in the South Pacific view death as a process whereby the life force leaves the body. However, this life force need not depart permanently at all times; it can depart when a person is asleep or is suffering from a very serious illness. Thus defined, it is possible for a person to die several times before his or her final departure. More significantly, it is possible to define someone as dead even when none of the eight criteria listed in the medical definition is met. A difference, though, is that a final disposition of the body (earth burial, entombment, and cremation) follows the medical definition whereas it does not in this case.

In a similar vein, the Trukese, a Micronesian society, believe that life ends when you are forty and death begins when you are forty. In this society, one is not considered as fully grown up until one reaches that pivotal age of forty, where one begins to have the maturity to make decisions and guide his or her life. The reason is that because this society does not have any industrial or technological facilities, people rely on physical strength and agility to undertake such tasks as paddling canoes and climbing trees. At forty, a person's physical strength begins to decline; sensing that life is ebbing away, the person then begins to prepare himself or herself for death (Kübler-Ross, 1975). The Trukese can thus be described as a death-affirming society. On the other hand, the

United States and most of the West are viewed as death-denying societies where people deny the dying process itself; people are reluctant to reveal their age, spend billions of dollars a year to conceal wrinkles, and feel uncomfortable talking about or preparing for death. These different perspectives on death have implications for how people in different societies view the dying process, bereavement, and the final rites that accompany death.

CAUSES OF DEATH

With the exception of the African region, ischemic heart disease and cerebrovascular disease rank among the top five killers in all the other regions of the world. Even in Africa, the percentage of death from noncommunicable diseases has been rising steadily over the years. In fact, the top three causes of death in the developed world—ischemic heart disease, cerebrovascular disease, and acute lower respiratory infections—are also among the top ten causes of mortality in the developing world. A recent potent killer has been HIV/AIDS, which is now the number one killer in Africa and ranks fourth worldwide (WHO, 1999). However, with new advances in treatment, more people are living longer with HIV-related diseases. This implies that even in the developing world fewer people are dying at an early age and that for most people, dying is likely going to be a long, drawn-out process.

WHERE DO WE DIE?

Data from the developing world are scanty, but anthropological accounts suggest that more people in most of these countries die at home. As suggested in Chapter 8, this may have to do with the fact that many of these countries have very few settings such as nursing homes and also because there is less access to standardized, Western-type health care facilities for the general public.

In the developing countries, the health facilities are not in sufficient numbers, and the few that exist are found predominantly in the urban centers. In addition, the cost of getting desirable treatment is so high that many people cannot afford these services. Governments in certain countries have tried to establish government-owned hospitals and clinics, but these are often underfunded, inefficiently run, or both. In extreme cases, family members of the sick person are required to buy the hospital instruments needed for certain procedures. Moreover, most of the developing countries do not have any elaborate health insurance programs, and there is still a substantial reliance on traditional healers.

When old age becomes a factor in death, culture is a significant variable in determining where a person dies. In a majority of developing countries, the norm is that family members are supposed to take care of their elderly (Apt, 1996). People who are placed in these institutions may perceive themselves as being abandoned and their last days may be lived in considerable misery. Besides, there may be the factor of social disapproval from the other members of the community and some cultural practices that may play a role. For instance, in India, when it becomes obvious that a person is going to die, he or she is lifted out of bed and placed on the floor. This is aimed at fulfilling the Hindu symbolism of "earth to earth" and the notion that when death eventually comes it will be easier for the soul to depart if the body is placed on the floor (Laungani, 1997). It is unlikely that most hospitals will permit this practice of putting very ill people on the floor. For these and other related reasons, more people in the developing world die at home or in settings less formal than hospitals or nursing homes.

DEATH ANXIETY

In our discussion of death anxiety in the developed world section, we mentioned the fact that fear of death can be characterized in four ways: fear of death of oneself, fear of death of others, fear of dying of self, and fear of dying of others. There have been no direct studies comparing the developed world with the developing world in terms of death anxiety. What has been examined in the literature that may have bearing on differences between the two worlds is the association between religiosity and death anxiety. Duff and Hong (1995) surveyed 674 older adults and found death anxiety to be significantly associated with frequency of attending religious services. This factor was particularly related to the belief in life after death. For instance, Rasmussen and Johnson (1994) found that as the degree of certainty in life after death increased, levels of death anxiety decreased. Similarly, Alvarado, Templer, Bresler, and Thomson-Dobson (1995) found a strong negative correlation between death anxiety and belief in afterlife.

This belief in an afterlife notion was explored further in a study that compared participants of three different religions. Parsuram and Sharma (1992) compared groups of 20 Hindus, Muslims, and Christians living in India. They found that the Hindus, who had the greatest belief in life after death, also tested lowest in death anxiety, followed by the Muslims, while the Christians showed the highest death anxiety. More recently, Roshdieh, Templer, Cannon, and Canfield (1999) studied death anxiety and death depression among 1,176 Iranian Muslims who had war-related exposure during the Iran-Iraq war. They found that those who showed higher death anxiety were those who also had weaker religious beliefs, did not believe in life after death, and did not maintain that the most important aspect of religion is life after death. Extrapolating from these studies, we contend that there would be relatively lower death anxiety in the developing world compared to the developed world. This is largely because besides being predominantly Christian, there is a high rate of secularity in the developed world. In contrast, there is a high rate of religiosity in the developing world where most people proclaim membership in many of the dominant religions of Christianity, Islam, Hinduism, and Buddhism. Even when they practice traditional religions, these tend to incorporate elaborate notions of life after death, a reliable predictor of low death anxiety.

Besides religiosity, we propose that death anxiety will be relatively lower among death-affirming societies than among death-denying cultures. We cited the example of the Trukese as a death-affirming society where people start preparing for death at age 40 (Kübler-Ross, 1975). Similarly, among several Vietnamese groups, people, as soon as they start to age, begin to prepare for their deaths through such actions as buying their own coffins and setting aside money for a tomb. Some cautious villagers purchase their coffins when they are 40 or 50 years of age and could have a coffin lying around the house for upwards of 20 years (Ta & Chung, 1990). This action is somewhat similar to the "preneed" arrangement in developed societies, where funeral homes provide people with the opportunity to make down payments, sometimes with financing options, for their cemetery lots, caskets, and funeral ceremonies before death occurs. With the lack of opportunity structures in developing societies, such actions as those of the Vietnamese may reflect a low death anxiety.

THE DYING PROCESS

We discussed two theories of dying in the developed world section: the stage theory of dying and the phase of dying theory. Our goal in this section is to discuss the extent to which these theories apply to the developing world. Briefly stated, the stage theory of dying (Kübler-Ross 1969, 1981) suggests that the dying person undergoes five stages in reaction to his or her death: denial, anger and resentment, bargaining, depression, and acceptance. As mentioned earlier, the stage theory of dying suffers from the problem of almost all stage theories, and that is, not everyone systematically passes through these stages in a unidirectional fashion. Many people remain at only one stage such as denial or anger; others alternate between periods of calm, fear, hope, depression, anger, sadness, and withdrawal (Buckman, 1993). Moreover, the religious assumptions as well as the implied notions of life after death embedded in this theory puts into question its empirical usefulness and generalizability.

The component that we think should modulate the application of the stage theory to any society relates to a given culture's outlook on death. We have made a distinction between death-affirming and death-denying societies. The cognitive processes underlying some of the stages of the stage theory of dying, such as denial and anger, may very well apply to people in death-denying societies, mostly in the developed world. A person from a death-affirming society like the Trukese who believe that death begins at forty, may show evidence of only one stage, acceptance, or at best two stages: depression and acceptance. Thus the stage theory may be useful mainly as a helpful cognitive guide of possible ways of coping with impending death or loss and not as a fixed and universal sequence that precedes death. In addition, in order to go through the earlier Kübler-Ross's stages of denial, anger, and bargaining, there must be a medical diagnosis of an impending death, as in the case of the cancer patients Kübler-Ross studied. Unfortunately, with the problems enumerated earlier with the availability of and acceptance of Western medicine, most terminal illnesses usually go undiagnosed. Most people, especially in the rural areas where most elderly people dwell, turn to traditional healers who are usually ill equipped to carry out any medical diagnosis. Therefore it is hard to know if people in the developing world also go through the Kübler-Ross's stages of dying.

The phase of dying theory is somewhat related to the stage theory in the sense that it proposes three phases on dying: acute, chronic-living, and terminal phases. In terms of the physical components of progression through an illness condition, there is no reason to expect differences between the developed world and the developing world. However, cultural variables may play a role in the cognitive and emotional processes believed to underlie these phases. In that regard in death-affirming cultures, anger, denial, and other such emotions need not characterize the chronic phase.

The concept of the dying trajectory (Glaser & Strauss, 1968) deals with the pace of dying, which can be sudden or slow, regular or irregular. This is influenced by the condition causing death, as in the case of hypertension versus heart attack, and how much information has been given to the dying person (Marshall & Levy, 1990). The critical elements in the dying trajectories are duration and form: (a) certain death at a known time, (b) certain death at an unknown time, (c) uncertain death but a known time when the certainty will be determined, and (d) uncertain death and an unknown time when the uncertainty will be resolved. Like the stage theory, different cognitive and emotional experiences are presumed to characterize each trajectory. For example, the last two trajectories are believed to produce higher levels of anxiety due to the uncertainty of the outcome.

The problem this and other related theories share is that they have not been verified in different contexts (Kastenbaum & Thuell, 1995). Even within the developed world, the four death trajectories, for example, have been evaluated mainly within hospital and other institutional settings such as hospices and thus remain largely undeveloped and require further study (Copp, 1998). We are not aware of studies evaluating the phase of dying theory specifically within the context of the developing world. Any proposed application of the phase of dying theory or the stage theory would have to take into consideration a given person's perspectives and values, religiosity, as well as his or her sociocultural environment.

GRIEF AND BEREAVEMENT

According to Worden (1991) grief refers to the personal emotional reactions that accompany a loss as manifested by such responses as anger and guilt, while mourning is the process through which grief is expressed. As we have stated earlier, there is a wide variation across cultures in how people behave after a death and how they are expected to behave. In some societies, the requirements of dealing with a major loss are played out over the balance of the lifetime of the survivor. This could be in form of rituals, what is worn, how one is addressed by others, and one's rights and obligations to participate in various activities within the community (Rosenblatt, 1997). Despite these differences, there are also some similarities. For instance, grief reactions expressed in the form of crying, fear, and anger are so common as to be deemed universal (a reflection of the Global environmental dimension), and most cultures provide sanction for the expression of these emotions in rites of mourning that follow bereavement (Parkes, Laungani, & Young, 1997). Perhaps owing to these common themes, some authors have proposed an organized pattern as well as what is deemed a normal or abnormal way in which grief is experienced.

Normal versus Abnormal Grief Reactions

Worden (1991) identified four main categories under which a broad range of grief reactions could be classified: feelings, physical sensations, cognitions, and behaviors. Feelings include reactions of shock and numbness, sadness, anger, and anxiety. Physical sensations can include shortness of breath, tightness in the chest, and in some cases even feelings of depersonalization. Common cognitions are disbelief, preoccupation with thoughts of the deceased, and sometimes hallucination; these last two are usually transient. Behaviors include sleep disturbance, eating difficulties, and absentmindedness.

Abnormal or pathological grief reactions are said to occur when people display actions that are not statistically common or may express normal grief reactions for an extended period of time. Based on the criteria listed by Worden (1991) grief that is never expressed, grief that is expressed but is intense and goes on for too long, grief that involves threats to others, or that involves self-injury may be considered abnormal. However, while the concept of grief is universal, the specific way in which grief is expressed can vary widely across cultures. A mother in Egypt who is immersed in deep grief for seven years over the death of a child may not be behaving pathologically if judged by the standards of her community (Wikan, 1980). In contrast, overt expressions of sorrow are severely proscribed among the Balinese. Thus, a bereaved Balinese who appears to laugh off a death is also behaving appropriately, based on the standards of his or her culture (Wikan, 1990). In yet another society, a person who is possessed by the spirits of the dead may be within the limits of what is quite appropriate and common in bereavement in his or her own society (Rosenblatt, 1997). Thus, issues of normal and abnormal reactions will make sense only when they are viewed within the sociocultural and environmental framework of the people being evaluated.

Widowhood

Like in the developed world, widows outnumber widowers in the developing world, and based on the greater disparity in the ages of husbands and wives, many women become widows at relatively early stages of adulthood. Aside from the normal problems of loss shared by widows generally, there are certain prevailing economic conditions and unique cultural practices in some countries that impact negatively on widows in the developing world. As we discussed in Chapter 8 that focused on social policies, pension and other income programs are not fully established in the developing world, particularly among the predominant informal labor sector. The husband tends to be the primary breadwinner in most families in the developing world. When he dies, not only is there a drastic reduction in income, but this is compounded by certain cultural requirements and succession laws that further increase the hardship of the widow. However, given the cross-cultural environment of developing societies (Eyetsemitan, 2002a), Christian influence is enabling women to refuse traditional widow inheritance (remarriage) by their dead husbands' kin (Cattell, 1992).

In India, when a husband dies, his wife is expected to stay with his family and devote herself to the husband's legacy. However, since a widow is generally considered unlucky, she is usually isolated and ignored by her husband's family (Basu, 1996). In fact, until recently, in some parts of India, widows were expected to throw themselves on their husband's funeral pyres because such an action was believed to remove the sins of both the wife and her husband (Pujari & Kaushik, 1994). A widow who died in this way was known as *sati*, meaning "virtuous woman," and women were raised to believe that committing sati was an act of highest merit. Widowhood also results in a loss of participation in social and religious activities. Hindu women are entitled to marry with full rights only once, and even though the Widow Remarriage Act was passed since 1956, the Hindu society still does not fully accommodate widow remarriages. In contrast, a widower can marry with full rites as many times as he chooses (Basu, 1996).

The position of widows in many parts of Africa is equally, and sometimes even more, unfavorable not only because of economic insecurity but also the social problems that often accompany widowhood (Apt, 1996). As indicated earlier, the husband is usually the main breadwinner in the home. Not only is family income substantially reduced following his death, whatever is left is not guaranteed to go to his immediate family. Many people still do not write wills specifying how their assets and resources should be disbursed. Even when a will exists, it is sometimes discarded in favor of traditional laws of inheritance that affirm collectivistic values (Hofstede, 1980). The deceased's possessions are allocated to his parents, uncles, or brothers. Consequently, a widow and her children are left at the mercy of the surviving members of the deceased's family.

The widow is further subjected to certain forms of physical and psychological abuse, including mandatory seclusion and shaving of her hair, and in some communities, the widow is physically beaten under the pretext that she is supposed to cry sufficiently over the husband's death. In a few cases, the widow is expected to perform the *Ajaani* ritual whereby the chief priest of the god of *Ani* is expected to have carnal knowledge of the widow under the pretext that he is purifying her. In certain places, the widow is sometimes forced to drink the water from which her husband's corpse was washed. This inhumane act of being forced to drink the contaminated water is supposed to serve as proof that she was innocent of causing the husband's death (Nwandu, 1998). Little attention is paid to the welfare of the children who are supposed to be their own relatives, but are left with the widow alone to raise, despite the fact that she was already stripped of most of the immediate family's resources. Some women's groups and other church organizations have begun to focus on ways of securing legal empowerment for widows, but this is something that must receive urgent support and intervention from government in terms of legislation and enforcement.

Disenfranchised Grief and Stifled Grief

How will these two concepts, developed mainly within the Western perspective, apply to the developing world? Disenfranchised grief refers to a process whereby some bereaved people are not allowed, or are unable, to express grief because such grief is not officially sanctioned. Because every society has norms about acceptable links between people, it is our view that the general provisions of disenfranchised grief are applicable to the developing world, although the specific parameters will vary. In other words, differences that exist in the form that disenfranchised grief takes will be less due to the development status of a country and more to what is generally acceptable within every society. For example, even within the developed countries of the West, a country such as France may have less of disenfranchised grief with regard to cohabitation or extramarital partners. During the funeral of former president François Mitterrand, his mistress and illegitimate daughter had a public participation in the state funeral rites that were performed, and actually stood beside Mitterrand's wife at the funeral (McFeatters, 1998). A similar acceptance or tolerance will also be witnessed among many segments of countries in Africa where multiple wives are still permissible under certain customary arrangements. However, within these societies, grief of homosexual partners will very likely be disenfranchised. More research needs to be conducted in order to uncover the culture-specific patterns of restrictions on the expression of grief.

With regard to stifled grief, which refers to any kind of recognized grief that is denied its full course, we believe that this process will be more evident among the developed nations, especially if this is within the concept of the workplace. Weiss (1988) identified two types of relationships and how they affect the outcome of grief. The first is what he termed relationships of attachment, such as that which exists between parent and child, that are thought to trigger severe grief with persisting distress. The second type, termed relationship of community, is the type that exists between friends, neighbors, coworkers, and is believed not to elicit such severe grief reactions. In the effort to support the bereaved through the grief process, employers may assign more weight to the so-called relationships of attachment than to relationships of community when it comes to determining the amount of time assigned for grieving.

Due mainly to our informal personal experiences with many people in the developing world, we think that much more time is assigned for grief in the developing world than it is in the developed societies. In India, for example, most of the groups and religions require twelve days of grief and mourning by close relatives such as children or spouses of the deceased (Laungani, 1997), and many employers often grant a bereaved employee sufficient time off work to enable him or her to fulfill this obligation. This is why the concept of stifled grief in cross-cultural contexts is needed to determine just how serious a problem it constitutes in developing societies.

Taking time away from social obligations—in the case of people in developing societies it appears longer—is not the only way by which grief is resolved in both the developed and developing worlds. One other way is to maintain bonds with the dead loved one. Usually in developed society it takes the form of fighting a cause such as raising funds for breast cancer victims if that was what killed the person, pursuing the values of the dead person, setting up memorials in honor of the dead individual, or donating that person's organs to those who need them or the dead person's body to science. However, in developing societies, maintaining bonds with the deceased is through roles that also confer religious powers to that individual who performs the role (Klass & Walter, 2001); usually elderly people perform this role because they are deemed to be closer to the dead. We attribute this to the extended family relationships that are more prevalent in the developing world as well as to collectivism (Hofstede, 1983; Triandis, 1994) and to the extensive belief in the spirit world in developing societies. Collectivism is a value system that emphasizes the collective good, and where the individual views himself or herself as part of the larger unit. The person is thus more likely to be protected and insulated by the in-group. This concept has been found to be widely applicable to a variety of processes, including the methods in which people in different societies might choose in resolving conflicts (Gire, 1997).

SUMMARY

With improvements in health care, more people are living longer and dying from chronic, long-term illnesses that require specialized care. As a result, more people, especially in the developed world, are dying in hospitals and other institutionalized settings, even though most people would rather die at home. Dying gradually means more people are aware of their impending death. There are some theories that propose a sequence of cognitive and behavioral stages we follow in the dying process, but these have not been adequately evaluated in different contexts, putting into question their generalizability.

Thoughts of death often lead to death anxiety, but this is moderated by religiosity, especially belief in life after death, as well as culture. There appear to be common expressions of grief following the loss of a loved one through death. However, expressions of grief vary significantly, therefore what is termed normal or abnormal is mediated by cultural practices. Widows consti-tute a special group of bereaved people; they tend to outnumber widowers, and tend to be worse off financially. Widows in the developing world also experience unique hardships arising from unfavorable cultural practices.

Bereavement is sometimes denied its full expression either because the re-lationship between the deceased and the bereaved is not socially sanctioned, disenfranchised grief, or because grief is denied its full course, stifled grief. These are, however, interesting concepts that are yet to be cross-culturally validated.

10

Conclusion and Implications for the Future

Our objectives for this book were threefold. The first aim was to discuss the aging process and adult development in the developing world using Western theories and concepts, and in the process highlight both the appropriateness and inappropriateness of these theories for the developing world. The second goal was to identify, through empirical primary data collection, some psychosocial developmental milestones that demarcate, for the developing world, the three major stages of development: the early, middle, and late adulthood stages. Our third major goal was to suggest new perspectives for understanding aging and adult development in the developing world. In this chapter, we will take stock and present in summary form the extent to which we have attempted to accomplish the objectives for this book. We will begin with the major theories and concepts that have been discussed.

MAJOR THEORIES AND CONCEPTS

Development versus Westernization

We have decided to comment about these general twin concepts because of the tendency for many people to use them interchangeably. We have defined a society as developed or developing based on the scores that society or country attains on the United Nation's Human Development Index (HDI). Factors that lead to high scores on the HDI include the extent to which citizens of a given country live a long and healthy life, are educated, and have a decent standard of living. Because countries from the West have predominantly higher scores on the HDI, some have regarded Westernization as *the* standard for development.

One of the value attributes that underlie most of the nations of the West is individualism. We have argued that because countries such as Japan have been able to attain development while maintaining a collectivist orientation, other societies too need not adopt individualistic values in order to become developed. This general framework has guided our evaluation of the other theories relating to aging and adult development. Just as development can be accomplished using different models, we believe that successful aging can be attained through careful adaptations to different sociocultural environments. Against this premise, we will now examine some of the theories and concepts that are specific to the process of aging and adult development.

BIOLOGICAL THEORIES OF AGING

Five biological theories that attempt to explain the aging process were discussed. The wear-and-tear theory suggests that we use our organs and other body systems to function and over time the body simply wears out due to extensive use. The autoimmune theory posits that our immune system becomes less efficient as we age, and may not only fail to function efficiently, but may actually attack the body itself. The cross-linkage theory proposes that the aging process results from declines in the amount of collagen in the body. Cellular theories of aging suggest that there are a limited number of times that cells in the body can divide. As the number of divisions decrease, aging increases. According to the rate of living theory, people are born with a limited amount of a substance that can be used at a certain rate. As this substance is increasingly used, aging also increases.

It is our position that these theories are appropriate for understanding aging in the developing world, although consideration should be given to the specific sociocultural and physical environments in which they are applied. For instance, the extent of wear and tear due to exposure to identical physical elements may be quite different for a person from the tropics than it may be for a person from the temperate regions. But even of greater significance may be the perceived or psychological impact of whatever the declines may be. Beall and Goldstein (1986) found that among Nepalese men (aged 50–88) vision and hearing impairments affected the frequency of their outing and social contacts, perhaps because of a lack of adaptive devices like glasses and hearing aids. In addition, they were also more likely to lose their esteemed role as head of household. However, Barker (1997) reported that similar impairments among the Niue, a Polynesian society, did not prevent elderly persons from providing words of wisdom and spiritual advice to the young. Thus, even though the basic underlying mechanisms through which physical aging occurs may be the same for all societies, the rate and nature of the triggering mechanism and the sociocultural impact of such changes may differ widely and should be taken into consideration.

PSYCHOLOGICAL THEORIES AND CONCEPTS

Personality Theories

Two main personality theories were considered in detail. The first is Erikson's theory of psychosocial development. This theory covers all the stages of the life span, and three of the eight stages are presumed to occur during adulthood. Early adulthood is a period of intimacy versus isolation, generativity versus stagnation is assumed to characterize the middle adulthood stage, while the late adulthood stage is marked by ego integrity versus despair. The theory essentially assumes a similar experience for all people. The second theory, the five-factor model, dubbed the Big Five, has viewed personality from the trait perspective, suggesting stability across the life span. These five basic traits are neuroticism, extraversion, openness, agreeableness, and conscientiousness.

Based on an extensive review of cross-cultural literature, Church and Lonner (1998) found no cross-cultural support for Erikson's personality stages, particularly the higher level ones. Therefore, it is uncertain whether or not the postulations of the theory may be appropriate for the developing world. The Big-Five model, in contrast, has been used extensively in cross-cultural contexts, and the basic traits have been replicated. However, even with the Big-Five model, there still exist some questions as to its suitability in the developing world. This is because the underlying notion in the Big-Five approach implies an independent view of personality. However, much of the developing world is collectivist, where construction of personality may be viewed as an interdependent entity, which is imbedded in, and not separate from, a context (Markus & Kitayama, 1998). Therefore, an interdependent view of personality that takes into account the manner in which the individual interfaces with social structures and interpersonal frameworks such as family and work groups may be required. Such a framework is yet to be fully conceptualized and empirically tested, but is sorely needed.

The Self

Even though the self is an aspect of personality, it is so prominent that it requires a focus by itself. The self encompasses a multilevel structure of cognitive, affective, and somatic representations that have implications for that person's experiences, activities, and well-being—in a nutshell, a person's view of himself or herself. Of all the theories and concepts discussed in this book, the one with perhaps the most questionable unmodified applicability to the developing world is the self-concept. As mentioned briefly in the discussion of personality theories above, Western nations tend to have an individualistic value orientation. This is where attention is focused on individual autonomy and interest. A simple but elegant method to view differences in this conceptualization comes from responses to a question such as "Who am I?" People from individualistic societies answer this question with reference to themselves, whereas those from collectivist societies define themselves in the context of the social groups to which they belong.

This is not to suggest that people in the developing world (largely collectivist) do not demonstrate a self that is separate from others. They do, especially when it comes to matters of self-preservation. Factors such as competition and jealousy can induce unfavorable wishes and intentions for even members of the in-group. The difference is in magnitude. Selfhood in developing societies is complex and can be expressed in many ways. These self-expressions are rooted in roles, statuses, as well as in-group memberships. In contrast, the self in Western societies is mainly a manifestation of traits enveloped in the individual. The implication of these differing conceptualizations for aging and adult development is that as people in the developing world age, they may become dependent on their children for support (Kagitcibasi, 1996b; Nsamanang, 1992) with minimal impact on their self-worth. In fact, they may still retain leadership roles in the community. A similar process will not only have negative consequences on the self-worth of the elderly in the developed world, but will likely lead to a loss in status. Thus, conceptions of self do not only differ between people from the developed and developing worlds, the implications these differences have in how people view the world and their experiences of aging are enormous.

Cognition

The focus on the discussion of cognition has been on intelligence. A distinction is often made between two types of intelligence: fluid intelligence and crystallized or pragmatic intelligence. The former refers to basic information processing mechanisms such as attention, memory, and reasoning and is presumed to decline across the life span. Crystallized or pragmatic intelligence, on the other hand, refers to general knowledge and acquired information and is generally believed to increase over time. Age-related cognitive losses in fluid intelligence may be relatively similar across cultures. However, cognitive gains in crystallized intelligence may be more subject to cultural influences.

The cultural meaning of intelligence is different in developing societies and may affect how cognitive declines and gains are measured. Dasen (1984), for instance, pointed to the relevance of culture in the conception of intelligence, and in a study among the Baoule of Ivory Coast, found a strong social component to intelligence, for example, obedience and respect. Even though aspects of intelligence such as memory and attention are important, they are useful only so long as they are of service to the social group. In like manner, Gill and Keats (1980) found that whereas Australian participants rated academic skills, writing, and reading very highly, their Malay counterparts placed more emphasis on social and practical skills. Thus, an examination of cognitive processes in the developing would necessarily have to incorporate these differences in the focus on crystallized intelligence.

SOCIAL THEORIES

These categories of theories are somewhat similar and include role, age-stratification, activity, disengagement, continuity, labeling, and aging as subculture theories. Role and age-stratification theories basically contend that the roles we are engaged in seem to be tied to different stages and thus will change as we move through different stages. The activity theory posits that the best way to age is to remain active, however, the value placed on being active could be tied to age norms for each stage. Disengagement theory suggests that the best way to age is to gradually relinquish roles and concentrate on the inner self. Continuity theory proposes that aging will be successful to the extent to which people experience continuity in their roles. One way to do this is to replace lost roles with similar ones. Labeling theory suggests that labels given to people in society will influence how they think about themselves and how people relate to them. Aging as a subculture contends that elderly persons interact more with themselves than with other members of society because they share common experiences, interests, etc.

With slight modifications, most of these theories are appropriate in explaining aging and adult development in the developing world. They help to explain such activities as marriage, parenthood, intergenerational relationships, work career, and retirement that typify various stages of adulthood. For example, although its onset may occur earlier in the developing world, marriage is typically associated with early adulthood stage in both the developed and the developing world. And in both groups of societies, roles and responsibilities assumed as a result of marriage include parenting and discipline.

Another example of similar underlying processes with appropriate modifications is intergenerational relationships. In both the developed world and the developing world, adult children often provide support for elderly parents and this support tends to be in the form of financial assistance and coresidency arrangements. However, whereas support for the elderly in the developed world is likely to be based on need, support for elderly parents in the developing world is more likely to be based on expectations. Thus, if modifications attend to the different nuances of each type of society, these social theories will be helpful in understanding the social aspects of aging in the developing world.

PERSON-ENVIRONMENT THEORIES

The Competence and Environmental Press Model

This theory suggests that a person's behavior is determined by his or her given level of competence operating in an environment of a particular press level. That is, if a person is operating in a challenging environment but has the resources to cope with these challenges, that person would function well. Remove the coping mechanisms and negative consequences would result. Because of the contingency nature of the theory, we deem it appropriate to the developing world. With specific reference to the elderly, this theory would suggest that declines that accompany aging need not reduce competence, to the extent that the individual is availed the necessary resources to address these declines. However, a person who is in the early to middle adulthood stages with little or no physical declines might still not operate at an optimum level of functioning so long as the environment is lacking in the basic facilities needed to attain competence.

The Congruence Model

This model proposes that we all have needs, but these needs vary among people. In the same manner, environments differ in terms of their ability to satisfy the needs of different people. When there is a congruence between a person's needs and the resources the environment has, the person is happy and contented. Incongruence results when the environment is not able to satisfy the needs of the person. This theory is also appropriate to the developing world because it takes into consideration the different needs that people have as well as the environments in which they function. This means that even if an elderly person in the developing world does not have sufficient income but exists in a setting where the social structure mandates that members of the family provide for this person, that person is very likely to be contented. The same person in similar financial standing but who lives in an environment that does not provide that support would experience stress and discomfort.

THEORIES OF DYING

Two main theories of dying were discussed: the stage theory of dying and the concept of the dying trajectory. Kübler-Ross (1969, 1981) suggested that a dying person goes through five stages: denial, anger and resentment, bargaining, depression, and acceptance. The problem with the theory is that many people do not go through these stages in the sequence suggested by the theory; some may actually shuttle back and forth across stages while others may remain at only one stage. Also, it has not been tested extensively across cultures, especially in the developing world. One of the variables that may be worth noting before its application in the developing world is the distinction between death-affirming and death-denying societies. In a society where people accept the notion of death and are ready for it, many of the cognitive processes in these stages may not apply.

The dying trajectory (Glaser & Strauss, 1968) deals with the pace of dying, the important aspects being duration and form. Also important is the element of uncertainty; if a person is not sure whether or not he or she may likely die, that person has a greater tendency to display signs of anxiety, even if the duration is long. Like the stage theory, this concept of dying has not been widely tested, even in the developed world (Copp, 1998). Societal differences in death affirmation or denial may also play a part. Furthermore, the postulations imply that the dying person knows reasonably ahead of time that he or she is dying. This may work in the developed world where improvements in health care systems afford people an opportunity of early diagnosis. In much of the developing world, especially in places where exposure to Westernized health care is limited, people may not have sufficient information about their impending death for the assumptions in the theory to apply. Appropriateness of this theory may need empirical validation in appropriate settings.

In the preceding section, we have attempted to evaluate the appropriateness of the major theories and perspectives discussed in the book in addressing aging and adult development processes in the developing world. The common theme that ties all the theories we deemed suitable for the developing world is the contingency provisions in each theory. This has reinforced a theme we have tried to emphasize throughout the book; it will be meaningless to discuss aging and adult development issues devoid of the sociocultural context within which they exist. In the next section, we summarize the major milestones and roles that appear to demarcate the various stages of adulthood.

EMPIRICAL STUDY ON BOUNDARIES AND CHARACTERISTICS OF ADULTHOOD STAGES

Using the Western model of early, middle, and late adulthood stages, the developing world shares certain common characteristics that are typical for each of the stages. The early adulthood stage is marked by marriage and children for females, but not for males. Starting a job is typical for males, but not for females. However, both males and females are expected to be physically strong. The middle adulthood stage is characterized by assuming increased responsibilities in the family and in the community. These responsibilities include taking care of the financial needs of parents, of siblings, and other relatives, serving as community leader and as spiritual leader, and providing advice in resolving family and community disputes. Leadership roles at ceremonies are expected and the perception of being wise is attributed to this stage.

Despite modernization influences, the late adulthood stage is also perceived as the period for leadership roles in the family and in the community. People are expected to retire from their jobs, and to be grandparents, a role more typical of the middle adulthood stage in developed societies. Interestingly, our survey of university students who are exposed to modernization influences yet acknowledge the leadership roles of the elderly, attests to how individuals choose to interact with their cross-cultural environment.

There is role continuity from the middle adulthood stage to the late adulthood. As Barker (1997) in her study of Polynesian societies noted, political and social influences are acquired by the middle age and maintained in later life by a competent person, even when significant physical and mental declines set in. Also in discussing role loss among the elderly in Africa, Eyetsemitan (1997) noted that the elderly still retain their roles, and the only difference is that there are now more individuals engaged in those roles that include deserving young people. According to the role continuity theory, in order to maintain an integrated personality in old age, roles that are similar to the ones dropped should be adopted. But being able to retain middle adulthood roles will help elderly people in the developing world in this respect because of the limited choices available to them compared to their counterparts in the developed world.

From our survey, people are reported to appear physically strong only during the early and middle adulthood stages. Although individuals are said to look old in late adulthood stage, we do not know the declines that occur, for example, with regards to height, vision, taste, sex, hearing, memory, and speed. Subsequent studies, taking the Functional approach, may explore the specific kinds of changes that are experienced and when in the late adulthood stage those changes take place. For example, it is possible that people could perceive declines in vision to start at the beginning of the late adulthood stage while hearing impairment could be presumed to begin toward the end of the late adulthood stage.

NEW PERSPECTIVE FOR UNDERSTANDING AGING AND ADULT DEVELOPMENT IN THE DEVELOPING WORLD

The prevailing theme in this book has been the need to consider specific environment-individual interactions that would enhance the understanding of aging and adult development processes, and in the process we have pointed to some new perspectives. While we have consistently made reference to the developed world and the developing world as though each group constituted a homogenous entity, there are many differences in the level of development among the countries comprising the developing world and several differences even within countries. However, we suggest that the countries of the developing world have a cross-cultural environment that consists of the Global, Developed, and Developing world dimensions. Thus in aging and adult development, the individual exercises interactions with any or a combination of those dimensions. Culture should be considered in discrete forms or as elements rather than as whole units (Triandis, 1990). Therefore, we suggest that the different environmental dimensions should be represented by elements. For example, the Global dimension by senescence, the Developed dimension by Western medicine, and the Developing dimension by native medicine or beliefs in the spirit world.

In interacting with the Developed dimension, the individual is exposed to Western acculturation experience. The existing models on Western acculturation are based on studies that include immigrants, refugees, and sojourners in Western societies. We find such models inadequate for explaining the experiences of the indigenous peoples living in the developing world. First, immigrants, refugees, and sojourners are likely to be more motivated or feel pressured to integrate the culture of their host societies. Second, when such models are used with the indigenous people in the developing world it was hard to know if the people shifted toward the Western acculturation experience (Mishra, Sinha & Berry, 1996). There are aspects of Western culture that enhance or facilitate human development but even so developing world people can choose to interact with them (education, language, and health care). As an alternative to understanding Western acculturation experiences of the indigenous peoples of the developing world, we have suggested a psychoeconomic model based on a *supply* and *demand* dynamic.

Because of the dominance of Western culture, aided by travels and different types of communication, the cross-cultural environment provides a more fitting framework for explaining the trajectories of the people living in the developing world, rather than the cultural environment. A dominant culture (Western), as we have demonstrated in this book from the review of Western concepts and perspectives, can influence both the understanding and conception of aging and adult development in non-dominant societies (non-Western). But the cross-cultural environment of the developing world is made up of other dimensions as well. As we have suggested, it is made up of the Global, the Developed (Western), and the Developing (non-Western) dimensions, and therefore it is important to emphasize that the individual can interact, based on *supply* and *demand*, with any of, or a combination of, these dimensions (Eyetsemitan, 2002b).

The *Global world dimension* represents the universal cultural standards that the United Nations identifies as indexes for human development. In addition to efforts toward universal cultural changes that impact on human development by the United Nations, biological experiences that are universally shared, such as senescence and death, also help to create a global experience. These biological experiences help to periodize the life span more or less uniformly across different cultures (Baltes, Staudinger, & Lindenberger,1999). For instance, across all societies the typical age to marry and to have children would biologically favor the early adulthood stage rather than the late adulthood stage while retirement timing or slowing down from work would typically occur in the late adulthood stage because of biological declines.

The other dimension is the *Developed world dimension*, made up of Westernization influences such as education, language, technology, medicine, and individualism (Cowgill & Holmes, 1972: modernization influences). Although Cowgill and Holmes (1972) suggest that elderly people in non-Western societies lose their high status and respect as a result of modernization influences, the same modernization influences, for example, biomedical technology, can also help to extend life expectancy in those societies as they have indeed done in the developed world.

The developing world dimension includes native medicine and spiritualism, indigenous languages, non-Western education, simple technology, and collectivism. It is erroneous to attempt to understand aging and adult development only from this dimension because of the likely influence of the other environmental dimensions mentioned earlier. The three dimensions of the cross-cultural environment, however, provide a range of possible interaction outcomes between the individual and his or her environment, based on a *supply and demand* dynamic. "Accommodation behavior" has been well documented among developing world people (Kagiticibasi, 1996a: "autonomous-relational self"; J. B. P. Sinha, 1980: "nurturant-task leader"; and Kwan, Bond, & Singelis, 1997: "relationship harmony"; see also Steen & Mazonde, 1999). But "accommodation behavior" is only one of such likely outcomes as there are others, like the following:

The Individual and the Developing dimension: An example would be a person who relies solely on a native healer for medical treatment.

The Individual and the Developed dimension: An example would be a person who relies exclusively on Western medicine for medical treatment.

The Individual and the Developing and Developed dimension: An example would be a person who combines both Western and native medical treatments—"accommodation behavior."

The Individual and the Developing and Global dimensions: An example would be a person who is literate only in his native language, for example, Urdu.

The Individual and the Developed and Global dimensions: An example would be a person who is literate only in a Western language, for example, English.

The Individual and the Developing, Developed, and Global dimensions: An example would be a person who is literate in both his or her native language and English.

The framework of the cross-cultural environment provides a new perspective for 1) classifying the environment of the people of the developing world; and 2) understanding the various patterns of aging and adult development that could occur in nondominant cultures like those of the developing world (Eyetsemitan, 2002a).

References

Abd el-Fattah, K. A. (1984). *The psychology of working women.* Beirut: Dar el-Nahada el-Arabia.

Ackerman, S., Zuroff, D. C., & Moskowitz, D. S. (2000). Generativity in midlife and young adults: Links to agency, communion, and subjective well-being. *International Journal of Aging and Human Development, 50,* 17–41.

Adair, J. G. (1992). The indigenous psychology bandwagon: Cautions and considerations. *Paper presented at the 14th Asian Regional IACCP Conference,* Kathmandu, Nepal.

Adi, R. (1982). *The aged in the homes for the aged in Jakarta: Status and perceptions.* Pusat Penelitian, Universitats Katolik Indonesia Atma Jaya, Jakarta, Indonesia.

Agarwal, R., & Mistra, G. (1986). A factor analytical study of achievement goals and means: An Indian view. *International Journal of Psychology, 21,* 717–731.

Agency for Health Care Policy and Research (AHCPR) (1993). *Management of cataract in adults: Clinical practice guidelines.* AHCPR Publication # 93-0543. Rockville, MD: Author.

Agronick, G. S., & Duncan, L. E. (1998). Personality and social change: Individual differences, life path, and importance attributed to the women's movement. *Journal of Personality and Social Psychology, 74,* 1545–1555.

Albert, S. M., & Cattell, M. G. (1994). *Old age in global perspective.* New York: G. K. Hall.

Aldwin, C. M. (1994). *Stress, coping and development: An integrative perspective.* New York: Guilford.

Alvarado, K. A., Templer, D. I., Bresler, C., & Thomas-Dobson, S. (1995). The relationship of religious variables to death depression and death anxiety. *Journal of Clinical Psychology, 51,* 202–204.

Anthony, J. C., & Aboraya, A. (1992). The epidemiology of selected mental disorders in later life. In J. E. Birren, R. B. Sloane, & G. D. Cohen (Eds.), *Handbook of mental health and aging* (2nd ed., pp. 27–72). San Diego: Academic Press.

Apt, N. A. (1988). Aging in Africa. In E. Gort (Ed.), *Aging in cross-cultural perspective* (pp. 17–32). New York: The Phelps-Stokes Fund.

———. (1992). Family support to the elderly in Ghana. In H. L. Kendig, A. Hashimoto, & L. C. Coppard (Eds.), *Family support for the elderly* (pp. 201–212). New York: Oxford University Press.

————. (1996). *Coping with old age in a changing Africa: Social change and the elderly Ghanaian*. Aldershot, UK: Avebury.

Aycan, Z. (2000). Cross-cultural industrial and organizational psychology: Contributions, past developments, and future directions. *Journal of Cross-Cultural Psychology, 31,* 110–128.

Azer, A. (1988). Dilemmas of formal and informal social security in a developing country: The case of Egypt. In F. von Benda-Beckmann, K. von Benda-Beckmann, E. Casino, F. Hirtz, G. R. Woodman, & H. F. Zacher (Eds.), *Between kinship and the state: Social security and law in developing countries* (pp. 419–436).Providence, RI: Foris Publications.

Azuma, H. (1984). Psychology in a non-Western country. *International Journal of Psychology, 19,* 45–56.

Baihua, J. (1987). An urban old people's home. *China Reconstructs, 36,* 32–33.

Baltes, P. B. (1993). The aging mind: Potentials and limits. *The Gerontologist, 33,* 580–594.

————. (1997). On the incomplete architecture of human ontogeny: Selection, optimization, and compensation as foundation of developmental theory. *American Psychologist, 52,* 366–380.

Baltes, P. B., & Baltes, M. M. (1990). Psychological perspectives on successful aging: The model of selective optimization with compensation. In P. B. Baltes, & M. M. Baltes (Eds.), *Successful aging: Perspectives from the behavioral sciences* (pp. 1–34). Cambridge, England: Cambridge University Press.

Baltes, M. M., & Carstensen, L. L. (1999). Social-psychological theories and their applications to aging: From individual to collective. In V. L. Bengtson, & K. W. Schaie (Eds.), *Handbook of theories of aging* (pp. 209–226). New York: Springer.

Baltes, P. B., Reese, H. W., & Lipsitt, L. P. (1980). Lifespan developmental psychology. *Annual Review of Psychology, 31,* 65–110.

Baltes, P. B., & Smith, J. (1997). A systemic holistic view of psychological functioning in very old age: Introduction to a collection of articles from the Berlin Aging study. *Psychological Aging, 12,* 395–409.

Baltes, P. B., Staudinger, U. M., Maercker, A., & Smith, J. (1995). People nominated as wise: A comparative study of wisdom-related knowledge. *Psychology and Aging, 10,* 155–166.

Baltes, P. B., Staudinger, U. M., & Lindenberger, U. (1999). Lifespan psychology: Theory and application to intellectual functioning. *Annual Review of Psychology, 50,* 471–507.

Banaji, M., & Prentice, D. (1994). The self in social contexts. *Annual Review of Psychology, 45,* 297–332.

Bandura, A. (1982). *Social foundations of thought and action: A social cognitive theory.* Englewood Cliffs, NJ: Prentice-Hall.

Barber, C. E. (1997). Olfactory acuity as a function of age and gender: A comparison of African and American samples. *International Journal of Aging and Human Development, 44,* 317–334.

Barker, J. C. (1997). Between humans and ghosts: The decrepit elderly in a Polynesian society. In J. Sokolovsky (Ed.), *The cultural context of aging* (2nd ed., pp. 407–424). Westport, CT: Bergin & Garvey.

Barry, H., Child, I., & Bacon, M. (1959). Relations of child training to subsistence economy. *American Anthropologist, 61,* 51–63.

Basu, S. (1996). Pioneering Hindu women: Overcoming barriers and claiming their places in today's society. In K. D. Arnold, K. D. Noble, & R. F. Subotnik (Eds.), *Remarkable women: Perspectives on female talent development* (pp. 81–92). Cresskill, NJ: Hampton Press, Inc.

Baugher, E., & Lamison-White, L. (1996). Poverty in the United States: 1995. *U. S. Bureau of the Census, Current Population Reports, Consumer Income,* (pp. 60–194). Washington, DC: U. S. Government Printing Office.

Baumrind, D. (1972). An exploratory study of socialization effects on Black children: Some Black–White comparisons. *Child Development, 43,* 261–267.

———. (1983). Rejoinder to Lewis's reinterpretation of parental firm controls effects: Are authoritative families really harmonious? *Psychological Bulletin, 94,* 132–142.

Bauserman, R. (1997). International representation in the psychological literature. *International Journal of Psychology, 32,* 107–112.

Beall, C., & Goldstein, M. C. (1986). Age differences in sensory and cognitive functioning in elderly Nepalese. *Journal of Gerontology, 41,* 387–389.

Beall, C. M. (1983). Ages at menopause and menarche in a high altitude Himalayan population. *Annals of Human Biology, 10,* 365–370.

Beall, C. M., & Weitz, C. A. (1989). The human population biology of aging. In M. A. Little, & J. D. Hass (Eds.), *Human population biology: A transdisciplinary science* (pp.189–200). Oxford: Oxford University Press.

Becker, E. (1973). *The denial of death.* New York: Free Press.

Belsky, J., Lang, M. E., & Rovine, M. (1985). Stability and change in marriage across the transition to parenthood: A second study. *Journal of Marriage and the Family, 47,* 855–865.

Bengtson, V. L. (1969). Cultural and occupational differences in level of present role activity in retirement. In R. J. Havighurst, J. M. A. Munnichs, B. L. Neugarten, & H. Thomae (Eds.), *Adjustment to retirement: A cross-national study* (pp. 35–53). Assen, Netherlands: Van Gorkum.

Berg, R. L., & Cassels, J. S. (1992). *The second fifty years: Promoting health and preventing disability.* Washington, DC: Institute of Medicine, National Academy Press.

Berry, J. W. (1976). *The human ecology and cognitive style.* Beverly Hills, CA: Sage.

———. (1979). A cultural ecology of social behavior. In L. Berkowitz (Ed.), *Advances in experimental social psychology* (Vol. 12, pp. 177–207). New York: Academic Press.

Berry, J. W., Poortinga, Y. H., Segall, M. H., & Dasen, P. R. (1992). *Cross-cultural psychology: Research and applications.* Cambridge, UK: Cambridge University Press.

Berry, J. W., & Sam, D. (1997). Acculturation and adaptation. In J. W., Berry, M. H. Segall, & C. Kagitcibasi (Eds.), *Handbook of cross-cultural psychology. Vol. 3. Social behavior and applications* (2nd ed., pp. 291–326). Boston: Allyn & Bacon.

Best, D. L., & Williams, J. E. (1996). Anticipation of aging: A cross-cultural examination of young adults' views of growing old. In J. Pandey, D. Sinha, & D. P. S. Bhawuk (Eds.), *Asian contributions to cross-cultural psychology* (pp. 274–288). New Delhi, India: Sage.

Bhatt, G. S. (1991). *Women and polyandry in Rawain-Jaunpur.* Jaipur: Rawat.

Biegel, D. E., Sales, E., & Schulz, R. (1991). *Family caregiving in chronic illness: Alzheimer's disease, cancer, heart disease, mental illness, and stroke.* Newbury Park, CA: Sage.

Binstock, R. H. (1994). Changing criteria in old age programs: The introduction of economic status and need for services. *Gerontologist, 34,* 726–730.

Bjorksten, J. (1974). Crosslinkage and the aging process. In M. Rockstein, M. L. Sussman, & J. Chesky (Eds.), *Theoretical aspects of aging.* New York: Academic Press.

Blanchard-Fields, F. (1998). The role of emotion in social cognition across the adult life span. In K. W. Schaie, & M. P., Lawton (Eds.), *Annual Review of Gerontology and Geriatrics. Vol. 17: Focus on emotion and adult development* (pp. 238–265). New York: Springer.

Bloom, B. S. (1964). *Stability and change in human characteristics.* New York: Wiley.

Blumberg, J. B. (1996). Status and functional impact of nutrition in older adults. In E. L. Schneider and J. W. Rowe (Eds.), *Handbook of the biology of aging* (4th ed.; pp. 393–414). New York: Van Nostrand.

Bortz, W. M. IV, & Bortz, W. M. II. (1996). How fast do we age? Exercise performance as a biomarker. *Journal of Gerontology Medical Science, 51A,* M223–M225.

Brandon, C. (1996). Confronting the growing problem of pollution in Asia. *Journal of Social, Political & economic Studies, (Summer),* 199–204.

Brandtstadter, J. (1998). Action perspectives on human development. In R. M. Lerner (Ed.), *Handbook of child psychology: Vol 1.Theoretical models of human development* (5th ed., pp. 807–866). New York: Wiley.

Brandtstadter, J., & Greve, W. (1994). The aging self: Stabilizing and protective processes. *Developmental Review, 14,* 1–29.

Brody, J. E. (1992, August 4). How the taste bud translates between tongue and brain. *The New York Times,* pp. C1, C8.

Bronfrenbrenner, U. (1979). *The ecology of human development: Experiments by nature and design.* Cambridge, MA: Harvard University Press.

————. (1993). The ecology of cognitive development: Research models and fugitive findings. In R. H. Wozniak & K. W. Fischer (Eds.), *Development in context: Acting and thinking in specific environments* (pp. 3–44). Hillsdale, NJ: Lawrence Erlbaum.

Brown, R. (1984). Medicare and Medicaid: The process, value and limits of health care reform. In M. Minkler & C. Estes (Eds.), *Readings in the political economy of aging* (pp. 117–143). New York: Baywood.

Buckman, R. (1993). Communication in palliative care: A practical guide. In D. Doyle, G. W. C. Hanks, & N. MacDonald (Eds.), *Oxford textbook of palliative medicine* Oxford: Oxford Medical Publications.

Busse, E. W. (1969). Theories of aging. In E. W. Busse & E. Pfeiffer (Eds.), *Behavior and adaptation in later life* (pp. 17–32). Boston: Little, Brown.

Campbell, E. (1991). Sex preferences for offspring among men in the western area of Sierra Leone. *Journal of Biosocial Science, 23,* 337–342.

Canadian Society of Health and Aging Workshop Group (1994). Canadian study of health and aging: Study methods and prevalence of dementia. *Canadian Medical Association Journal, 150,* 899–913.

Cantor, M. (1991). Family and community: Changing roles in an aging society. *The Gerontologist, 31,* 337–346.

Carstensen, L. L. (1992). Social and emotional patterns in adulthood: Support for so-cioemotional selectivity theory. *Psychology and Aging, 7*, 331–338.

Cartwright, L. K., & Wink, P. (1994). Personaliy change in women physicians from medical student years to mid-40s. *Psychology of Women Quarterly, 18*, 291–305.

Cassidy, C. M. (1991). The good body: When big is better. *Medical Anthropology, 13*, 181–213.

Cattell, M. G. (1992). Praise the Lord and say no to men: Older women empowering themselves in Samia, Kenya. *Journal of Cross-Cultural Gerontology, 7*, 307–330.

———. (1997). The discourse of neglect: Family support for the elderly in Samia. In T. S. Weisner, C. Bradley, & P. L. Kilbride (Eds.), *African families and the crisis of social change* (pp. 157–183). Wesport, CT: Bergin & Garvey.

Chan, J. (1996). Chinese intelligence. In M. H. Bond (Ed.), *The handbook of Chinese psychology* (pp. 93–108). New York: Oxford University Press.

Chandra, V., Dekosky, S. T., Pendav, R., Belle, S. H., Ratchiff, G., & Ganguli, M. (1998). Neurologic factors associated with cognitive impairment in a rural elderly popu-lation in India: The Indo–US cross-national dementia epidemiology study. *Jour-nal of Geriatric Psychiatry & Neurology, 11*, 11–17.

Chao, R. K. (1994). Beyond parental control and authoritarian parenting style: Under-standing Chinese parenting through the cultural notion of training. *Child De-velopment, 65*, 1111–1119.

Checkoway, B. (1994). Empowering the elderly: Gerontological health promotion in Latin America. *Ageing & Society, 14*, 75–95.

Chen, G. (1995). Differences in self-disclosure patterns among Americans versus Chi-nese: A comparative study. *Journal of Cross-Cultural Psychology, 26*, 84–91.

Chiriboga, D. A. (1989). Mental health at the midpoint: Crisis, challenge, or relief? In S. Hunter, & M. Sundel (Eds.), *Midlife myths: Issues, findings, and practice applications* (pp. 116–144). Newbury Park, CA: Sage.

Choi, N. G. (1991). Racial differences in the determinants of living arrangements of widowed and divorced elderly women. *The Gerontologist, 31*, 496–504.

Choi, S.-J. (1992). Ageing and social welfare in South Korea. In D. R. Phillips (Eds.), *Ageing in east and south-east Asia* (pp. 148–166). London: Edward Arnold.

Chuanyi, Z. (1989). Mutual assistance funds expand in China. *Ageing International, 16*, 21–22.

Church, A. T., & Lonner, W. J. (1998). The cross-cultural perspective in the study of personality: Rationale and current research. *Journal of Cross-Cultural Psychol-ogy, 29*, 32–62.

Cicirelli, V. G. (1983). Adult children and their elderly parents. In T. H. Brubaker (Ed.), *Family relationships in later life* (pp. 31–46). Beverly Hills, CA: Sage.

Cohen, L. (1994). Old age: Cultural and critical perspectives. *Annual Review in An-thropology, 23*, 137–158.

Cohen, S. (1991). Social support and physical health: Symptoms, health behaviors, and infectious disease. In E. M. Cummings, A. L. Greene, & K. H. Karraker (Eds.), *Life-span developmental psychology: Perspectives on stress and coping* (pp. 213–234). Hillsdale, NJ: Erlbaum.

Congressional Budget Office. (1997). *Long-term budgetary pressures and policy op-tions.* Washington, DC: Government Printing Office.

Conwell, Y. (1995). Suicide among elderly people. *Psychiatric Services, 46,* 563–564.

Cook, P. (1994). Chronic illness beliefs and the role of social networks among Chinese, Indian, and Angloceltic Canadians. *Journal of Cross-Cultural Psychology, 25,* 452–465.

Copp, G. (1998). A review of current theories of death and dying: Integrative literature reviews and meta-analyses. *Journal of Advanced Nursing, 28,* 382–390.

Costa, P. T., Jr., & McCrae, R. R. (1980). Still stable after all these years: Personality as a key to some issues in adulthood and old age. In P. B. Baltes, & O. G. Brim, Jr. (Eds.), *Life-span development and behavior* (Vol. 3, pp. 65–102). New York: Academic Press.

Costa, P. T., Jr., & McCrae, R. R. (1984). Personality as a life-long determinant of well-being. In C. Z. Malatesta, & C. E. Izard (Eds.), *Emotion in adult development* (pp. 141–158). Beverly Hills, CA: Sage.

Costa, P. T., Jr., & McCrae, R. R. (1988). Personality in adulthood: A six-year longitudinal study of self-reports and spouse ratings on the NEO Personality inventory. *Journal of Personality and Social Psychology, 54,* 853–863.

Costa, P. T., Jr., & McCrae, R. R. (1994). Set like plaster? Evidence for the stability of adult personality. In T. F. Heatherton & J. L. Weinberger (Eds.), *Can personality change?* (pp. 21–40). Washington, DC: American Psychological Association.

Counts, D. A., & Counts, D. R. (1985). I'm not dead yet! Aging and death: Processes and experiences in Kalia. In D. A. Counts & D. R. Counts (Eds.), *Aging and its transformations* (pp. 131–156). Lanham, MD: University of America Press.

Cowgill, D. O., & Holmes, L. (1972). *Aging and modernization.* New York: Appleton-Century-Crofts.

Craik, F. I. M., & Jennings, J. M. (1992). Human memory. In F. I. M. Craik, & T. A. Salthouse (Eds.), *The handbook of aging and cognition* (pp. 51–110). Hillsdale, NJ: Lawrence Erlbaum.

Crews, D. E. (1990). Anthropological issues in biological gerontology. In R. Rubinstein (Ed.), *Anthropology and aging: Comprehensive reviews* (pp. 11–38). Dordrecht: Kluwer.

Cumming, E., & Henry, W. E. (1961). *Growing older: The process of disengagement.* New York: Basic Books.

Dannefer, D., & Uhlenberg, P. (1999). Paths of the life course: A typology. In V. L. Bengtson, & K. W. Warner (Eds.), *Handbook of theories of aging* (pp. 306–326). New York: Springer.

Darling, J., & Lawrence, J. A. (1994). Australian women writers' experience of early career dreams and mentoring. *Paper presented at Eight National Human Development conference,* Melbourne, July.

Dasen, P. (1984). The cross-cultural study of intelligence: Piaget and the Baoule. *International Journal of Psychology, 19,* 407–434.

Davis, C. T. M. (1979). Thermoregulation during exercise in relation to sex and age. *Journal of Applied Physiology, 42,* 71–79.

Davis, K. (1986). Paying the health care bills of an aging population. In A. Pifer & L. Bronte (Eds.), *Our aging society* (pp. 299–318). New York: Norton.

Dekovic, M., & Janssens, J. M. (1992). Parents' child-rearing style and child's sociometric status. *Developmental Psychology, 28,* 925–932.

Denga, D. I. (1982). Childlessness and marital adjustment in northern Nigeria. *Journal of Marriage and the Family, 44,* 799–802.

———. (1983). The effect of mobile group counseling on nomadic Fulanis' attitudes toward formal education. *Journal of Negro Education, 52,* 170–175.

Devereux, G. (1963). Two types of modal personality models. In B. Kaplan (Ed.), *Personality viewed cross-culturally* (pp. 227–241). New York: Norton.

de Vos, S. (1990). Extended family living among the older people in six Latin American countries. *Journal of Gerontology, 45,* S8–S94.

Diamond, J. (1997). *Male menopause.* Naperville, IL: Sourcebooks.

Diaz-Guerrero, R. (1993). Mexican ethno-psychology. In U. Kim, & J. W. Berry (Eds.), *Indigenous psychologies: Research and experience in cultural context* (pp. 44–55). Newbury Park, CA: Sage

Diel, M., Coyle, N., & Labouvie-Vief, G. (1996). Age and sex differences in strategies of coping and defense across the life span. *Psychology and aging, 11,* 127–139.

Dixon, R. A., & Backman, L (Eds.). (1995). *Compensating for psychological deficits and declines: Managing losses and promoting gains.* Mahwah, NJ: Lawrence Erlbaum.

Dixon, R. A., & Lerner, R. M. (1988). A history of systems in developmental psychology. In M. H. Bornstein, & M. E. Lamb (Eds.), *Developmental Psychology: An advanced textbook* (2nd ed., pp. 3–50). Hillsdale, NJ: Lawrence Erlbaum.

Doka, K. (1987). Silent sorrow: Grief and the loss of significant others. *Death Studies, 10,* 441–449.

———. (1989). Disenfranchised grief. In K. J. Doka (Ed.), *Disenfranchised grief: Recognizing hidden sorrow* (pp. 3–11). Lexington, MA: Lexington Books.

Domingo, L. J. (1995). The elderly and the family in selected Asian countries. *Bold, 5,* 29–39.

Domingo, L. J. & Asis, M. M. B. (1995). Living arrangements and the flow of support between generations in the Philippines. *Journal of Cross-Cultural Gerontology, 10,* 21–51.

Dowd, J. (1987). The reification of age: Age stratification theory and the passing of the autonomous subject. *Journal of Aging Studies, 1,* 317–335.

Draguns, J. (1997). Abnormal behavior patterns across cultures: Implications for counseling and psychotherapy. *International Journal of Intercultural Relations, 21,* 213–248.

Draper, P., & Harpending, H. (1994). Cultural considerations in the experience of aging: Two African cultures. In B. R. Bonder, & M. B. Wagner (Eds.), *Functional performance in older adults* (pp. 15–27). Philadelphia: F. A. Davis.

Dreher, G. F., & Bretz, R. D. (1991). Cognitive ability and career attainment: Moderating effects of early career success. *Journal of Applied Psychology, 76,* 392–397.

Duane, R., & Grusec, J. E. (2001). Correlates of authoritarian parenting in individualist and collectivist cultures and implications for understanding the transmission of values. *Journal of Cross-Cultural Psychology, 32,* 202–212.

Ducharme, F., & Corin, E. (1997). Widowed men and women—An exploratory study of the significance of widowhood and coping strategies. *Canadian Journal on Aging, 16,* 112–141.

Duff, R. W., & Hong, L. K. (1995). Age density, religiosity and death anxiety in retirement communities. *Review of Religious Research, 37,* 19–32.

Edman, J. L. & Kameoka, V. A. (1997). Cultural differences in illness schemas: An analysis of Filipino and American illness attributions. *Journal of Cross-Cultural Psychology, 28,* 252–265.

Encyclopedia Britannica Online (1994–1999). *Bahrain* (http://search.eb.com/bol/topic?artcl = 11789&seq_nbr = 1&page = n&isctn = 2). Author.

Enriquez, V. G. (Ed.). (1990). *Indigenous psychologies.* Quezon City: Psychology Research & Training House.

Ekman, P., & Friesen, W. V. (1986). A new pan-cultural facial expression of emotion. *Motivation and Emotion, 10,* 159–168.

Ekman, P., Friesen, W. V., O'Sullivan, M., Chan, A., Diacoyanni-Tarlatzis, I., Heider, K., Krause, R., LeCompte, W. A., Pitcairn, T., Ricci-Bitti, P. E., Scherer, K. R., Tomita, M., & Tzavaras, A. (1987). Universals and cultural differences in the judgments of facial expressions of emotion. *Journal of Personality and Social Psychology, 53,* 712–717.

Ekman, P., & Heider, K. G. (1988). The universality of a contempt expression: A replication. *Motivation and Emotion, 12,* 303–308.

Erikson, E. H. (1950). *Childhood and society.* New York: Norton.

———. (1959). *Identity and the life cycle.* New York: Norton (Reissued 1980).

———. (1982). *The life cycle completed.* New York: Norton.

Erikson, E. H., Erikson, J. M., & Kivnick, H. Q. (1986). *Vital involvement in old age.* New York: Norton.

Esping-Anderson, G. (1990). *The three worlds of welfare capitalism.* Cambridge, U. K.: Polity Press.

Evans, D. A., Funkenstein, H., Albert, M. S., Scherr, P. A., Cook, N. R., Chown, M. J., Herbert, L. E., Hennekens, C. H., & Taylor, J. O. (1989). Prevalence of Alzheimer's disease in a community population of older persons. *Journal of the American Medical Association, 262,* 2551–2556.

Evers, S. E., Orchard, J. W., & Haddad, R. G. (1985). Bone density in postmenopausal North American Indian and Caucasion females. *Human Biology, 57,* 719–726.

Eyetsemitan, F. (1991). The Black experience and wisdom: Any link? *Minority Voices, 7,* 27–32.

———. (1997). Age, respect, and modernization in Africa: Toward a psycho-sociological understanding. *Western Journal of Black Studies, 21,* 142–145.

———. (1998). Stifled grief in the workplace. *Death Studies, 22,* 469–479.

———. (2000). Care of elderly persons in the family: An approach based on a developmental model. *Psychological Reports, 86,* 281–286.

———. (2002a). Suggestions regarding cross-cultural environment as context for human development and aging in non-Western cultures. *Psychological Reports, 90,* 823–833.

———. (2002b). Perceived elderly traits and young people's perception of helping tendencies in the U. S., Ireland, Nigeria & Brazil. *Journal of Cross-Cultural Gerontology, 17,* 57–69.

Eyetsemitan, F. & Eggelston, T. (2002). The faces of deceased persons as emotion-expressive behaviors: Implications for mourning trajectories. *Omega: Journal of Death & Dying, 44,* 151–167.

Eysenck, H. J., & Eysenck, S. B. G. (1975). *Manual of the Eysenck Personality Questionnaire.* San Diego, CA: Edits.

Fant, R. V., Pickworth, W. B., & Henningfield, J. E. (1999). Health effects of tobacco. In R. T. Ammerman, P. J. Ott, & R. E. Tarter (Eds.), *Prevention and societal impact of drug and alcohol abuse* (pp. 93–106). Mahwah, NJ: Lawrence Erlbaum.

Feld, S., & George, L. K. (1994). Moderating effects of prior social resources on the hospitalizations of elders who become widowed. *Aging and Health, 6,* 275–295.

Field, M. J. (1960). *Search for security: An ethno-psychiatric study of rural Ghana.* London: Faber and Faber.

Finch, C. E. (1996). Biological bases for plasticity during aging of individual life histories. In D. Magnusson (Ed.), *The life-span development of individuals: Behavioral, neurobiological and psychosocial perspective* (pp. 488–511). Cambridge, UK: Cambridge University Press.

Fischer, K. W., & Ayoub, C. (1994). Affective splitting and dissociation in normal and maltreated children: Developmental pathways for self in relationships. In D. Cicchetti & S. L. Toth (Eds.), *Rochester symposium on developmental psychopathology: Vol. 5. Disorders and dysfunctions of the self* (pp. 147–222). Rochester, NY: Rochester University Press.

Fleeson, W., & Heckhausen, J. (1997). More or less "me" in past, present, and future: Perceived lifetime personality during adulthood. *Psychology and Aging, 12,* 125–136.

Flynn, J. R. (1987). Massive IQ gains in 14 nations. What IQ tests really measure. *Psychological Bulletin, 101,* 171–191.

———. (1994). IQ gains over time. In R. J. Sternberg (Ed.), *Encyclopedia of human intelligence* (Vol. 1., pp. 617–623). New York: Macmillan.

Fortes, M. (1984). Age, generation and social structure. In D. I. Kertzer, & J. Keith (Eds.), *Age and anthropological theory* (pp. 99–122). San Diego, CA: Academic Press.

Freeman, M. A. (1997). Demographic correlates of individualism and collectivism: A study of social values in Sri Lanka. *Journal of Cross-Cultural Psychology, 28,* 321–341.

Friedman, A. (1987). Getting powerful with age: Changes in women over the life cycle. *Israel Social Science Research, 5,* 76–86.

Fry, C. L. (1999). Anthropological theories of age and aging. In V. L. Bengtson, & K. W. Schaie (Eds.), *Handbook of theories of aging* (pp. 271–286). New York: Springer.

Fuchs, M. (1983). Health insurance systems in Africa. In P. Oberender, H. J. Diesfeld, & W. Gitter (Eds.), *Health and development in Africa* (p. 345). Frankfurt.

———. (1988). Social security in Third World countries. In In F. von Benda-Beckmann, K. von Benda-Beckmann, E. Casino, F. Hirtz, G. R. Woodman, & H. F. Zacher (Eds.), *Between kinship and the state: Social security and law in developing countries* (pp. 39–51). Providence, RI: Foris Publications.

Fulcher, D. (1982). *The organization and administration of medical care under social security.* The ILO/Norway African Regional Training Course, Geneva.

Gabrielidis, C., Stephan, W. G., Ybarra, O., Pearson, V. M., & Villareal, L. (1997). Preferred styles of conflict resolution: Mexico and the United States. *Journal of Cross-Cultural Psychology, 28,* 661–677.

Galt, C. P., & Hayslip, B., Jr. (1998). Age differences in levels of overt and covert death anxiety. *Omega: Journal of Death and Dying, 37,* 187–202.

Gardiner, H. W., & Gardiner, O. S. (1991). Women in Thailand. In L. L. Adler (Ed.), *Women in cross-cultural perspective* (pp. 174–187). New York: Praeger.

Gardiner, H. W., Mutter, J. D., & Kosmitzki, C. (1998). *Lives across cultures: Cross-cultural human development.* Boston, MA: Allyn & Bacon.

Gatz, M., Kasl-Godley, J. E., & Karel, M. J. (1996). Aging and mental disorders. In J. E. Birren, & K. W. Schaie (Eds.), *Handbook of the psychology of aging* (pp. 365–381). San Diego, CA: Academic Press.

Geary, D. C., Salthouse, T. A., Chen, G.-P., & Fan, L. (1996). Are east Asian versus American differences in arithmetical ability a recent phenomenon? *Developmental Psychology, 32*, 254–262.

Gilchrest, B. A. (1982). Skin. In J. W. Rowe and Besdine, R. W. (Eds.), *Health and disease in old age* (pp. 381–392). Boston: Little, Brown.

Gill, R., & Keats, D. M. (1980). Elements of intellectual competence: Judgments by Australian and Malay university students *Journal of Cross-Cultural Psychology, 11*, 233–243.

Gire, J. T. (1997). The varying effect of individualism-collectivism on preference for methods of conflict resolution. *Canadian Journal of Behavioural Science, 29*, 38–43.

Glaser, B., & Strauss, A. (1968). *Time for dying.* Chicago: Aldine.

Gochman, D. S. (1997). Health behavior research: Definitions and diversity. In D. S. Gochman (Eds.), *Handbook of health behavior research 1: Personal and social determinants* (pp. 3–20). New York: Plenum Press

Goodnow, J. J., Cashmore, J., Cotton, S., & Knight, R. (1984). Mothers' developmental time-tables in two cultural groups. *International Journal of Psychology, 19*, 193–205.

Gordon-Salant, S. (1996). Hearing. In J. E. Birren (Ed.), *Encyclopedia of gerontology* (Vol. 1, pp. 643–653). San Diego: Academic Press.

Gould, R. (1978). *Transformations: Growth and change in adult life* . New York: Simon & Schuster.

———. (1980). Transformation during early and middle adult years. In N. J. Smelser, & E. H. Erikson (Eds.), *Themes of work and love in adulthood* (pp. 213–237). Cambridge, MA: Harvard University Press.

Graves, T. (1967). Psychological acculturation in a tri-ethnic community. *South-Western Journal of Anthropology, 23*, 337–350.

Greenfield, P. M. (1994). Independence and interdependence as developmental scripts: Implications for theory, research, and practice. In P. M. Greenfield, & R. R. Cocking (Eds.), *Cross-cultural roots of minority child development* (pp. 1–37). Hillsdale, NJ: Lawrence Erlbaum.

———. (1997a). Culture as process: Empirical methods for cultural psychology. In J. W. Berry, Y. H. Poortinga, & J. Pandey (Eds.), *Handbook of cross-cultural psychology: Vol. 1. Theory and method* (2nd ed., pp. 301–346). Boston, MA: Allyn & Bacon.

———. (1997b). You can't take it with you: Why ability assessments don't cross cultures. *American Sociologist, 52*, 1115–1124.

Greenfield, P. M., Suzuki, L. (1998). Culture and human development: Implications for parenting, education, pediatrics, and mental health. In E. Sigel & K. A. Renninger (Eds.), *Handbook of child psychology: Vol. 4. Child psychology in practice* (5th ed., pp. 1059–1109). New York: Wiley.

Grolnick, W. S., & Ryan, R. M. (1989). Parent styles associated with children's self-regulation and competence in school. *Journal of Educational Psychology, 81*, 143–154.

Gross, J. J. (1998). The emerging field of emotion regulation: An integrative view. *Review of General Psychology, 2,* 271–299.

Gudykunst, W. B., Ting-Toomey, S., & Chua, E. (1988). *Culture and interpersonal communication.* Newbury Park, CA: Sage.

Guralnik, J. M., Land, K. C., Blazer, D., Fillenbaum, G. G., & Branch, L. G. (1993). Educational status and active life expectancy among older blacks and whites. *New England Journal of Medicine, 329,* 110–116.

Gutmann, D. (1975). Parenthood: A key to the comparative study of the life cycle. In N. Datan, & L. H. Ginsber (Eds.), *Life-span developmental psychology: Normative life crises.* (pp. 167–184). New York: Academic Press.

Haan, N., Millsap, R., Hartka, E. (1986). As time goes by: Change and stability in personality over fifty years. *Psychology and Aging, 1,* 220–232.

Haidt, J., & Rodin, J. (1999). Control and efficacy as interdependent bridges. *Review of General psychology, 3,* 317–337.

Harmon, A. B. (1996). Ignoring the missionary position (retention of pre-Christian beliefs in the south sea islands). *New Statesman, 12,* 20–21.

Harris, P. (1996). Sufficient grounds for optimism? The relationship between perceived controllability and optimistic bias. *Journal of Social & Clinical Psychology, 15,* 9–52.

Harrison, D. E. (1985). Cell and tissue transplantation: A means of studying the aging process. In C. E. Finch, & E. L. Schneider (Eds.), *Handbook of the biology of aging* (2nd ed., pp. 322–356). New York: Van Nostrand Reinhold.

Harteneck, P., & Carey, D. J. (1994). The new direction in South American pension plans. *Journal of International Compensation & Benefits,* March/April, 25–30.

Hashimoto, A. (1991). Living arrangements of the aged in seven developing countries: A preliminary analysis. *Journal of Cross-Cultural Gerontology, 6,* 359–381.

Hayflick, L. (1994). *How and why we age.* New York: Ballantine Books.

Hayflick, L., & Moorehead, P. S. (1961). The serial cultivation of human diploid cell strains. *Experimental Cell Research, 25,* 285–621.

Heath, G., Hagberg, J., Ehrani, A. A., & Holloszy, J. O. (1981). Physical comparison of young and old endurance athletes. *Journal of Applied Physiology, 51,* 634–640.

Heintz, K. M. (1976). *Retirement communities.* New Brunswick, NJ: Rutgers University Center for Urban Policy research.

Helson, R. (1998). Personality change in all people, some people, and in individuals. *Paper presented at the 9th European conference on personality.* Surrey, England, July.

Helson, R., Stewart, A. J., & Ostrove, J. (1995). Identity in three cohorts of midlife women. *Journal of Personality and Social Psychology, 69,* 544–557.

Helson, R., & Wink, P. (1992). Personality change in women from the early 40s to the early 50s. *Psychology and Aging, 7,* 46–55.

Herzog, A. R., & Markus, H. R. (1999). The self-concept in life span and aging research. In V. L. Bengtson, & K. W. Schaie (Eds.), *Handbook of theories of aging* (pp. 227–252). New York: Springer.

Ho, D. Y. F. (1993). Relational orientation in Asian social psychology. In U. Kim, & J. W. Berry (Eds.), *Indigenous psychologies: Research and experience in cultural context* (pp. 240–259). Newbury Park, CA: Sage.

Hochschild, A. R. (1973). *The unexpected community.* Englewood Cliffs, NJ: Prentice-Hall.

Hofstede, G. (1980). *Culture's consequences: International differences in work-related values.* Beverly Hills, CA: Sage.

———. (1983). Dimensions of national cultures in fifty countries and three regions. In B. Deregowski, S. Dziurawiec, & R. C. Annis (Eds.), *Expiscations in cross-cultural psychology* (pp. 335–355). Lisse, The Netherlands: Swets and Zeitlinger.

Holden, K, & Smeeding, T. (1990). The poor, the rich and the insecure elderly caught in between. *Millbank Quarterly, 68,* 191–219.

Holland, J. L. (1992). *Making vocational choices: A theory of vocational personalities and work environments (2nd ed.).* Odessa, FL: Psychological Assessment Resources.

Hong, Y., Wong, S., & Lee, K. (1996). Effects of cultural knowledge activation on intergroups perceptions. *Paper presented at the annual convention of the American Psychological Association,* San Francisco.

Hooker, K. & Kaus, C. R. (1992). Possible selves and health behaviors in later life. *Journal of Aging & Health, 4,* 390–411.

Hooker, K., & Kaus, C. R. (1994) Health-related possible selves in young and middle adulthood. *Psychology & Aging, 9,* 126–133.

Hooyman, N., & Kiyak, H. A. (1999). *Social gerontology: An interdisciplinary perspective* (Fifth Edition). Boston: Allyn & Bacon.

Hortacsu, N., Bastug, S. S., & Muhammetberdiev, O. B. (2001). Desire for children in Turkmenistan and Azerbaijan: Son preference and perceived instrumentality for value satisfaction. *Journal of Cross-Cultural Psychology, 32,* 309–321.

Howell, N. (1979). *Demography of the Dobe !Kung.* New York: Academic Press.

Hoyer, W. J., & Rybash, J. M. (1994). Characterizing adult development *Journal of Adult Development, 1,* 7–12.

Hoyert, D. L., & Seltzer, M. M. (1992). Factors related to the well-being and life activities of family caregivers. *Family Relations, 41,* 74–81.

Hudson, R. B. (1978). The "graying" of the federal budget and its consequences for old age policy. *Gerontologist, 18,* 428–440.

Hui, C. H., & Triandis, H. C. (1986). Individualism-Collectivism: A study of cross-cultural researchers. *Journal of Cross-Cultural Psychology, 17,* 225–248.

Hultsch, D. F., Hammer, M., & Small, B. J. (1993). Age differences in cognitive performance in later life: Relationships to self-reported health and activity lifestyle. *Journal of Gerontology, 48,* P1–P11.

Hynie, M. (1998). The AIDS/HIV pandemic. In F. E. Aboud, *Health psychology in global perspective* (pp. 94–122). Thousand Oaks, CA: Sage.

Ide, B. A., & Sanli, T. (1992). Health beliefs and behaviors of Saudi women. *Women & Health, 19,* 97–113.

Iglehart, J. (1992). Health policy report: The American health care system—Medicare. *The New England Journal of Medicine, 327,* 1467–1472.

Ikels, C. (1991). Aging and disability in China: Cultural issues in measurement and interpretation. *Social science and Medicine, 32,* 649–655.

Ilgen, D. R. (1990). Health issues at work: Opportunities for industrial/organizational psychology. *American Psychologist, 45,* 273–283.

Ingstad, B., Bruun, F. J., & Tlou, S. (1997). AIDS and the elderly Tswana: The concept of pollution and consequences for AIDS prevention. *Journal of Cross-Cultural Gerontology, 12,* 357–372.

International Labour Office (1993). *World Reports.* Geneva: Author.

Izard, C. E., & Haynes, O. M. (1988). On the form and universality of the contempt expression: A challenge to Ekman and Friesen's claim of discovery. *Motivation and Emotion, 12,* 1–16.

Jackson, B., Taylor, J., & Pyngolil, M. (1991). How age conditions the relationship between climacteric status and health symptoms in African American Women. *Research in Nursing and Health, 14,* 1–9.

Jacobs, J. (1974). *Fun city: An ethnographic study of a retirement community.* New York: Holt, Rinehart, & Winston.

Jacobs, J. (1975). *Older persons and retirement communities.* Springfield, IL: Charles C. Thomson.

Jacques, P. F., Chylack, L. T., & Taylor, A. (1994). Relationships between natural antioxidents and cataract formation. In B. Frei (Ed.), *Natural antioxidents in human health and disease* (pp. 515–533). San Diego: Academic Press.

Jarallah, J. S. & Al-Shammari, S. A. (1999). Factors associated with health perception of Saudi elderly. *Journal of Cross-Cultural Gerontology, 14,* 323–334.

Jazwinski, S. M. (1996). Longevity, genes, and aging. *Science, 23,* 54–59.

Jeffko, W. C. (1979, July 9). Redefining death. *Commonweal,* 394–397.

Johansson, B., & Zarit, S. H. (1995). Prevalence and incidence of dementia in the oldest old: A study of a population based sample of 84–90 year olds in Sweden. *International Journal of Geriatric Psychiatry, 10,* 359–366.

Kagitcibasi, C. (1996a). The autonomous-relational self: A new synthesis. *European Psychologist, 1,* 180–186.

———. (1996b). *Family and human development across cultures: A view from the other side.* Mahwah, NJ: Lawrence Erlbaum.

———. (1997). Individualism and collectivism. In J. W. Berry, M. H. Segall, & C. Kagitcibasi (Eds.), *Handbook of cross-cultural psychology: Vol. 3. Social behavior and applications* (pp. 1–51). Boston: Allyn & Bacon.

Kahana, E. (1982). A congruence model of person-environment interaction. In M. P. Lawton, P. G. Windley, & T. O. Byerts (Eds.), *Aging and the environment: theoretical approaches* (pp. 97–121). New York: Springer.

Kahn, S. B., Alvi, S., Shaukat, N., Hussain, M. A., & Baig, T. (1990). A study of the validity of Holland's theory in a non-Western culture. *Journal of Vocational Behavior, 36,* 132–146.

Kakar, S. (1978). *The inner world: A psychoanalytical study of childhood and society in India.* Delhi: Oxford University Press.

Kalish, R. A. (1984). *Death, grief, and caring relationships* (2nd ed.). Pacific Grove, CA: Brooks/Cole.

———. (1985). The social context of death and dying. In R. H. Binstock & E. Shanas (Eds.), *Handbook of aging and the social sciences* (2nd ed., pp. 149–170). New York: Van Nostrand Reinhold.

———. (1987). Death and dying. In P. Silverman (Ed.), *The elderly as modern pioneers* (pp. 320–334). Bloomington: Indiana University Press.

Kastenbaum, R. (1975). Is death a life crisis? On the confrontation with death in theory and practice. In N. Datan & L. Ginsberg (Eds.), *Life-span developmental psychology: Normative life crises* (pp. 19–50). New York: Academic Press.

———. (1985). Dying and death: A life-span approach. In J. E. Birren & K. W. Schaie (Eds.), *Handbook of the psychology of aging* (2nd ed., pp. 619–643). New York: Van Nostrnad Reinhold.

———. (1991). *Death, society and human experience* (4th ed.). New York: Macmillan/ Merrill.

Kastenbaum, R. & Theull, S. (1995). Cookies baking, coffee brewing: Toward a contextual theory of dying. *Omega: Journal of Death & Dying, 31,* 175–187.

Kawachi, I. (1999). Physical and psychological consequences of weight gain. *Journal of Clinical Psychiatry, 60 (Suppl. 21),* 5–9.

Kay, D. W. K. (1995). The epidemiology of age-related neurological disease and dementia. *Reviews of Clinical Gerontology, 5,* 39–56.

Keller, H., & Greenfield, P. M. (2000). History and future of development in cross-cultural psychology. *Journal of Cross-Cultural Psychology, 31,* 14–32.

Keller, J. W., Sherry, D., & Piotrowski, C. (1984). Perspectives on death: A developmental study. *Journal of Psychology, 116,* 137–142.

Kessler, R. C., Foster, C., Webster, P. S., & House, J. S. (1992). The relationship between age and depressive symptoms in two national surveys. *Psychology & Aging, 7,* 119–126.

Kilbride, P. L., & Kilbride, J. C. (1997). Stigman, role overload, and decolonization among contemporary Kenyan women. In T. S. Weisner, C. Bradley, & P. L. Kilbride (Eds.), *African families and the crisis of social change* (pp. 208–226). Wesport, CT: Bergin & Garvey.

Kim, U. (1990). Indigenous psychology: Science and applications. In R. Brislin (Ed.), *Applied cross-cultural psychology* (pp. 142–160). Newbury Park, CA: Sage.

Kim, U., Triandis, H. C., Kagitcibasi, C., Choi, S., & Yoon, G. (1994). *Individualism and collectivism: Theory, method, and applications.* Thousand Oaks, CA: Sage.

Kinsella, K. (1988). *Aging in third world* (U. S. Bureau of the Census International Report No. 79). Washington, DC: U. S. Government Printing Office.

Kinsella, K., & Gist, Y. J. (1995). *Older workers, retirement, and pensions: A comparative international chartbook.* Washington, DC: U. S. Department of Commerce and Bureau of the Census.

Kiyak, H. A. (1996). Communication in the practitioner-aged patient relationship. In P. Holm-Pedersen & H. Loe (Eds.), *Textbook of geriatric dentistry* (2nd ed., pp. 150–161). Copenhagen: Munksgaard.

Klass, D. & Walter, T. (2001). Processes of grieving: How bonds are continued. In M. S. Stroebe, & Hansson, R. O. (Eds.), *Handbook of bereavement research: Consequences, coping, and care* (pp. 431–448). Washington, DC: American Psychological Association.

Kliegl, R., Smith, J., & Baltes, P. B. (1989). Testing the limits and the study of adult age differences in cognitive plasticity of a mnemonic skill. *Developmental Psychology, 25,* 247–256.

Knodel, J., Saengtienchai, C., & Sittitrai, W. (1995). Living arrangements of the elderly in Thailand: Views of the populace. *Journal of Cross-Cultural Gerontology, 10,* 79–111.

Koff, T. H. (1981). *Hospice: A caring community.* Cambridge, MA: Winthrop.

Kohli, M. (1986). The world we forgot: A historical view of the life course. In V. W. Marshall (Ed.), *Later life: The social psychology of aging* (pp. 271–303). Beverly Hills, CA: Sage.

Krippner, S., & Glenney, S. (1997). The Kallawaya healers of the Andes. *Humanistic Psychologist, 25,* 212–229.

Kübler-Ross, E. (1969). *On death and dying.* New York: Macmillan.

———. (1974). *Questions and answers on death and dying.* New York: Macmillan.

———. (1975). *Death: The final stage of growth.* Englewood Cliffs, NJ: Prentice-Hall.

———. (1981). *Living with dying.* New York: Macmillan.

Kumar, U. (1991). Life stages in the development of the Hindu woman in India. In L. L. Adler (Ed.), *Women in cross-cultural perspective* (pp. 143–159). New York: Praeger.

Kwan, V. S. Y., Bond, M. H., & Singelis, T. M. (1997). Pancultural explanations for life satisfaction: Adding relationship harmony to self-esteem. *Journal of Personality and Social Psychology, 73,* 1038–1051.

Labouvie-Vief, G. (1998). Cognitive-emotional integration in adulthood. In K. W. Schaie & M. P. Lawton (Eds.), *Annual Review of Gerontology and Geriatrics, Vol. 17: Focus on emotion and adult development* (pp. 206–237). New York: Springer.

Lake, A. J., Staiger, P. K., Glowinski, H. (2000). Effect of Western culture on women's attitudes to eating and perceptions of body shape. *International Journal of Eating Disorders, 2,* 83–89.

Langer, E. J. (1983). *The psychology of control.* Beverly Hills, CA: Sage.

Langer, E. J., & Rodin, J. (1976). The effects of choice and enhanced personal responsibility for the aged: A field experiment in an institutional setting. *Journal of Personality and Social Psychology, 34,* 191–198.

Langer, E. J., Rodin, J., Beck, P., Weinman, L., & Spitzer, J. (1979). Environmental determinants of memory improvements in late adulthood. *Journal of Personality & Social Psychology, 37,* 2003–2013.

Larue, A., Koehler, K. M., Wayne, S. J., Chiulli, S. J., Haaland, K. Y., & Garry, P. J. (1997). Nutritional status and cognitive functioning in a normally aging sample: A 6-year reassessment. *American Journal of Clinical Nutrition, 65,* 20–29.

Laungani, P. (1997). Death in a Hindu family. In C. M. Parkes, P. Laungani, & B. Young (Eds.), *Death and bereavement across cultures* (pp. 54–72). London: Routledge.

Lawton, M. P. (1996). Quality of life and affect in later life. In C. Magai, & S. H. McFadden (Eds.), *Handbook of emotion, adult development, and aging* (pp. 327–348). San Diego: Academic Press.

Lawton, M. P., Moss, M., & Moles, E. (1984). The supra-personal neighborhood context of older people: Age heterogeneity and well-being. *Environment & Behavior, 16,* 89–109.

Lawton, M. P., & Nahemow, L. (1973). Ecology and the aging process. In C. Eisdorfer & M. P. Lawton (Eds.), *The psychology of adult development and aging* (pp. 619–674). Washington, DC: American Psychological Association.

Lazarus, R. S. (1991). *Emotion and adaptation.* Oxford: Oxford University Press.

Lee, G. R., Dwyer, J. W., & Coward, R. T. (1993). Gender differences in parent care. Demographic factors and same gender preferences. *Journal of Gerontology: Social Sciences, 48,* S9–S16.

Lee, M., Lin, H., & Chang, M. (1995). Living arrangements of the elderly in Taiwan: Qualitative evidence. *Journal of Cross-Cultural Gerontology, 10,* 53–78.

LeGoff, J. (1984). *The birth of purgatory.* Chicago: University of Chicago Press.

Lerner, R. M. (1991). Changing organism-context relations as the basic process of development: A developmental contextual perspective. *Developmental Psychology, 27,* 27–32.

Levenson, R. W., Carstensen, L. L., Friesen, W. V., & Ekman, P. (1991). Emotion, physiology, and expression in old age. *Psychology and Aging, 6,* 28–35.

Levine, R., Sato, S., Hashimoto, T., & Verma, J. (1995). Love and marriage in eleven cultures. *Journal of Cross-Cultural Psychology, 26,* 554–571.

Levinson, D. J. (1986). A conception of adult development. *American Psychologist, 41,* 3–13.

Lewin, K. (1936). *Principles of topological psychology.* New York: McGraw-Hill.

Li, H. & Tracy, M. B. (1999). Family support, financial needs, and health care of rural elderly in China. A field study. *Journal of Cross-Cultural Gerontology, 14,* 357–371.

Light, P. C. (1985). *Artful work: The politics of social security reform.* New York: Random House.

Lightfoot, C., & Valsiner, J. (1992). Parental belief systems under the influence: Social guidance of the construction of personal cultures. In E. Sigel, A. McGillycuddy, & J. Goodnow (Eds.), *Parental belief systems* (pp. 393–414). Hillsdale, NJ: Lawrence Erlbaum.

Liker, J. K., & Elder, G. H. (1983). Economic hardship and marital relations in the 1930s. *American Sociological Review, 48,* 343–359.

Lindemann, E. (1944). Symptomatology and management of acute grief. *American Journal of Psychiatry, 101,* 141–149.

Lindenberger, U., & Baltes, P. B. (1994). Sensory functioning and intelligence in old age. *Psychology and Aging, 9,* 339–355.

Lindenberger, U., Baltes, P. B. (1997). Intellectual functioning in old and very old age: Crosssectional results from the Berlin Aging Study. *Psychology and Aging, 12,* 410–432.

Lund, D. A. (1993). Widowhood: The coping response. In R. Kastenbaum (Ed.), *Encyclopedia of adult development* (pp. 537–541). Phoenix, AZ: Oryx Press.

Lund, D. A., Caserta, M., & Dimond, M. (1993). The course of spousal bereavement in later life. In M. Stroebe, W. Stroebe, & R. Hanson (Eds.), *Handbook of bereavement: Theory, research and intervention* (pp. 240–254). New York: Cambridge University Press.

Lund, D. A., Dimond, M. S., Caserta, M. F., Johnson, R. J., Poulton, J. L., & Connelly, J. R. (1985–86). Identifying elderly with coping difficulties after two years of bereavement. *Omega: Journal of Death & Dying, 16,* 213–224.

Maas, H. S., & Kuypers, J. A. (1974). *From thirty to seventy.* San Francisco: Jossey-Bass.

Maddox, G. L. (1964). Disengagement theory: A critical evaluation. *Gerontologist, 6,* 80–82.

Madu, S. N., & Adebayo, O. E. (1996). Anxiety and retirement among some workers in Nigeria and some considerations for counseling and psychotherapy. In S. N. Madu, P. K. Baguma, & A. Pritz (Eds.), *Psychotherapy in Africa: First investigations* (pp. 197–205). Vienna, Austria: Association of New York City Teachers of Special Education.

Magnusson, D. (Ed.). (1996). *The life-span development of individuals: Behavioural, neurobiological and psychosocial perspectives.* Cambridge, UK: Cambridge University Press.

Mann, J. M. (1991). Global AIDS: Critical issues for prevention in the 1990s. *International Journal of Health Services, 21,* 553–559.

Margolis, R. (1990). *Risking old age in America.* Boulder, CO: Westview.

Markus, H. R., Holmberg, D., Herzog, A. R., & Franks, M. M. (1994). Self-making in adulthood. *Symposium presented at the annual meeting of the Gerontological Society of America,* Atlanta.

Markus, H. R., & Kitayama, S. (1991). Culture and the self: Implications for cognition, emotion, and motivation. *Psychological Review, 98*, 224–253.

Markus, H. R., & Kitayama, S. (1998). The cultural psychology of personality. *Journal of Cross-Cultural Psychology, 29*, 63–87.

Marmor, T., Mashaw, J. L., & Harvey, P. (1990). *America's misunderstood welfare state.* New York: Basic Books.

Marsella, A. J. (1980). Depressive experience and disorder across cultures. In H. C. Triandis, & J. G. Draguns (Eds.), *Handbook of cross-cultural psychology* (Vol. 6, pp. 233–262). Boston: Allyn & Bacon.

Marsella, A., DeVos, G., & Hsu, F. L. K. (1985). *Culture and self.* London: Tavistock.

Marsella, A. J., Sartorious, N., Jablensky, A., & Fenton, F. (1985). Cross-cultural studies of depressive disorders: An overview. In A. Klienman, & B. Good (Eds.), *Culture and depression: Studies in the anthropology and cross-cultural psychiatry of affect and disorders* (pp. 299–324). Berkeley, CA: University of California Press.

Marshall, V. (1980). *Last chapters: A sociology of aging and dying.* Pacific Grove, CA: Brooks/Cole.

Marshall, V., & Levy, J. (1990). Aging and dying. In R. Binstock, & L. George (Eds.), *Handbook of aging and the social sciences* (3rd ed., pp. 254–260). New York: Academic Press.

Martin-Matthews, A. (1996). Widowhood and widowerhood. *Encyclopedia of Gerontology, 2*, 621–625.

McAdams, D. P., & de St. Aubin, E. (1992). A theory of generativity and its assessment through self-report, behavioral acts, and narrative themes in autobiography. *Journal of Personality and Social Psychology, 62*, 1003–1015.

McCrae, R. R., & Costa, P. T., Jr. (1990). *Personality in adulthood.* New York: Guilford Press.

McCrae, R. R., Costa, P. T., Jr., Pedroso de Lima, M., Simtes, A., Ostendorf, F., Angleitner, A., Marusi, I., Bratko, D., Caprara, G. V., Barbaranelli, C., Chae, J.-H., & Piedmont, R. L. (1999). Age differences in personality across the adult life span: Parallels in five cultures. *Developmental Psychology, 35*, 466–477.

McCue, J. D. (1995). The naturalness of dying. *Journal of the American Medical Association, 273*, 1039–1043.

McFeatters, D. (1998, February 8). French take own slant on Clinton affair. *Reporternews.com.* Scripps Howard News Service. (http://www.reporternews.com/opinion/dale0208.html).

McGrath, J. W., Rwabukwali, C. B., Schumann, D. A., Pearson-Marks, J., Nakayiwa, S., Namande, B., Nakyobe, L., & Mukasa, R. (1993). Anthropology and AIDS: The cultural context of sexual risk behavior among urban Baganda women in Kampala, Uganda. *Social Science & Medicine, 36*, 1383–1395.

Medvedev, Z. A. (1990). An attempt at a rational classification of theories of aging. *Biological Review, 65*, 375–398.

Mehta, K., Osman, M. M.; & Alexander, L. E. Y. (1995). Living arrangements of the elderly in Singapore: Cultural norms in transition. *Journal of Cross-Cultural Gerontology, 10*, 113–143.

Meinz, E. J., & Salthouse, T. A. (1998). The effects of age and experience on memory for visually presented music. *Journal of Gerontology: Psychological Sciences, 53B*, P60–69.

Mesquita, B., & Frijda, N., Scherer, K. (1997). Culture and emotion. In J. W. Berry, P. R. Dasen, T. S. Saraswathi (Eds.), *Handbook of cross-cultural psychology: Vol. 2. Basic processes and human development* (pp. 255–298). Boston: Allyn & Bacon.

Meyer, M. H., & Bellas, M. L. (1995). U. S. old-age policy and the family. In R. Blieeszner & V. H. Bedford (Eds.). *Handbook of aging and the family* (pp. 263–283). Westport, CT: Greenwood Press.

Miller, G. (1996). Hospice. In C. Evashwick (Ed.), *The continuum of long term care: An integrated systems approach* (pp. 97–108). Albany, NY: Delmar Publishers.

Miller, K. (1984). The effects of industrialization on men's attitudes toward the extended family and women's rights: A cross-national study. *Journal of Marriage and the Family, 46,* 153–160.

Mishra, R. C., Sinha, D., & Berry, J. W. (1996). *Ecology, acculturation and psychological adaptation.* Thousand Oaks, CA: Sage.

Monczunski, J. (1991). The incurable disease. *Notre Dame Magazine, 20(1),* 37.

Morris, M. W., Nisbett, R. E., & Peng, K. (1995). Causal attributions across domains and cultures. In D. Sperber, D. Premack, A. J. Premack (Eds.), *Causal cognition: A multidisciplinary debate* (pp. 557–614). New York: Oxford University Press.

Morris, M. W., & Peng, K. (1994). Culture and cause: American and Chinese attributions for social and psychological events. *Journal of Personality and Social Psychology, 67,* 949–971.

Morrow, D. G., Leirer, V. O., & Altieri, P. A. (1992). Aging, expertise, and narrative processing. *Psychology and Aging, 7,* 376–388.

Mueller, W. H., Deutsch, M. I., & Malina, R. M. (1986). Subcutaneous fat topography: Age changes and relationships to cardiovascular fitness in Canadians. *Human Biology, 58,* 955–973.

Mundy-Castle, A. (1974). Social and technological intelligence in Western and non-Western cultures. *Universitas, 4,* 46–52.

Mundy-Castle, A., & Bundy, R. (1988). Moral values in Nigeria. *Journal of African Psychology, 6,* 25–40.

Murphy, C. (1986). Taste and smell in the elderly. In H. L. Meiselman & R. S. Rivlin (Eds.), *Clinical measurement of taste and smell* (pp. 343–371). New York: Macmillan.

Muse, C. J. (1991). Women in western Samoa. In L. L. Adler (Ed.), *Women in cross-cultural perspective* (pp. 221–241). New York: Praeger

National Center for Health Statistics (1995). Current estimates from the National Health Interview survey: U.S. 1994. *Vital and Health Statistics, series 10, #193.* Washington, DC: U.S. Department of Health and Human Services.

Neisser, U. (Ed.). (1998). *The rising curve.* Washington, DC: American Psychological Association.

Nektarios, M. (1982). *Public pensions, capital formation, and economic growth.* Boulder, CO: Westview.

Neugarten, B. L. (1968). *Middle age and aging.* Chicago: University of Chicago Press.

Neugarten, B. L., Moore, J. W., & Lowe, J. C. (1965). Age norms, age constraints, and adult socialization. *American Journal of Sociology, 70,* 710–717.

Neugarten, B. L., Wood, V., Kraines, R. J., & Loomis, B. (1963). Women's attitudes toward the menopause. *Vita Humana, 6,* 140–151.

Neugarten, D. A. (Ed.). (1996). *The meanings of age: Selected papers of Bernice L. Neugarten.* Chicago: University of Chicago Press.

Newman, A. P. (1982). Twenty lives revisited: A summary of a longitudinal study. *Reading Teacher, 35,* 814–818.

Niles, F. S. (1989). Parental attitudes toward female education in northern Nigeria. *Journal of Social Psychology, 129,* 13–20.

Niles, S. (1998). Achievement goals and means: A cultural comparison. *Journal of Cross-Cultural Psychology, 29,* 656–667.

Nigeria (1983). *Bulletin on aging, 8,* 28.

Norgan, N. G. (1987). Fat patterning in Papua New Guineans: Effects of age, sex, and acculturation. *American Journal of Physical Anthropology, 74,* 385–392.

Nsamenang, A. B. (1992). *Human development in cultural context: A third world perspective.* Newbury Park, CA: Sage.

Nsamenang, A. B. (1995). Theories of developmental psychology from a cultural perspective: A view from Africa. *Psychology and Developing Societies, 7,* 1–19.

Nwandu, T. (1998, February 21). Nigerian widows cry for succor. *Post Express Wired Online* (http://www.postexpresswired.com/postexpre...1a9e4ab5848525664700 57e6fc?OpenDocument).

Nydegger, C. N. (1991). The development of paternal and filial maturity. In K. Pillemer, & K. McCartney (eds.), *Parent-child relations throughout life* (pp. 93–112). Hillsdale, NJ: Lawrence Erlbaum.

O'Bryant, S., & Morgan, C. (1991). Recent widows' kin support and orientation to self-sufficiency. *The Gerontologist, 30,* 391–398.

O'Rand, A. (1996). The precious and the precocious: The cumulation of disadvantage and advantage over the life course. *Gerontologist, 36,* 230–238.

Orubuloye, I. O., Caldwell, J. C., & Caldwell, P. (1993). African women's control over their sexuality in an era of AIDS: A study of the Yoruba of Nigeria. *Social Science & Medicine, 37,* 859–872.

Orwoll, L., & Achenbaum, W. A. (1993). Gender and the development of wisdom. *Human Development, 36,* 274–296.

Park, D. C., Nisbett, R., & Hedden, T. (1999). Aging, culture, and cognition. *Journal of Gerontology, 54,* P75–P84.

Parkes, C. M. (1972). *Bereavement: Studies of grief in adult life.* New York: International Universities Press.

Parkes, C. M., Laungani, P., & Young, B. (1997). Introduction. In C. M. Parkes, P. Laungani, & B. Young (Eds.), *Death and bereavement across cultures* (pp. 3–9). London: Routledge.

Parkes, C. M., & Weiss, R. (1983). *Recovery from bereavement.* New York: Basic Books.

Parsuram, A., & Sharma, M. (1992). Functional relevance in belief in life-after-death. *Journal of Personality & Clinical Studies, 8,* 97–100.

Patterson, J. (1996). Participation in leisure activities by older adults after a stressful life event: The loss of a spouse. *International Journal of Aging and Human Development, 42,* 123–142.

Pattison, E. M. (1977). The dying experience—retrospective analysis. In E. M. Pattison (Ed.), *The experience of dying* (pp. 303–315). Englewood Cliffs, NJ: Prentice-Hall.

Peltzer, K. ((1989). Psycho-social contexts of retirement in Nigeria and their comparison with USA. *Pakistan Journal of Psychological Research, 4,* 27–42.

Pervin, L. A. (1996). *The science of personality.* New York: John Wiley.

Petri, P. A. (1982). Income, employment, and retirement policies. In R. H. Binstock, W. S. Chow, & J. H. Schultz (Eds.), *International perspectives on aging: Population and policy challenges* (pp. 75–126). New York: United Nations Fund for Population Activities.

Phalet, K., & Claeys, W. (1993). A comparative study of Turkish and Belgian Youth. *Journal of Cross-Cultural Psychology, 24,* 319–343.

Plato, C. C. (1987). The effects of aging on bioanthropological variables: Changes in bone mineral density with increasing age. *Colloqium in Anthropology, 11,* 59–72.

Pleck, J. (1977). The work-family role system. *Social Problems, 24,* 417–427.

Pollack, M. L., Foster, C., Knapp, D., Rod, J. L., & Schmidt, D. H. (1987). Effect of age and training on aerobic capacity and body composition of master athletes. *Journal of Applied Physiology, 62,* 725–731.

Pujari, P., & Kaushik, V. K. (1994). *Women power in India* (Vol. I, II, & III). New Delhi: Kanishka.

Punyahotra, S., & Dennerstein, L. (1997). Menopausal experiences of Thai women: Part 2. The cultural context. *Maturitas, 26,* 9–14.

Quadagno, J. (1988). *The transformation of old age security: Class and politics in the American welfare state.* Chicago: University of Chicago Press.

Quadagno, J., & Reid, J. (1999). The political economy perspective in aging. In V. L. Bengtson, & K. W. Schaie (Eds.), *Handbook of theories of aging* (pp. 344–360). New York: Springer.

Quadagno, J. & Reid, J. (1999). The political economy perspective in aging. In V. L. Bengtson, & K. W. Schaie (Eds.), *Handbook of theories of aging* (pp. 344–360). New York: Springer.

Rabbitt, P., Donland, C., Watson, P., McInnes, L., & Bent, N. (1995). Unique and interactive effects of depression, age , and socioeconomic advantage, and gender on cognitive performance of normal healthy older people. *Psychology and Aging, 10,* 307–313.

Rao, A. V. (1973). Depressive illness and guilt in Indian cultures. *Indian Journal of Psychiatry, 26,* 99–221.

Rasmussen, C. H., & Johnson, M. E. (1994). Spirituality and religiosity: Relative relationships to death anxiety. *Omega: Journal of Death & Dying, 29,* 313–318.

Regan, P. C., Snyder, M., & Kassin, S. M. (1995). Unrealistic optimism: Self-enhancement or person positivity? *Personality & Social Psychology Bulletin, 21,* 1073–1082.

Reifler, B. V. (1994). Depression: Diagnosis and comorbidity. In L. S. Schneider, C. F. Reynolds, III, et al. *Diagnosis and treatment of depression in late life: Results of the NIH consensus development conference.* (pp. 55–59). Washington, DC: American Psychiatric Press.

Reinke, B. J., Holmes, D. S., & Harris, R. L. (1985). The timing of psychosocial changes in women's lives: The years 25 to 45. *Journal of Personality & Social Psychology, 48,* 1353–1364.

Rentsch, J. R., & Heffner, T. S. (1994). Assessing self-concept: Analysis of Gordon's coding scheme using "Who am I?" responses. *Journal of Social Behavior and Personality, 9,* 283–300.

Reskin, B. (1993). Sex segregation in the workplace. *Annual Review of Sociology, 19,* 241–270.

Reykowski, J. (1994). Collectivism and individualism as dimensions of social change. In U. Kim, H. C., Triandis, C. Kagitcibasi, S. C., Choi, & G. Yoon (Eds.), *Individualism and collectivism: Theory, method, and applications* (pp. 276–293). Thousand Oaks, CA: Sage.

Riley, M. W. (1971). Social gerontology and the age stratification of society. *Gerontologist, 11,* 79–87.

Riley, M. W., Foner, A., & Riley, J. W. (1999). The aging and society paradigm. In V. L. Bengtson, & K. W. Schaie (Eds.), *Handbook of theories of aging* (327–343). New York: Springer.

Roberts, P., & Newton, P. M. (1987). Levinsonian studies of women's adult development. *Psychology and Aging, 2,* 154–163.

Rodin, J., & Langer, E. J. (1977). Long-term effects of a control-relevant intervention with the institutionalized aged. *Journal of Personality and Social Psychology, 35,* 897–902.

Rose, A. M. (1965). A current theoretical issue in social gerontology. In A. M. Rose, & W. A. Peterson (Eds.), *Older people and their social worlds* (pp. 359–366). Philadelphia: F. A. Davis.

Rosenberg, H. G. (1997). Complaint discourse, aging and caregiving among the Ju/hoansi of Botswana. In J. Sokolovsky (Ed.), *The cultural context of aging: Worldwide perspectives* (pp. 33–55). Westport, CT: Bergin & Garvey.

Rosenberg, I. H. (1989). Summary comments: Epidemiological and methodological problems in determining nutritional status of older persons. *American Journal of Clinical Nutrition, 50,* 1231–1233.

Rosenblatt, P. C. (1997). Grief in small-scale societies. In C. M. Parkes, P. Laungani, & B. Young (Eds.), *Death and bereavement across cultures* (pp. 27–51). London: Routledge.

Roshdieh, S., Templer, D. I., Cannon, W. G., & Canfield, M. (1999). The relationship of death anxiety and death depression to religion and civilian war-related experiences in Iranians. *Omega: Journal of Death & Dying, 38,* 201–210.

Rosow, I. (1967). *Social integration of the aged.* New York: Free Press.

———. (1974). *Socialization to old age.* Berkeley, CA: University of California Press.

Rotter, J. B. (1966). Generalized expectancies for internal versus external control of reinforcement. *Psychological Monographs, 80* (1, Whole No. 609).

Rudman, D., Drinka, P. J., Wilson, C. R., Mattson, D. E., Scherman, F., Cuisinier, M. C., & Schultz, S. (1991). Relations of endogenous anabolic hormones and physical activity to bone mineral density in elderly men. *Clinical Endocrinology, 40,* 653–661.

Ryff, C. D. (1991). Possible selves in adulthood and old age: A tale of shifting horizons. *Psychology and Aging, 6,* 286–295.

Rykken, D. E. (1987). Sex in later years. In P. Silverman (Ed.), *The elderly as modern pioneers* (pp. 125–144). Bloomington: Indiana University Press.

Rylands, K. & Rickwood, D. J. (2001). Ego-integrity versus ego-despair: The effect of "accepting the past" on depression in older women. *International Journal of Aging and Human Development, 53,* 75–89.

Salthouse, T. A. (1993). Speed mediation of adult age differences in cognition. *Developmental Psychology, 29,* 722–738.

————. (1994). The nature of the influence of speed on adult age differences in cognition. *Developmental Psychology, 30*, 240–259.

————. (1999). Theories of cognition. In V. L. Bengtson, & K. W. Schaie (Eds.), *Handbook of theories of aging* (pp. 196–208). New York: Springer.

Salthouse, T. A., Babcock, R. L., Skovronek, E., Mitchell, D. R. D., & Palmon, R. (1990). Age and experience effects in spatial visualization. *Developmental Psychology, 26*, 128–136.

Salthouse, T. A., & Mitchell, D. R. D. (1990). Effects of age and naturally occurring experience on spatial visualization performance. *Developmental Psychology, 26*, 845–854.

Sanders, C. M. (1993). Risk factors in bereavement outcome. In M. Stroebe, W. Stroebe, & R. O. Hanson (Eds.), *Handbook of bereavement: Theory, research and intervention* (pp. 255–267). New York: Cambridge University Press.

Schaie, K. W. (1996). *Intellectual development in adulthood: The Seattle longitudinal study.* New York: Cambridge University Press.

Schaie, K. W., & Willis, S. L. (1991). Adult personality and psychomotor performance: Cross-sectional and longitudinal analyses. *Journal of Gerontology: Psychological Sciences, 46*, P276–P284.

Schimmack, U. (1996). Cultural influences on the recognition of emotion by facial expressions: Individualistic or Caucasian cultures? *Journal of Cross-Cultural Psychology, 27*, 37–50.

Schlegel, A., & Barry III, H. (1991). *Adolescence: An anthropological enquiry.* New York: Free Press.

Schroots, J. J. F. (1991). Methaphors of aging and complexity. In G. M. Kenyon, J. E. Birren, & J. J. F. Schroots (Eds.), *Methaphors of aging in science and the humanities* (pp. 219–243). New York: Springer.

————. (1995). Gerodynamics: Toward a branching theory of aging. *Canadian Journal of Aging, 14*, 74–81.

Schroots, J. J. F., & Yates, F. E. (1999). On the dynamics of development and aging. In V. L. Bengtson, K. W. Schaie (Eds.), *Handbook of theories of aging* (pp. 417–433). New York: Springer.

Schulz, J. H. (1993). Chile's approach to retirement income security attracts worldwide attention. *Ageing International, 20*, 51–52.

Schultz, R. (1978). *The psychology of death, dying and bereavement.* Reading, MA: Addison-Wesley.

————. (1985). Emotion and affect. In J. E. Birren & K. W. Schaie (Eds.), *Handbook of the psychology of aging* (2nd ed., pp. 531–543). New York: Van Nostrand Reinhold.

Schwartz, S. H. (1990). Individualism–collectivism: Critique and proposed refinements. *Journal of Cross-Cultural Psychology, 21*, 139–157.

————. (1992). Universals in the content and structure of values. Theoretical advances and empirical tests in 20 countries. In M. Zanna (Ed.), *Advances in experimental and social psychology* (vol. 25, pp. 1–65). Orlando: Academic Press.

————. (1994). Beyond individualism and collectivism: New cultural dimensions of values. In U. Kim, H. C. Triandis, C. Kagitcibasi, S.-C. Choi, & G. Yoon (Eds.), *Individualism and collectivism: Theory, method, and applications* (pp. 85–119). Thousand Oaks, CA: Sage.

Schwartz, S. H., & Bilsky, W. (1987). Toward a psychological structure of human values. *Journal of Personality and Social Psychology, 53,* 550–562.

Schwartz, S. H., & Bilsky, W. (1990). Toward a theory of the universal content and structure of values: Extensions and cross-cultural replications. *Journal of Personality and Social Psychology, 58,* 878–891.

Seligman, M. E. P. (1991). *Learned optimism.* New York: Knopf.

Selkoe, D. J. (1997). Alzheimer's disease: Genotypes, phenotypes, and treatments. *Science, 25,* 630–631.

Settersten, R. A., Jr., & Hagestad, G. O. (1996a). What's the latest? Cultural age deadlines for family transitions. *Gerontologist, 36,* 178–188.

Settersten, R. A., Jr., & Hagestad, G. O. (1996b). What's the latest? Cultural age deadlines for educational and work transitions. *Gerontologist, 36,* 602–613.

Shanan, J., & Sagiv, R. (1982). Sex differences in intellectual performance during middle age. *Human Development, 25,* 24–33.

Sherwood, S., Ruchlin, H. S., & Sherwood, C. C. (1990). CCRCs: An option for aging in place. In D. Tilson (Ed.), *Supporting the frail elderly in residential environments* (pp. 125–164). Glenview, IL: Scott, Foresman & Company.

Shifren, K. (1996). Individual differences in the perception of optimism and disease severity: A study among individuals with Parkinson's disease. *Journal of Behavioral Medicine, 19,* 241–271.

Shifren, K., & Hooker, K. (1995). Stability and change in optimism: A study among spouse caregivers. *Experimental Aging Research, 21,* 59–76.

Shock, N. W., Greulich, R. C., Andres, R., Arenberg, D., Costa, P. T., Jr., Lakatta, E. G., & Tobin, J. D. (1984). *Normal human aging: The Baltimore longitudinal study of aging.* NIH Publication # 84-2450. Washington, DC: U. S. Government Printing Office.

Shuchter, S. R., & Zissok, S. (1986). Treatment of spousal bereavement: A multidimensional approach. *Psychiatric Annals, 16,* 295–305.

Silverman, P. (1987). Community settings. In P. Silverman (Ed.), *The elderly as modern pioneers* (pp. 185–210). Bloomington: Indiana University Press.

Singelis, T. M. (2000). Some thoughts on the future of cross-cultural social psychology. *Journal of Cross-Cultural Psychology, 31,* 76–91.

Singhal, U., & Mrinal, N. R. (1991). Tribal women of India: The Tharu women. In L. L. Adler (Ed.), *Women in cross-cultural perspective* (pp. 160–174). New York: Praeger.

Sinha, D. (1965). Integration of modern psychology with Indian thought. In A. J. Sutchi, & M. A. Vick (Eds.), *Readings in humanistic psychology* (pp. 265–279). New York: Free Press.

———. (1986). *Psychology in a third world country: The Indian experience.* New Delhi: Sage.

———. (1993). Indigenization of psychology in India and its relevance. In U. Kim, J. W. Berry (Eds.), *Indigenous psychologies: Research and experience in cultural context* (pp. 30–43). Newbury Park, CA: Sage.

Sinha, J. B. P. (1980). *The nurturant task leader.* New Delhi, India: Concept.

Smith, A. D. (1996). Memory. In J. E. Birren, & W. K. Schaie (Eds.), *Handbook of the psychology of aging* (4th ed., pp. 236–250). San Diego, CA: Academic Press.

Smith, P. B., Bond, M. H. (1993). *Social psychology across cultures.* Hartfordshire, England: Harvester/Wheatsheaf.

Sobal, J. (1991). Obesity and socioeconomic status: A framework for examining relationships between physical and social variables. *Medical Anthropology, 13,* 231–247.

Social Security Administration (1992). *Social security bulletin and annual statistical supplement.* Washington, DC: U. S. Department of Health and Human Services.

Social Security Administration (1997). *Social security programs throughout the world—1997* (Research Report #65). Washington, DC: U. S. Government Printing Office.

Sodowsky, G. R., Maguire, K., & Johnson, P. (1994). Worldviews of white American, mainland Chinese, Taiwanese and African students: An investigation into between group differences. *Journal of Cross-Cultural psychology, 25,* 309–324.

Solomon, L. (1979). Bone density in aging Caucasian and African populations. *Lancet, 1,* 326–1329.

Spitze, G. (1988). Women's employment and family relations: A review. *Journal of Marriage and the Family, 50,* 595–618.

Staudinger, U. M., Marsiske, M., Baltes, P. B. (1995). Resilience and reserve capacity in later adulthood: Potentials and limits of development across the life span. In D. Cicchetti, D. Cohen (Eds.), *Vol. 2. Developmental psychopathology: Risk, disorder, and adaptation* (pp. 801–847). New York: Wiley.

Steen, T. W., & Mazonde, G. N. (1999). Ngaka ya setswana, ngaka ya sekgoa or both? Health seeking behavior in Botswana with pulmonary tuberculosis. *Social Sciences and Medicine, 48,* 163–172.

Stephens, M. A. P., Franks, M. M., & Atienza, A. A. (1997). Where two roles intersect: Spillover between parent care and employment. *Psychology and Aging, 12,* 30–37.

Stevens, J. C., & Cain, W. S. (1987). Old-age deficits in the sense of smell as gauged by thresholds, magnitude matching, and odor identification. *Psychology of Aging, 2,* 36–42.

Stevenson, H. W., & Stigler, J. W. (1992). *The learning gap: Why our schools are failing and what we can learn from Japanese and Chinese education.* New York: Summit Books.

Stipek, D. (1998). Differences between Americans and Chinese in the circumstances evoking pride, shame, and guilt. *Journal of Cross-Cultural Psychology, 29,* 616–629.

Strauss, A. L., & Glaser, B. G. (1970). *Anguish.* Mill Valley, CA: Sociology Press.

Street, D. (1996). The politics of pension. *Unpublished doctoral dissertation.* Department of Sociology, Florida State University, Tallahassee, FL.

Strehler, B. L. (1986). Genetic instability as the primary cause of human aging. *Experimental Gerontology, 21,* 283.

Sue, D. W., & Sue, D. (1977). Barriers to effective cross-cultural counseling. *Journal of Counseling Psychology, 24,* 420–429.

Suominen, H., Heikkinen, E., Parkatti, T., Forsberg, S., & Kiiskinen, A. (1980). Effects of lifelong physical training on functional aging in men. *Scandinavian Journal of the Society of Medicine, 14 (Suppl.),* 225–240.

Ta, M., & Chung, C. (1990). Death and dying: A Vietnamese cultural perspective. In J. K. Parry (Ed.), *Social work practice with the terminally ill: A transcultural perspective* (pp. 191–204). Springfield, IL: Charles C. Thomas.

Tamburi, G. (1985). Social security in Latin America: Trends and outlook. In C. Mesa-Lago (Ed.), *The crisis of social security and health care: Latin American experiences and lessons* (pp. 57–83). Pittsburgh: Center for Latin American Studies.

Tayeh, A., Cairncross, S., & Maude, G. H. (1996). The impact of health education to promote cloth filters on dracunuliasis prevalence in the northern region, Ghana. *Social Science & Medicine, 43,* 1205–1211.

Thompson, I. (1994). Woldenburg Village: An illustration of supportive design for older adults. *Experimental Aging Research, 20,* 239–244.

Thorson, J. A., & Powell, F. C. (1990). Meanings of death and intrinsic religiosity. *Journal of Clinical Psychology, 46,* 379–391.

Tracy, B. T. (1991). *Social policies for the elderly in the Third World.* Westport, CT: Greenwood Press.

Trafimow, D., Silverman, E. S., Fan, R. M., & Law, J. S. F. (1997). The effects of language and priming on the relative accessibility of the private self and the collective self. *Journal of Cross-Cultural Psychology, 28,* 107–123.

Triandis, H. C. (1988). Collectivism v. individualism: A reconceptualization of a basic concept in cross-cultural social psychology. In G. K. Verma, & C. Bagley (Eds.), *Cross-cultural studies of personality, attitudes and cognition* (pp. 60–95). New York: Macmillan.

———. (1990). Cross-cultural studies of individualism and collectivism. In J. Berman (Ed.), *Cross-cultural perspectives: Nebraska Symposium on Motivation, 1989* (pp. 41–133). Lincoln, NE: University of Nebraska Press.

———. (1994). *Culture and social behavior.* New York: McGraw-Hill.

———. (1995). *Individualism and collectivism.* Boulder, CO: Westview.

Triandis, H. C., & Bhawuk, D. P. S. (1997). Culture theory and the meaning of relatedness. In P. C. Earley & M. Erez (Eds.), *New perspectives on international industrial/organizational psychology* (pp. 13–52). San Francisco, CA: The New Lexington Press.

Triandis, H. C., McCuster, C., & Hui, C. H. (1990). Multimethod probes of individualism and collectivism. *Journal of Cross-Cultural Gerontology, 24,* 366–383.

Tuddenham, R. D. (1948). Soldier intelligence in World Wars I and II. *American Psychologist, 3,* 54–56.

UNESCO Courier (1999). Helping the elderly help themselves. *UNESCO Courier, 52,* 24.

United Nations Development Programme. (1997). *Human Development Report.* New York: Author.

United Nations Development Programme (1998). *Statistics from the 1998 Human Development Report.* New York: Author.

United Nations Programme on HIV/AIDS (UNAIDS) (2000). Report on the global HIV/AIDS epidemic, June. Geneva: Author.

U.S. Bureau of the Census. (1989). *Current population reports* (Series P-23, No. 162). Washington, DC: U.S. Government Printing Office.

U.S. Bureau of the Census (1999). World population profile: 1998. http://www.census.gov/

U.S. House Select Committee on Aging (1988). *An assault on Medicare and Medicaid in the 1980s: The legacy of an administration* (Publication No. 100-679). Washington, DC: U.S. Government Printing Office.

Valsiner, J. (1989). *Human development and culture*. Lexington, MA: D. C. Heath.

Valsiner, J. & Lawrence, J. (1997). Human development in culture across the life span. In J. W. Berry, Dasen, P. R., & Saraswathi, T. S. (Eds.), Handbook of cross-cultural psychology: Vol 2. Basic processes and human development (2nd ed., pp. 69–106). Boston: Allyn & Bacon.

van de Vijver, F. (1997). Meta-analysis of cross-cultural comparisons of cognitive test performance. *Journal of Cross-Cultural Psychology, 28*, 678–709.

van de Vijver, F. J. F., & Leung, K. (2000). Methodological issues in psychological research on culture. *Journal of Cross-Cultural Psychology, 31*, 33–51.

Van Nostrand, J. F., Furner, S. E., & Suzman, R. (1993). Health data on older Americans: United States, 1992. *Vital and Health Statistics, series 3: Analytic and Epidiemological Studies, No. 27, DHHS Publication 93-1411*. Hyattsville, MD: NCHS.

van Willigen, J., Chadha, N. K., Kedia, S. (1995). Personal networks and sacred texts: Social aging in Delhi, India. *Journal of Cross-Cultural Gerontology, 10*, 175–198.

Verbrugge, L. M., Lepkowski, J. M., & Konkol, L. L. (1991). Levels of disability among U. S. adults with arthritis. *Journal of Gerontology: Social Sciences, 46*, S71–S83.

Walker, A. (1999). Public policy and theories of aging: Constructing or reconstructing old age. In V. L. Bengtson & K. W. Schaie (Eds.), *Handbook of theories of aging* (pp. 361–378). New York: Springer.

Wallace, S. (1990). Race versus class in the health care of African American elderly. *Social Problems, 37*, 517–534.

Walsh, E. K., & Cavanaugh, J. C. (1984, November). Does hospice meet the needs of dying clients? *Paper presented at the meeting of the Gerontological Society of America*, San Antonio.

Weisman, A. D. (1972). *On dying and denying*. New York: Behavioral Publications.

Weiss, R. S. (1988). Loss and recovery. *Journal of Social Issues, 44*, 37–52.

Wikan, U. (1980). *Life among the poor in Cairo*. London: Tavistock.

———. (1982). *Behind the veil in Arabia*. Chicago: University of Chicago Press.

———. (1990). *Managing turbulent hearts: A Balinese formula for living*. Chicago: University of Chicago Press.

Whitbourne, S. K. (1985). *The aging body*. New York: Springer.

Wolinsky, F. D., & Johnson, R. J. (1991). The use of health services by older adults. *Journal of Gerontology, 46*, S345–S357.

Wolinsky, F. D., Stump, T. E., & Clark, D. O. (1995). Antecedents and consequences of physical activity and exercise among older adults. *Gerontologist, 35*, 451–462.

Worden, J. W. (1976). *Personal death awareness*. Englewood Cliffs, NJ: Prentice-Hall.

———. (1991). *Grief counseling and grief therapy: A handbook for the mental health practitioner*. New York: Springer.

World Bank (1994). Averting the old age crisis (A World Bank Policy Research Report). New York: Oxford University Press.

World Health Organization (1999). *The world health report 1999: Making a difference*. Author.

Worobey, J. L., & Angel, R. J. (1990). Functional capacity and living arrangements of unmarried elderly persons. *Journal of Gerontology: Social Sciences, 45*, S95–S101.

Wurtman, J. J., Liberman, H., Tsay, R., & Nader, T. (1988). Caloric and nutrient intakes of elderly and young subjects measured under identical conditions. *Journal of Gerontology, Biological Sciences, 43*, 174–180.

Yates, F. E., & Benton, L. A. (1995a). Loss of integration and resiliency with age: A dissipative destruction. In E. J. Masoro (Ed.), *Handbook of physiology; Section 11. Aging* (pp. 591–610). New York: Oxford University Press.

Yates, F. E., & Benton, L. A. (1995b). Rejoinder to Rosen's comments on biological senescence. Loss of integration and resilience. *Canadian Journal of Aging, 14,* 125–130.

Yu, A.-B., & Yang, K.-S (1994). The nature of achievement motivation in collectivistic societies. In U. Kim, H. C. Triandis, C. Kagitcibasi, S.-C. Choi, & G. Yoon (Eds.), *Individualism and collectivism: Theory, method, and applications* (pp. 239–250). Thousand Oaks, CA: Sage.

Yu, L. C., & Carpenter, L. (1991). Women in China. In L. L. Adler (Ed.), *Women in cross-cultural perspective* (pp. 189–204). New York: Praeger.

Zarit, S. H., & Zarit, J. M. (1998). *Mental disorders in older adults: Fundamentals of assessment and treatment.* New York: Guilford Press.

Zebian, S., & Denny, J. P. (2001). Integrative cognitive style in Middle Eastern and Western groups: Multidimensional classification and major and minor property sorting. *Journal of Cross-Cultural Psychology, 32,* 58–75.

Name Index

Name Index

Subject Index

About the Authors

FRANK E. EYETSEMITAN is Professor of Psychology, McKendree College, Illinois.

JAMES T. GIRE is Associate Professor of Psychology and Lieutenant Colonel at the Virginia Military Institute, Lexington.